Murphy's Eight Great Steps
beneath the Shee

1. **Pick the right function for the job.** Beware of differences between functions that have similar purposes (ROUND and TRUNC, AVERAGE and MEDIAN, to name some of the worst offenders).

2. **Watch for common sources of error.** Avoid division by zero, rounded or truncated values used in multiplication formulas, and circular references.

3. **Make sure to feed a function everything it wants.** Enclose text values that are used as arguments in quotation marks, but don't use quotation marks with range names or with TRUE or FALSE. Use parentheses in matching pairs. If you're not sure what arguments a function wants, press Ctrl-A after typing the equal sign and the function name in the formula bar.

4. **Use the right stuff.** Make sure that arguments refer to cells or ranges that hold the values needed by the function. Use range names for clarity, but don't assume that the name refers to the correct range until you recheck it. Select the range you think is named and look in the cell reference box (top left of the screen) to see if the name appears there. Don't use the name of a cell that holds a formula unless you fully understand the formula's math. Use absolute and relative addressing correctly to prevent errors that might creep in if you edit the sheet later.

5. **Test each formula.** Watch for error messages (there's a list in Chapter 2) and incorrect results. Revise your formulas until the sheet works as expected.

6. **Test the sheet.** Generating graphs from ranges in the sheet can be a quick visual check on the reasonableness of results.

7. **If you make changes to the sheet, recheck and retest it.**

8. **If you think Excel goofed, think again.**

Smart Advice with a Smile
The Murphy's Laws Computer Book Series

Let's face it. Most computer books just don't feature the "can't put it down" excitement of an Ian Fleming spy novel or the heart-palpitating romance of Danielle Steele. But they don't have to put you to sleep, either. **The Murphy's Laws Computer Book Series** gives you the answers you need and keeps you entertained at the same time.

Written with wit and filled with useful information, **The Murphy's Laws Computer Book Series** *helps everyone*, even the most reluctant computer users, get the best of their computer and computing. In the series, there are books on word processing, spreadsheets, PCs, and operating systems—and even more books are planned. Every book in the series promises to give you the information you need on the software you use without boring you into oblivion.

Always smart, never stuffy. Every computer user will want to use **The Murphy's Laws Computer Book Series** whenever there are questions about the computer.

Look for **The Murphy's Laws Computer Book Series** at your favorite bookstore.

For a complete catalog of our publications:

SYBEX Inc.
2021 Challenger Drive, Alameda, CA 94501
Tel: (510) 523-8233/(800) 227-2346 Telex: 336311
Fax: (510) 523-2373

Murphy's Laws of Excel

Murphy's Laws of

EXCEL

Gerald E. Jones

SYBEX®   San Francisco   Paris   Düsseldorf   Soest

Acquisitions Editor: Dianne King
Series Editor: Sharon Crawford
Editor: Sarah Wadsworth
Technical Editor: Bruce Gendron
Book Designer: Claudia Smelser
Production Artist: Ingrid Owen
Screen Graphics and Technical Art: John Corrigan
Typesetter: Thomas Goudie
Proofreader/Production Assistant: Janet K. MacEachern
Indexer: Nancy Anderman Guenther
Cartoonist and Front Cover Illustrator: Robert Kopecky
Cover Designer: Ingalls + Associates
Special icon font created by Len Gilbert.
Screen reproductions produced with Collage Plus and SnapPro.

Library of Congress Card Number: 93-84306
ISBN: 0-7821-1294-3

Manufactured in the United States of America
10 9 8 7 6 5 4 3 2 1

Acknowledgments

I didn't do this all by myself. Some of the blame goes to the gang at SYBEX, including Dianne King, Acquisitions Editor; Sharon Crawford, Series Editor; Sarah Wadsworth, Editor; and Bruce Gendron, Technical Reviewer.

Take special note of Pete Nathan, Senior PC Systems Analyst at Paramount Pictures, for suggesting some of the more bizarre examples. Fred Gallegos of the U.S. General Accounting Office first introduced me to the worry of worksheets in his book *Audit and Control of Information Systems*, and his personal example convinces me that at least some G-men still wear white hats.

Personal thanks to Georja Oumano Jones, who picks me up whenever Murphy knocks me down.

Contents at a Glance

Table of Contents

Part 2   Giving Orders to Your Math Slave

4 ☞ THIS FORMULA ISN'T FOR BABIES   81

Part 3   Making a Public Appearance

Part 5 Who Said This Stuff is Hard?

Introduction

Murphy's Law: Anything that can go wrong will go wrong.

As I reread Murphy's famous law, I realize that it's not just an observation; it's *a promise*! I strongly suspect that this Murphy person played a role in the invention of the computer, and he (or she?) was certainly on the team when they thought up spreadsheet software. Maybe it all started as a game of tic-tac-toe that got way out of hand...

This book is dedicated to a simple idea—keeping you out of trouble. At least, when you're using Excel.

Microsoft Excel is the most popular spreadsheet software on the planet. Using Excel is like having a math whiz trapped inside your computer. This whiz lives to take orders from you alone. And besides a few pennies' worth of electricity, it asks for nothing in return (once you've popped for the purchase price). Excel is easy to learn, easy to use, and it presents the results of the math it does for you in neatly printed tables and colorful charts.

So, what's the big deal? If so many people are happily using Excel, *what could possibly go wrong?*

Watch Where You Point That Thing!

It could well be a Murphyism that the pen is mightier than the sword. When you turn on your computer instead of picking up a pen, your chances of doing some real damage are about ten guzzillion times greater.

Lest you think I exaggerate, consider the following horror stories. All of them are supposedly true, but they have attained the status of computer-inspired folklore. Each one demonstrates the potentially huge impact of a single error in a worksheet formula (the kind of math problem you give Excel):

☞ A financial analyst for a bank used the wrong formula for compound interest in preparing a projection of profits from an investment portfolio. As a result, the profits were overstated. A few months later when the profits didn't materialize, the customer and the bank's officers were disappointed, to put it mildly. Last I heard, the analyst was flipping burgers.

☞ A national sales manager included price discounts in one product line but neglected to include them in a formula that produced the sales forecast for related products. Because of the discounts, the actual sales for these products was much higher than the forecast. The company started to lose business, however, because the production quotas were too low and they could not keep up with demand. The sales manager—and the forecast—are history.

☞ Engineers at a firm that was bidding on a multimillion-dollar project overlooked the effect of rounding in their formulas. Their bid—which took them over a year to prepare— was way off, and somebody else got the contract. The engineers of the biggest write-off in the life of the firm took pay cuts and thought themselves lucky.

☞ Don't try this at home: In a classic case of computer fraud, a bank programmer tried to use a rounding formula to his advantage. He had the fractional parts of pennies left over from interest calculations deposited to his own account, which grew rapidly to a substantial sum. The bank eventually caught on, and now the only numbers he's allowed to work with are on license plates.

Whether you're using Excel to balance your checkbook or the national budget (and in that effort we wish you well), the tips in this book should give you more confidence in your numbers.

How Not to Use This Book

The stuff in this book has been written to provide answers quickly and in plain English. You don't have to read it all, or in any particular order.

Most of the stuff that you really ought to know for getting started with Excel is in the first chapter. If you want, you can read that and learn the rest as you go, by trial and error. Just remember that the instructor for Trial and Error 101 is none other than the renowned Professor Murphy.

You'll find a Reader's Digest condensed version of the main points in the book in the *last* chapter (Chapter 15). If you're perplexed, but unsure of the cause (you don't know which topic to look up in the index), you might skim the tips in this chapter, then look up the cross-references to other chapters for more information.

Inside each chapter, I break up the material into small chunks. That's partly because I have a short attention span, and every now and then something strikes me as funny or weird or both, and I can't resist putting it in. But this way of organizing stuff also helps you find what you're looking for so you can get to the information you need fast.

Some chunks of text have little pictures in the margin beside them. These pictures help you determine whether you want to give that information any of your attention. Here's what the pictures mean:

This guy points you to informative advice that you should probably pay attention to. I might be pointing out an aggravation-preventing, Murphy-thwarting shortcut—or maybe I'm just covering myself against the dreaded Attack of the Propeller-Heads!

This frigid character marks optional stuff that I think is nifty, slick, clever, or otherwise Excel-lent. You might not agree, and that's okay.

Here's an alert that Murphy may be breathing down your neck. Usually there's a distinct possibility of screwing things up where you see this guy.

Ignore this stuff at your peril. Something majorly stupid may be in the offing, from which there might be no recovery without pain.

What little technical stuff there is in this book goes here. Usually you can ignore this stuff, unless, like me, you occasionally get off on that kind of thing.

Read this if you're having a Murphy-inspired Mac Attack. The examples in this book focus on Excel for Windows, but most of it applies just as well to Apple-crunchers. If there's something special about the Mac way of doing things, it's pointed out here. (Shorter Mac tips are buried in the main text between parentheses.)

You Can Skip This Stuff

If something gets really involved, I set it off in a clearly marked box so that you can read around it. If you're trying to find background information or exceptions to the rules, you should look in here.

Don't let any of this stuff throw you. To lighten things up, there's an occasional tip or observation from the ubiquitous Murphy.

> **Murphy's Law of Jargon:** If you don't understand a technical term, ignore it. The sentence will make perfect sense without it.

Care to Sing Along?

All of the explanations of procedures are presented as step-by-step examples. You don't have to do them on the computer yourself, since the important menus and screens are usually shown right in the book.

But you might find it amusing and instructive to follow along, reading the book as you fiddle with Excel. Since most of the screen displays that result from the steps are shown in the book, you can compare what you did and see that things work as advertised. (All of the screens were produced with the Windows version of Excel, but the Mac displays look much the same.)

By the way, anything that you have to type at the keyboard is shown in **bold** in this book. And I've used a kind of shorthand for certain keys on the keyboard. The Enter key (the Return key on the Macintosh) is represented by the ↵ symbol. The Control key is abbreviated Ctrl (both Mac and PC).

The Command key on the Macintosh is represented in this book by the ⌘ symbol.

There's also a special shorthand for sequences of menu selections. Instead of saying, "Select Open from the File menu," I'll just say, "Select File ➤ Open." Commands strung together with the ➤ symbol are always given in the order you choose them. Also, where appropriate, I mention alternative instructions for maestros of the keys who dislike or otherwise avoid mice.

In many cases, there are several ways of doing the same thing in Excel. The first time I discuss something, I'll show you either the quickest way or the way that's easiest to remember. Along the way, I point out shortcuts. In fact, there's a whole chapter on shortcuts (Chapter 9).

Sometimes, when there are several ways of doing something, and I've already covered the various options, I'll describe the procedure in a weasel-worded way that covers all the possibilities. For example, I'm fond of saying "select OK" instead of "click the OK button or press ⏎." In effect, what I'm saying is, do it any way that feels good.

If you are familiar with Excel 3.0 for the Macintosh, version 4.0 gives you some more choices for shortcut keys. In version 3.0, many shortcut key combinations use the ⌘ key (the Command key, also called the Apple key). For example, you could press ⌘-X instead of choosing Edit ➤ Cut and ⌘-V instead of Edit ➤ Paste.

In version 4.0, these shortcut key combinations still work. But, if you prefer, you can use the Control key instead of the ⌘ key. In this book, wherever you see a shortcut reference to the Ctrl key on the PC, you can generally use either the ⌘ key or the Control key on the Mac in the same combination. So, if you see Ctrl-Z, you can press either ⌘-Z or Control-Z on the Mac to do the same thing.

What Else Do You Need to Know?

I don't expect you to have any previous experience with Excel. But it would be a big help if the program were already installed on your computer.

If it's not, the short version of the installation procedure is to start Windows, put the first installation disk in drive A, select File ➤ Run in Program Manager, then type **a:setup** and select OK. The Setup program will do the rest, asking you to insert the other disks when it needs them. Follow the program's suggestions on options unless you have a good reason not to. If it gets more complicated than that, ask for help and don't call me.

To install Excel on the Mac, insert the first distribution diskette and then double-click on the Microsoft Excel Setup icon when it appears on the screen.

You only need to know the basics about Windows (or System 7 on the Mac) and how to run programs. You'll spare yourself some grief if you already know how to make your mouse work for you. Know how to click, drag, and double-click (although I explain dragging when you need to do it in the early chapters). You should also know how to select commands from pull-down menus and how to set options in dialog boxes, although much of this gets explained in specific examples along the merry way.

Talk Back!

I could not have written this book without a sincere and sober appreciation of Murphy's influence in my own work. If you think I could make something clearer (or more entertaining) or if I just plain screwed up, please write:

Gerald Jones
c/o SYBEX Inc.
2021 Challenger Drive
Alameda, CA 94501

I'll try to incorporate your suggestions, including particularly colorful Murphyisms, in the next edition of this book.

Uh-oh...Where's Murphy?

Okay, you'd better get going. I hear Murphy's had a head start!

PART 1

If you're pressed for time, have a look at Chapter 1, the short course in Excel miracles. Then, if you dare, you can learn the rest by trial and error. Just remember that the instructor for Trial and Error 101 is none other than the renowned Professor Murphy. Check out Chapter 2 if you're trying to digest your first formula. If you're having trouble finding your way around, there's help in Chapter 3.

A PEEK BENEATH THE SHEETS

Chapter 1

STUFF YOU GOTTA KNOW

Murphy's Advice: If you know how to calculate compound interest, they'll put you in charge of the dip at the office party.

THE IDEA OF this book is to give you a case of the warm fuzzies about Excel. Excel is a computer program that, among other things, can keep track of lots of numbers and do all kinds of math with them. It can do this even while you sleep or otherwise goof off. Think of Excel as your own personal math slave.

Excel does its thing beneath the sheets. *Sheet* is short for *worksheet*—like a sheet of paper. But don't worry about the work part. Think of that sheet as the homework you don't have to do— the stuff you hand to the marvelously subservient Excel to do for you.

Summon Your Math Slave

Let us not waste words. See for yourself. Here's a quick way to start Windows and Excel on a PC: After that C:> do-hickey on the computer screen, type

```
win excel
```

Excel will start, and soon you will be staring at a blank sheet. The program is ready to submit to your every command and fulfill your fondest wish (or at least do your math).

To get things started on the Mac, open the Excel folder, then double-click the Excel program icon.

Running Naked through
Streets and Alleys, Columns and Rows

Remember the playground game "Streets and Alleys?" Sheets are arranged with streets and alleys, or columns and rows. The streets—columns—go up and down. The alleys—rows—go across. (Just kidding about the naked part.)

Now this orderly arrangement is not just because some computer programmer got fussy about laying out the screen. It's a way of storing things so that you—and your programmed math slave—can find them again. And to help you figure out where you are, Excel provides a *cell pointer*, which moves around the worksheet as you move the mouse (Figure 1.1).

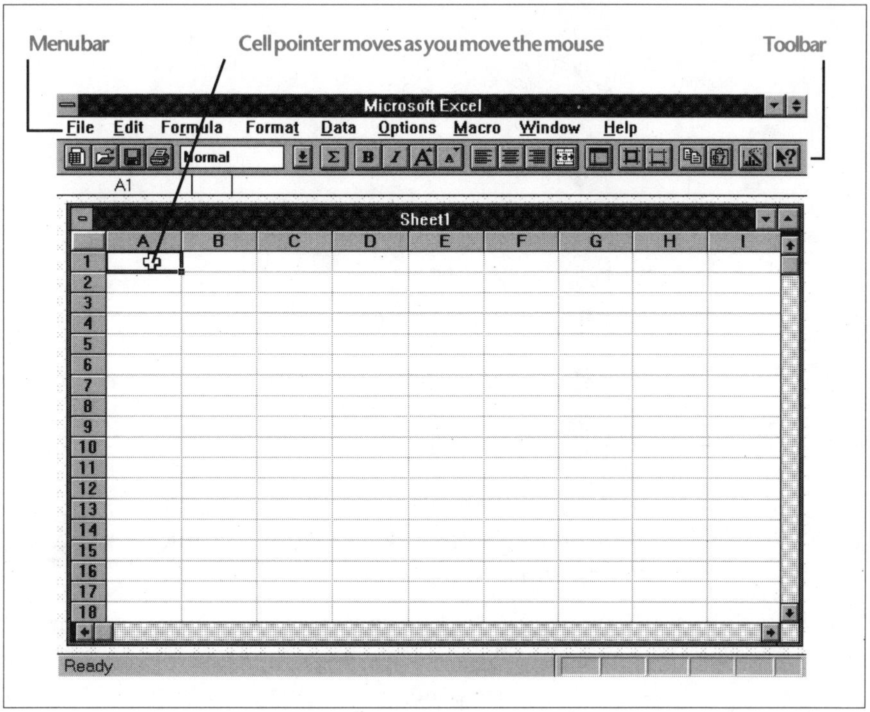

Figure 1.1:
A blank Excel worksheet. The line of icons above the sheet is called the *Toolbar*. The row of commands above the Toolbar is the *menu bar*.

I've Got the Number, I Need the Address

Columns are identified by letters, starting with A, across the top of the sheet:

Rows are identified by number, starting with 1 and running down the left side of the sheet:

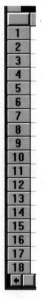

Notice in Figure 1.1 that the intersection of each street and each alley forms a little square. (Actually, I think it's a rectangle, but geometry wasn't my best subject.)

That little square is the dreaded *cell* you've heard about. Hey, relax. You don't have to live there. It's just a place to store your stuff. They should have called it a cubbyhole.

Each cell—every intersection of a street and an alley—has an *address*. The address of a cell is the letter of its column and the number of its row, the column always first. So the address of the top left cell in the sheet is A1.

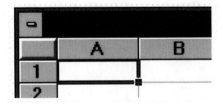

See the method to this madness? Each cell has its own address, and no two cells have the same address. If you tell Excel that you want the stuff you stored in cell D5, the program will know that you mean the little square at the intersection of column D and row 5.

Wrapping Your Stuff in a Sheet

The stuff that you store in a cell can be numbers, letters of the alphabet, a mixture of numbers and letters, or some of that math you want Excel to do for you. Each cell can only store *one piece* of stuff—one number value, for example. If I gave you $10 (and I'm not saying I will), you could record that amount in a cell.

Entering an Unfamiliar Cell

"How do you put a number into a cell?," you ask (or should ask, if you want to get with the program). To enter your stuff, you just

☞ Point

☞ Click

☞ Type

☞ Press ↵ (the Enter or Return key)

When the mouse pointer is inside the sheet, it becomes the cell pointer—a fat plus sign:

Move the pointer to cell B2 and click the mouse button. Now there's an outline around the cell (called the *cell highlight*), indicating that you've selected it to hold your stuff. Press the number keys **1** and then **0**.

When you press ↵, the number value shows up in the cell:

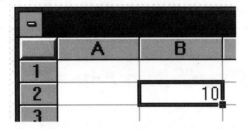

With my (okay, your) $10 in it, the little cell is all filled up. It can't hold any more. That's fine, because you want to be able to keep track of the different amounts you receive from me, and there are lots and lots of cells to store them in. So, if I gave you $20 more (I'd have to be out of my mind), you'd record that in a *different* cell.

To keep things nice and neat, you might enter your receipts in a column. So, click the next cell down (B3), type **20**, and press ↵:

Mouse Maniacs vs. Krazy Keyboardists

If you're a maestro of the keyboard, you will be happy to learn that rather than clicking your cell selection with the mouse you can move the cell highlight around the sheet by pressing the arrow keys: ← → ↑ ↓. You can do what you want. Mice don't have a union yet.

As I keep handing you money (assuming that I've lost all rational control of my actions), the cells in the column are going to fill up:

	A	B
1		
2		10
3		20
4		5
5		10
6		10
7		

The Sum of My Fears

At this point, I pause in my dizzy spending spree and I ask you, "How much have I given you so far?"

If you say, "I don't know. Let me get my calculator," return this book for a full refund. (Good luck.)

Before you head back to the bookstore, click the place where the answer would normally go—at the foot of the column—say, cell B8.

	A	B	
1			
2		10	
3		20	
4		5	
5		10	
6		10	
7			
8			
9			

Then, find this button in the Toolbar at the top of the screen (just below the word Data in the menu bar) and double-click it:

Σ

If you don't see the Toolbar, you (or somebody else who was playing with your computer) hid the thing. To display it again, select Options ➤ Toolbars. Make sure that the name Standard is highlighted in the Toolbars dialog box, then select the Show button. The standard set of tools should come out of hiding.

The button with the Greek letter sigma (Σ) is called the *AutoSum* tool, and it did just that: It <u>auto</u>matically <u>sum</u>med, or added, the numbers in the column above the cell you selected to hold the answer (see Figure 1.2).

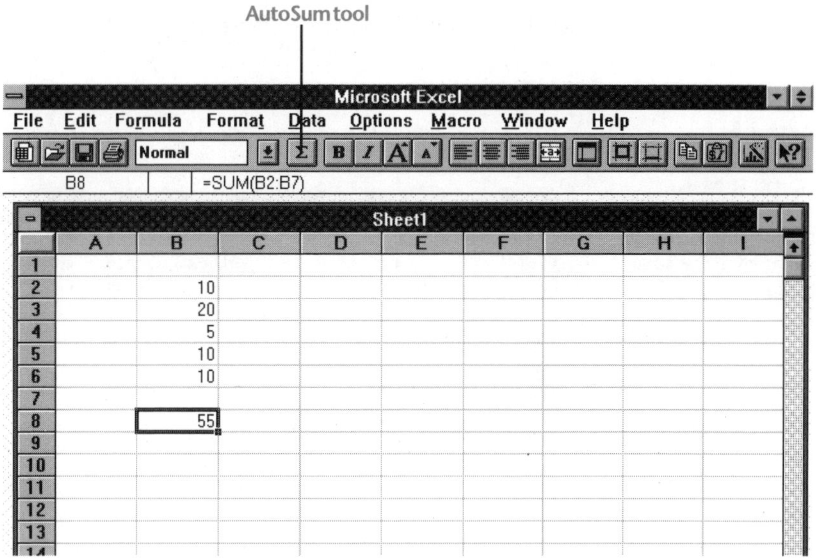

Figure 1.2:
You can add a column of numbers by selecting a cell at the bottom of the column and then double-clicking the AutoSum tool with your mouse.

Murphy's Rule of AutoSum

To generate a total, you can select a cell and *double-click* the AutoSum tool only if the selected cell is at the foot of a column or the end of a row and you want to include all the numbers in that column or row. In short, you can double-click AutoSum if you want the bottom line.

If the total is not at the bottom or at the side, click AutoSum *once*, then drag the moving dotted line around the group of cells you want summed. Next, press ↵ or click the Confirm (✓) button. There's more about this in Chapter 2.

There Must Be Some Mistake: Excel, Recalculate!

Wait a minute, pal. That third bill I handed you was a fifty—not a five. Better fix that, pronto.

Click cell B4. Type **50** and press ↵. Faster than you can say Microsoft, Excel has recalculated the total (Figure 1.3).

Figure 1.3:
When you change one of the entries in a summed column, Excel automatically recalculates the total for you.

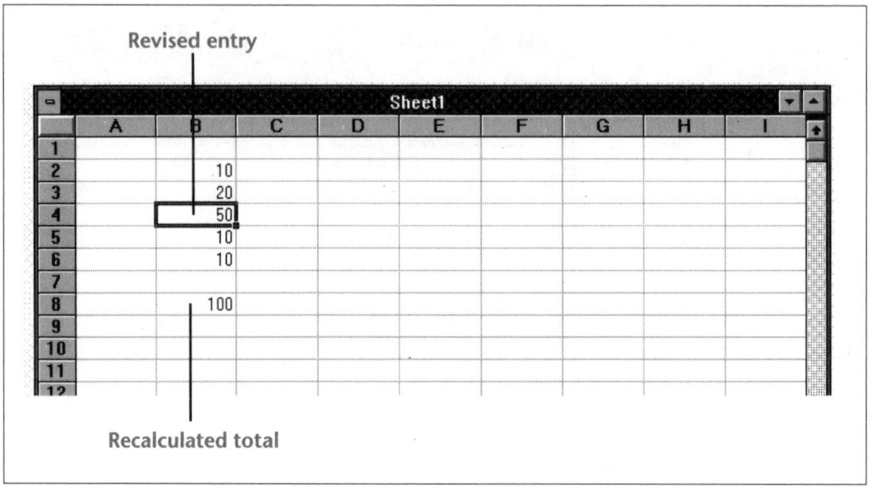

Revised entry

	A	B	C	D	E	F	G	H	I
1									
2		10							
3		20							
4		50							
5		10							
6		10							
7									
8		100							
9									
10									
11									
12									

Sheet1

Recalculated total

"Pret-ty nifty," you might say to yourself.

Ah, but that's just the beginning.

I've Got the Data, Now Give Me Information

In the jargon of computer hackers, the stuff you put in cells is *data*—one *data item*, or piece of data, in each cell. Data is not the same as *information*. A single data item has no meaning by itself. Information tells you something useful, for example

"How much do you owe me?"

Here's an illustration. It was shown to me in my youth in a back alley by an old computer programmer who didn't know any better.

This is data: 362436
This is information: 36-24-36

The total that Excel produced when you clicked the AutoSum tool is useful information when it appears along with the column of numbers it sums. That's the purpose of Excel—to generate information from the data you provide.

My Apology to the Citizens of Rome

The word "data" is the plural of the Latin *datum*, meaning "fact." So it would be perfectly correct to say, "The data are in Harvard Yard." However, even careful lexicographers admit that data can be a collective noun (referring to a group of more than one *datum*), in which case it would still be impeccable usage to say, "I went to Georgia Tech, and the data is wherever I say it is." In this book, I follow the crowd in saying "data is," but I will defend not quite to the death your right to say it either way.

Look at the Label, Mabel

Data can be letters as well as numbers. In Excel a group of letters in a cell is called a *label* because that's what such letters are typically used

Labels Aren't Just for Letters Anymore!

A label can include both letters and numbers, as in TOTAL1. For example, a label could be used for a model number— which might include special characters—such as SPEEDO-101. Number entries, or numeric data, cannot include any letters or special characters, except for

```
currency symbols ($100)
commas separating thousands (1,000,000)
leading plus or minus signs (+ or – in front of the
number)
decimal points (100.00), slashes (/), or hyphens (–)
month names in formatted dates (20-Jan)
in dates (1/2/99 or 1-2-99)
percent signs (%) after percentages
scientific notation (1E+08 in Excel-speak means $1.0 \times 10^8$)
```

for—to label the numeric entries in a sheet. (Another term for label is *text*. A good working definition of text is any entry that is the name of something, rather than an amount or a math problem.)

Remember when I was giving you all that money? Let's say I was giving you one payment per day. Perhaps you'd like to keep track of how much I give you each day, so that you could answer annoying questions like

```
"How much did I give you on Tuesday?"
```

You can add labels to the worksheet for the days of the week. And there's a *really* slick way to do it. Click cell A2. Type **Monday** and press ↵. The label Monday appears at the left edge of the cell:

Now here's the slick part. Move the pointer to the bottom right corner of the cell highlight. When the pointer is positioned over the small square in that corner, it will change to a solid plus sign:

With the pointer shaped like a solid plus sign, *drag* the right corner of the cell down to A6.

Basic Excel

How to Drag Your Mouse

It's not cruel and it can be fun: Grab the little critter and move it to the starting point. Press its button (on a PC, use the left mouse button) and *keep holding it down* as you move the mouse in a little race to the finish line. When you're there, let go of the button. (Dragging always involves movement from one location on the screen to another.)

Excel <u>auto</u>matically <u>fill</u>ed the cells you selected (by dragging over them) with the days of the week (see Figure 1.4). So some jargon-happy programmer has named this feature *AutoFill*, no doubt after its kissing cousin AutoSum.

Figure 1.4:
When you drag your mouse from the lower-right corner (fill handle) of the cell labeled *Monday* (A2) to the lower-right corner of A6, Excel fills in the other days of the week automatically.

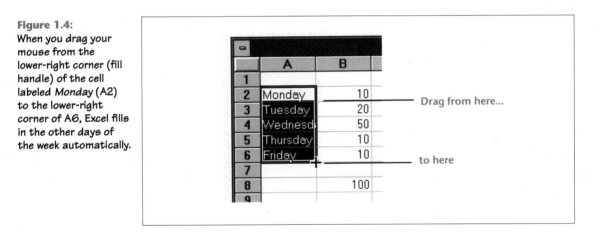

The small square in the bottom right corner of the cell highlight is called the **fill handle**. *Drag the fill handle away from the cell to copy its contents into adjacent cells (perhaps incrementing values in a series, as shown in the example). Or, drag the fill handle back up through the cell to clear (erase) its contents.*

Like other dandy inventions, such as Ginsu knives and Tupperware, the amazing new AutoFill has a thousand and one uses. Turn to Chapter 2 if you can't wait to find out what they are.

Narrow Cells Too Confining?

In the example shown here, the label Wednesday is too long. It won't all fit into cell A4. (Remember Wednesday in *The Addams Family*? She was a pain sometimes, too.) Rest assured that all of her is in there somewhere—you just can't see some of the letters because they *overflow* the cell. Here's a quick way to shove Wednesday into that cell and slam the door.

Move the pointer up to the right boundary in the column heading (the right edge of the column that's too narrow). The pointer will change into a vertical bar with a double arrow. Double-click and Excel will adjust the width of the column to accommodate the longest entry, as shown in Figure 1.5.

Figure 1.5:
When you move the mouse pointer to the right boundary of the column heading, the pointer changes into a double arrow. When you double-click, Excel adjusts the column width automatically so all the entries in the column will fit.

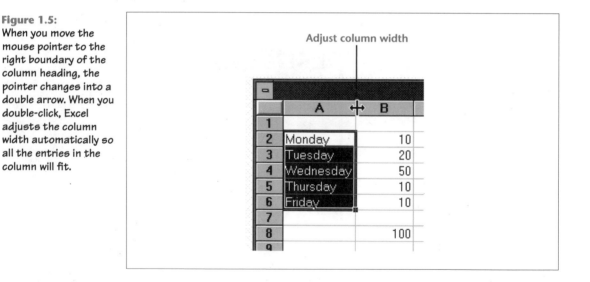

When the pointer has this double-arrow shape, you can also drag the column to any desired width. And you can adjust the height of a row by dragging the boundary below the row number (see Figure 1.6).

Figure 1.6:
You can adjust row height by dragging the double-arrow pointer up or down between the row numbers.

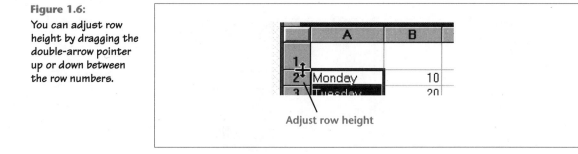

Adjust row height

Basic Excel

You Gotta Have Style

The numbers in the sheet look kind of naked. It would be nice to dress them up. For one thing, I'm worried that the numbers by themselves don't mean much. One hundred what? Since the value of the ruble isn't too stable these days, I'd like to make it clear that my generous contributions were in dollars.

Picking and Choosing

One of Murphy's Laws states that to do anything, you must do something else first. In Excel, you must *select* a thing before you can change it. Select a cell and its contents by clicking it. Select a column, a row, or several columns or rows by dragging the cell highlight from one corner of your selection to the other. And always select your underwear before you put on your pants.

To select the column of numbers in the sample sheet, drag the cell pointer (the fat plus sign) from cell B2 to cell B8, as shown in Figure 1.7.

Now, directly above the selected column, click the arrow button in the Toolbar (just beneath the word Format in the menu bar on the PC, or Formula on the Mac). This button activates the Style Box, which contains a list of *styles*, which control *number formats* (see Figure 1.8). From the list that drops down, click Currency.

Figure 1.7:
Drag the cell pointer from cell B2 to cell B8 to select the column of numbers.

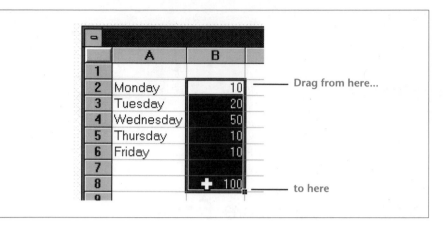

Drag from here...

to here

Figure 1.8:
After selecting the column of numbers, click the arrow button to open the Style Box (click and hold on the Mac). Then choose Currency from the drop-down list that appears.

Click here to open Style Box

File   Edit   Fo**r**mula   Format   Data

Currency

B2

Comma
Comma [0]
Currency
Currency [0]
Normal
Percent

	A	
1		
2	Monday	
3	Tuesday	
4	Wednesday	$50.00
5	Thursday	$10.00
6	Friday	$10.00
7		
8		$100.00

A number format *is an option that controls the display of numeric data on the screen and in printouts. A* style *includes preselected number formats, as well as other options that control appeerance, such as text font and color. There's more about this in Chapter 6.*

The numbers in the sheet are now shown in dollars and cents:

Dress It Up Some More

While we're on the subject of appearance, this sheet could use a couple of additional labels. Click cell A8, type **Total**, and press ↵. Click cell A1, type **How Much Do I Owe Gerald?**, and press ↵. (I never said it was a gift!)

	A	B	C	
1	How Much Do I Owe Gerald?			
2	Monday	$10.00		
3	Tuesday	$20.00		
4	Wednesday	$50.00		
5	Thursday	$10.00		
6	Friday	$10.00		
7				
8	Total	$100.00		
9				

The result is informative, but still rather plain. You can fix that. Drag the cell pointer from cell A1 to cell B8, highlighting the sheet that you've built. Then click this button:

Clicking the button <u>auto</u>matically <u>format</u>ted the selection, or dressed up its appearance. You guessed it: Meet AutoFormat, yet another member of the infamous Auto family.

The result is an improvement, but the text is all bunched up. To fix this, drag the right edge of column B about two column widths to the right, as shown in Figure 1.9.

Figure 1.9:

Drag the right edge of column B farther to the right to widen the column.

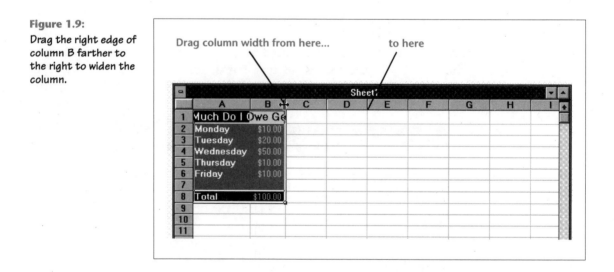

Get It on Paper!

While the formatted sheet is still selected (shown in reverse video), you can print it out so that we have a record of my contributions to your

Basic Excel

welfare. Make sure your printer is connected and switched on, then click the printer button:

To release the selection so that you can see it in normal colors on the screen, click anywhere outside the selected block of cells (see Figure 1.10).

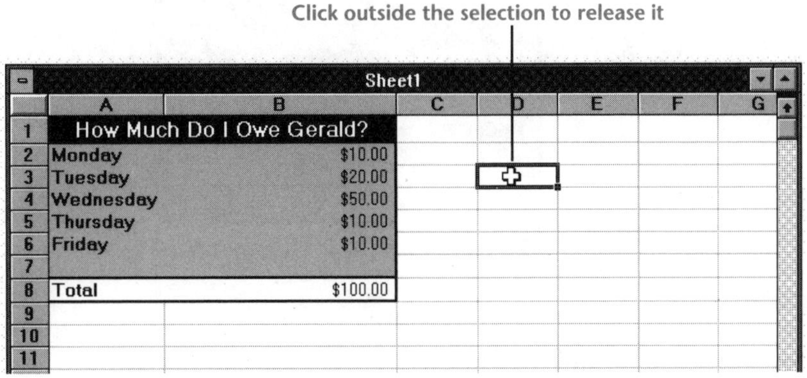

Figure 1.10:
To release you
selection, click
anywhere outside the
highlighted cells.

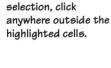

Click outside the selection to release it

The AutoFormat tool applies the last format you used. If you haven't tried format-ting yet, Excel will pick a format for you. This means that your result might not look the same as the example shown in Figure 1.10.

Clearing Your Obligations

I realize that I may have put you in an awkward position, financially speaking, and I would like to make amends. I take it all back.

Drag the cell pointer from B2 to B6, highlighting all of the money contributions. Move the pointer to the bottom right corner of cell B6 (the fill handle). The pointer should change to a solid plus sign. Now drag the plus sign up—back over the entries, from bottom to top, as if wiping the slate clean (see Figure 1.11).

Figure 1.11:
To remove the entries in column B, highlight the entries, move the pointer to the bottom right corner so that it changes to a solid plus sign, then drag the pointer up through the top entry.

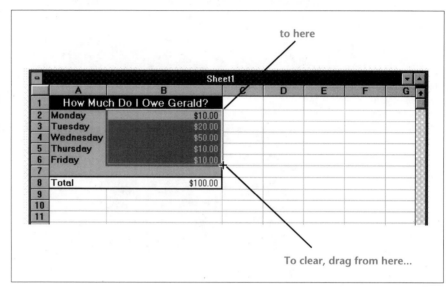

to here

To clear, drag from here...

Money, what money? The number values were *cleared*, or erased. The formatting remains, however. If I started giving you money again (watch out!), you could reuse this sheet rather than starting from scratch. Excel will even calculate the total without any further work on your part as long as you don't also erase the stuff that's in B8).

Never Trust Me If I Say Undo!

I'm fickle, I admit it. Choose Edit in the menu bar, then select Undo Clear (see Figure 1.12). There's my money again. Or is it yours?

Basic Excel

Figure 1.12:
The Edit menu. The pointer is over the Undo command, which will cancel the last thing you did (Clear, in this case).

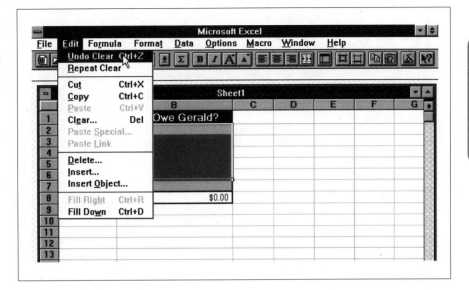

Save It—It Will Keep

Frankly, my head is spinning. Perhaps we could put off this discussion to a more mutually convenient time? But I hate for you to lose this valuable work, which, after all, has become the focus of a promising relationship.

To save this exemplary record of my cash outlay, click the button with a disk symbol on it:

When the Save As dialog box appears, click its OK button (Save on the Mac). Your work will be saved with the uninspiring file name SHEET1 (WORKSHEET1 on the Mac). (This is handy for people like me who would otherwise waste valuable playtime trying to come up with some clever name.)

Murphy Has the Last Word

In its eccentric way, this chapter has covered most of the tools and techniques you need to be productive with Excel right out of the box, as they say in Battle Creek. So go ahead. Flog your new math slave mercilessly. If you encounter something that strikes you as odd, or if you want to get really kinky with Excel, you might profitably consult the chapters that follow. Just remember—

Murphy's Extrasensory Perception: Those who can *do*. Those who can't *teach*. Those who write computer books must come from another planet.

Chapter 2

WHAT TO DO WHEN THINGS JUST DON'T ADD UP

Murphy's Complaint: Machines should work. People should think. Why is my life the other way around?

IN THIS CHAPTER you'll get acquainted with formulas. A *formula* is a math problem that you want Excel—your ever-helpful computer math slave—to solve.

Much of this chapter is about formulas in general—setting them up and getting them to work right. If you know this stuff already and you're itching to do serious math, you might skim this chapter and charge ahead to Chapter 4.

> ### Coming to Terms with Excel
>
> This chapter is sprinkled with definitions of Excel terminology that can be useful to you not only in reading this book, but also in consulting Excel's Help system.
>
> To access online help while using Excel, press F1 (% on the Mac). The program will display information on the task you're trying to do. You can click on any term that is highlighted in Excel's online help, and its definition will appear.

Don't Assume with AutoSum

Chapter 1 introduced the marvelous AutoSum tool, which provides a truly slick way to total a series of numbers—literally at the click of a button:

Σ

You just click the cell that will hold the answer and double-click this button. Right? Not necessarily. AutoSum generates a formula for the addition, and in some circumstances that formula may be incorrect if you blindly double-click.

You've probably heard the time-honored saying that sales managers are fond of repeating to trainees: "What does *assume* mean? It means making an ASS out of U and ME!" Translation: Don't assume. Double-check and get the facts.

Don't assume that using the AutoSum tool—or entering any other type of formula—will always give you a correct result. To determine whether AutoSum has produced a correct total, you have to know something about the formula it sneakily generates when you're not looking.

Look again at the sheet that recaps my cash disbursements to you (Figure 1.10). (Chapters in this book are like those envelopes from Ed McMahon: There could be money inside!) Start Excel. Click the File menu and then select the name of the sheet: SHEET1 (WORKSHEET1 on the Mac). (This file name should appear at the bottom of the menu among the sheets you used most recently. If the sheet isn't listed at the bottom of the File menu, select Open instead and double-click the file name.) When the sheet opens, click the cell that holds the total (B8).

Notice that the notation B8 appears in a box just above the sheet and to the left. This is the *cell reference box*, which shows the address of the currently selected cell (see Figure 2.1).

To the right of the cell reference box is the *formula bar*. It shows the contents of the cell you have selected. Right now, the resident of cell B8 looks suspiciously like math:

=SUM(B2:B7)

This is a formula. And, yes, it's math. But remember this is math *you* don't have to do. Excel will do the work—you just have to ask it nicely.

Figure 2.1:
The sample worksheet from Chapter 1 with cell B8 selected. The address of the selected cell appears in the cell reference box, and the contents of the selected cell are displayed in the formula bar.

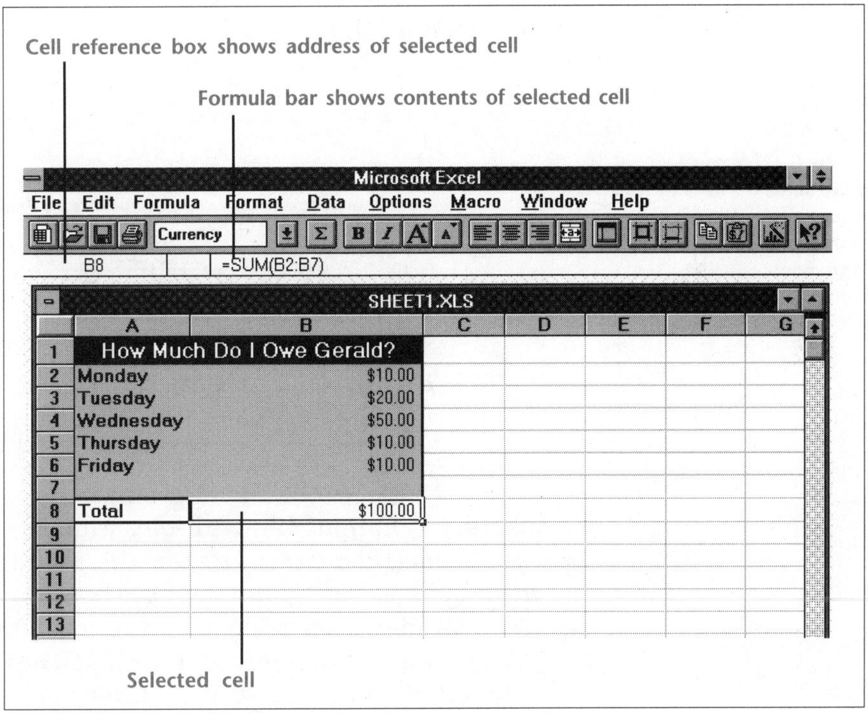

Cell reference box shows address of selected cell

Formula bar shows contents of selected cell

Selected cell

The **formula bar** *shows the stuff that's stored in the last cell you clicked. This can be a number, a label, or a math problem (a formula). (They may call it a "formula bar," but it's not just for formulas anymore.)*

When you want Excel to do something, you must ask nicely—Excel is very picky about syntax. *Syntax* is a specific way of writing something, or in this case, a precise way of entering formulas into cells. Why is syntax so important? You can expect the right answer only if you ask the right question.

Be Picky about Formulas and Excel Will Do Your Bidding

A formula in Excel is usually concocted of three nutritious ingredients. These are illustrated in Figure 2.2.

Figure 2.2:

Some Excel formulas have three parts: an equal sign, a function name, and an argument.

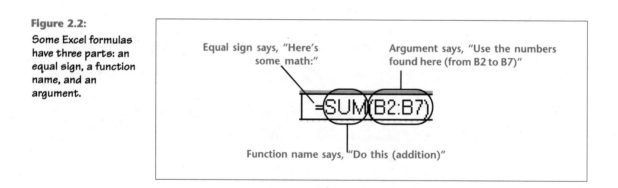

Equal sign says, "Here's some math:"

Argument says, "Use the numbers found here (from B2 to B7)"

=SUM(B2:B7)

Function name says, "Do this (addition)"

Equal sign   A formula always begins with an equal sign (=). It tells Excel in no uncertain terms, "Hey, do this math!" Those of you who are entering Excel from Lotusland have been trained to use the "at" sign (@) instead. Now, here's one thing about which Excel is not picky, but downright accommodating. If you enter @ to begin a formula, Excel will translate it automatically to =. It's just another way Excel eats Lotus for lunch. (Lotus programs chomp back, however, by translating = to @.)

Function name   A function name—SUM, in this case—is short-hand for a more complicated formula that Excel already knows how to do. This chapter covers SUM, which adds a series of numbers, and AVERAGE, which averages a series of numbers. Many more functions can be found in Chapters 4 and 5, where gourmet number crunchers can browse among a wide variety of tasty, ready-to-eat functions. (Excel is pickier about function names than it is about = and @. It likes the ones that are the same in Lotus—such as SUM—but it spits out the ones that are different—such as AVG instead of AVERAGE. Although Excel will translate functions when reading Lotus worksheets, you'll have trouble if you try to enter Lotus functions directly into an Excel sheet.)

Argument   The stuff enclosed in parentheses is called an *argument*. (Don't ask me why; apparently mathematicians are a contrary lot.) With functions such as SUM and AVERAGE, the arguments describe a group, or *range*, of cell values. (Read on for more about ranges.) In general, an argument gives Excel some numbers to chew on, or at least tells Excel where to find numbers to feed the hungry function. Some functions don't have arguments (more about this shortly).

A formula is a cell entry that says to Excel, "Here's math (=). Do this (function name) with that (argument specifying the data)." (Not all formulas have function names—just the lucky ones.)

In the example, AutoSum generated the formula

=SUM(B2:B7)

This strange conglomeration of signs and symbols simply means, "Sum the numbers in the range from cell B2 through and including B7." Excel does the work and puts the answer in the cell that contains the formula—B8, in this case.

Exploring the Open Range

The argument in the example above is the range B2:B7. When you specify a range, you are selecting the contents of its cells. The colon (:) means "and all cells through and including."

Yet Another Accommodation to Lotus Lovers

Excel will politely translate the .. syntax used in Lotus range definitions to the : it requires. So Lotus users can enter B2..B7 as compelled by force of habit, and Excel will translate the entry to B2:B7.

To summarize, *a range* is a rectangular block of cells defined by its first cell and its last cell. The first cell is in the upper-left corner of the range and the last cell is in the lower-right corner of the range. (You can specify any two opposite corners, but Excel will translate your entry to show the first and last cells—in that order.) Figure 2.3 shows the range B2:D4.

Figure 2.3:
The range B2:D4 is selected.

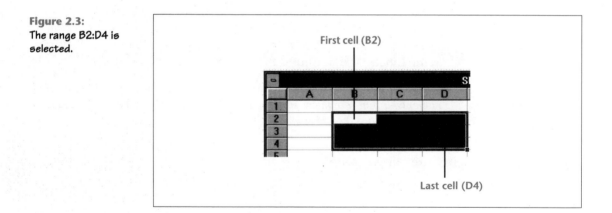

A range can also be a single column or row. In a column, the first cell is at the top and the last cell is at the bottom of the range, as it is in the AutoSum example. In a row, the first cell is at the left end and the last cell is at the right end of the range. Figure 2.4 shows the range B2:D2.

Figure 2.4:
The range B2:D2

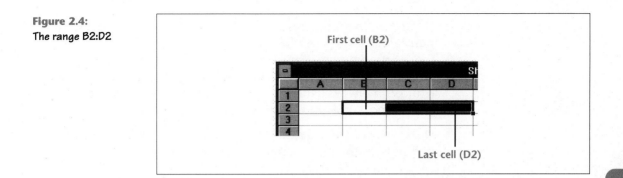

Beware the Hidden Formula!

Formulas in a sheet are usually hidden. In a cell containing a formula, Excel displays the *result* of the formula instead of the formula itself. However, the formula will appear above the sheet in the formula bar whenever you select (click) the cell that contains it. Think about what this means: By glancing at a sheet, *you can't tell which cells contain formulas!* Which numbers can you trust? Be guided by Murphy's First Law of Worksheets:

Murphy's First Law of Worksheets: In any sheet, the thing that you're positive is correct isn't.

Checking Up on Formulas

One way to tell whether a calculated answer is correct is to inspect the formula that produced it. It would be elementary, my dear Watson, to put the following questions:

☞ Does the formula begin with an equal sign? (All formulas generated by AutoSum will have this, but you want to be thorough.)

☞ Is the function name correct? (If you entered a correct function name, Excel will capitalize all its letters. If Excel doesn't capitalize the function name, it hasn't accepted the function.) Also, does it describe the result I want? Did I use the right function for the job? (AutoSum always generates SUM, so you'd be way off base if you were using AutoSum when you wanted an average.)

☞ Does the specified range contain the correct set of data? (This question may be the most important one with AutoSum.)

In the example, the range of numbers to be added extends from B2 to B7, which seems to be correct. However, AutoSum does not always pick the range so intelligently. In the next section, you'll learn how to avoid problems with AutoSum.

A Conservative's Guide to AutoSum

I confess that when I showed you how to use AutoSum in Chapter 1, I used a cheap, sleazy shortcut—namely, *double-clicking* on the tool. This is speedy and works fine—most of the time.

Murphy's Rule of AutoSum: *To generate a total, you can select a cell and double-click the AutoSum tool only if the selected cell is at the foot of a column or end of a row and you want to add all the numbers in that column or row.*

There's a more conservative approach to using AutoSum in which you select the range to be summed. In SHEET1 (WORKSHEET1 on the Mac), click cell B8 to select it. Then click the AutoSum tool just *once*. If Excel can find a column or row of numbers above or to the left of the selected cell, it will highlight the column or row with a moving dotted line, as shown in Figure 2.5. (The gang at Microsoft calls this "the crawling ants.")

You can drag the industrious little ants anywhere on the screen to define the range you want Excel to sum. The cell addresses in the formula (shown in the formula bar) will change as you drag the highlight.

When the crawling ants encircle the range you want, press ↵ to accept the formula or click the Confirm (✓) button just to the left of the formula

Figure 2.5:
The moving dotted line indicates the range to be summed.

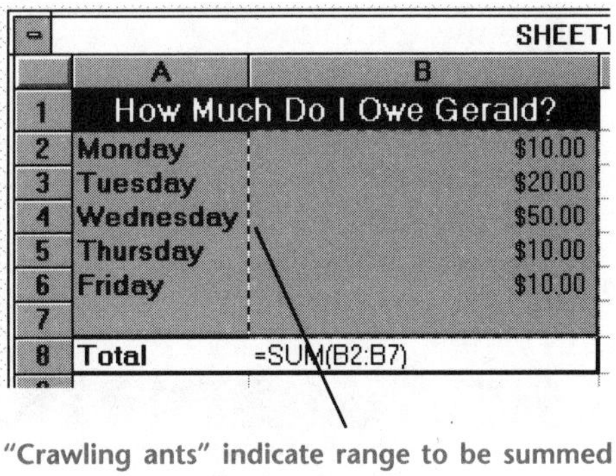

	A	B
1	How Much Do I Owe Gerald?	
2	Monday	$10.00
3	Tuesday	$20.00
4	Wednesday	$50.00
5	Thursday	$10.00
6	Friday	$10.00
7		
8	Total	=SUM(B2:B7)

SHEET1

"Crawling ants" indicate range to be summed

bar. To abort the operation—and reject the formula—click the Cancel (X) button:

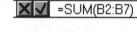

=SUM(B2:B7)

The two buttons to the left of the formula bar reject or accept the formula bar entry. Clicking Cancel (X) is the same as pressing Esc on the keyboard. Clicking Confirm (✓) is the same as pressing ↵.

Entering an Average Formula

As an example of a formula you type yourself, consider the scores of four people who bowled three games:

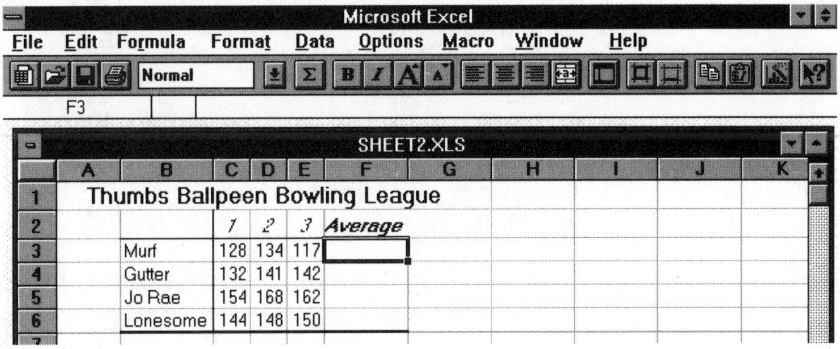

	Microsoft Excel										
File	Edit	Formula	Format	Data	Options	Macro	Window	Help			

Normal   Σ   B   I   A   A   ≡ ≡ ≡ ≡   □ □ □   ▣ ▣ ▣ ▨?

F3

SHEET2.XLS

	A	B	C	D	E	F	G	H	I	J	K
1	Thumbs Ballpeen Bowling League										
2			*1*	*2*	*3*	*Average*					
3		Murf	128	134	117						
4		Gutter	132	141	142						
5		Jo Rae	154	168	162						
6		Lonesome	144	148	150						
7											

To get the average for Murf's three games, you would click cell F3 and type this formula:

    =AVERAGE(C3:E3)

As you begin to type, your entry appears in the formula bar. (You can type formulas in either lowercase or uppercase letters—Excel doesn't care.) When you press ↵ or click ✓, the calculated average appears in the selected cell:

—						Microsoft Excel
File	**Edit**	**Formula**	**Format**	**Data**	**Options**	**Maci**
🖩 📂 🖫 🖨	Normal		↧ Σ	B	I	A⁺ A⁻ ☰
	F3			=AVERAGE(C3:E3)		

						SHEET2.XLS
	A	B	C	D	E	F	G
1	Thumbs Ballpeen Bowling League						
2			1	2	3	*Average*	
3		Murf	128	134	117	126.3333	
4		Gutter	132	141	142		
5		Jo Rae	154	168	162		
6		Lonesome	144	148	150		
7							

Chewing on the Formula Bar

Recall that the contents of a cell appear in the formula bar whenever you select the cell. There are several techniques you can use to edit the stuff in the formula bar:

☞ To insert a character into the stuff in the formula bar, click the exact insert location in the text or number you want to edit. A flashing vertical line will appear. Type the character(s) to be inserted, then press ↵ or click ✓.

☞ Drag across a group of characters that you want to replace. In the formula bar, the pointer becomes an I-beam-shaped cursor. Click the mouse button and hold it down as you drag the I-beam across a group of letters. The letters will become highlighted. Type the re-placement characters, then press ↵ or click ✓.

☞ Press Del to delete the character to the right of the insertion point. Press Backspace to delete the character to the left. Press either Del or Backspace to delete highlighted characters.

There's no Backspace key on the Mac. The Delete key removes the character to the left of the insertion point.

For example, suppose that an erstwhile Lotus user typed AVG in the for-mula bar instead of AVERAGE. To edit the formula name, drag the I-beam cursor over the letter G in the formula bar:

X ✓ =AVG(C3:E3)

Then type the replacement characters **ERAGE** and press ↵ or click ✓.

Another Use of the Amazing AutoFill

Recall from Chapter 1 that the little square in the lower-right corner of the cell highlight is called the *fill handle*. It's a mighty useful device. When you move the pointer to it, the pointer changes to a solid plus sign. Then, if you drag the handle into an adjacent cell (or cells), the contents of the first cell will be copied into the other cell(s).

This AutoFill feature can involve *automatic incrementing* of values as well as copying. This is demonstrated in Chapter 1. With the text *Monday* in the first cell, you can drag the fill handle to increment the copies in the adjacent cells. These adjacent cells become *Tuesday*, *Wednesday*, *Thursday*, and *Friday*.

Now let's return to the bowling scores example. Suppose you want to copy the Average formula so that Excel will calculate the average scores for the other bowlers. Drag the fill handle from cell F3 down to cell F6, as shown in Figure 2.6.

Here AutoFill increments the cell addresses in the formula so that each copy refers to the correct row. For example, if you click cell F6 and look

Basic Formulas

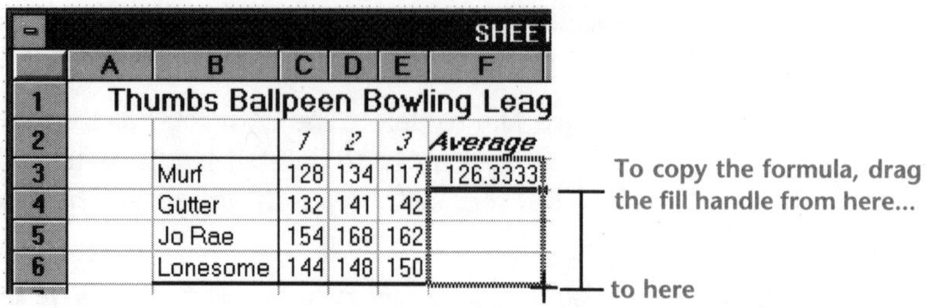

Figure 2.6:
Drag the fill handle down the column and Excel will copy the formula to the adjacent cells, automatically incrementing the cell addresses.

	A	B	C	D	E	F
1		Thumbs Ballpeen Bowling Leag				
2			*1*	*2*	*3*	*Average*
3		Murf	128	134	117	126.3333
4		Gutter	132	141	142	
5		Jo Rae	154	168	162	
6		Lonesome	144	148	150	

To copy the formula, drag the fill handle from here...

to here

in the formula bar, you will see that the copied formula has been adjusted to

    =AVERAGE(C6:E6)

The range C3:E3 in the original formula (which referred to Murf's scores) has been adjusted to refer to Lonesome's scores.

Murphy's Guide to AutoFill

To recap, when using AutoFill, if the first cell contains a date or a formula, it will be incremented as it is copied. If it contains a numeric value or text, it will simply be copied.

AutoFill will increment numeric values as well if your initial selection contains *two* values. The copies will be increased or decreased each time by the difference between these two values. If the value in the first cell is greater than the value in the second cell, the value of each copy will be decreased. If the value in the first cell is less than the value in the second cell, the value of each copy will be increased.

Here's how it works: Select two adjacent cells that contain values and drag the fill handle into the next column or row. The copies will be incremented by the difference between the two values. For example, if the first two values in a row were 2 and 4, you could select them and drag the fill handle to the right to fill the rest of the row with 6, 8, 10, 12, 14, 16, and so on to the end of the dragged range (see Figure 2.7).

Figure 2.7:

To use AutoFill, select two adjacent cells containing numeric values, then drag the fill handle to the right.

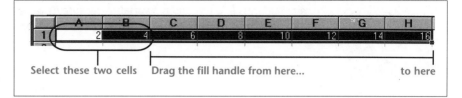

Select these two cells   Drag the fill handle from here...   to here

Some Very Useful Formulas Have No Function at All

There is no law of Excel that says a formula must include a function name. Functions are just shorthand for longer formulas. You can type a formula that does arithmetic, using the following symbols for each type of operation:

```
+     Addition
−     Subtraction
*     Multiplication
/     Division
m^n   Exponentiation (raise the value m to the nth
      power; 2^3 = 2³)
```

So, instead of =SUM(B2:B7), a keyboard maestro who forgot about the SUM function might have typed

```
=B2+B3+B4+B5+B6+B7
```

His Love Isn't Constant, but Her Number Is

A cell address (such as B2) in a formula refers to the stuff stored in that cell. You can also include specific number values in formulas, such as

```
=B2+1
```

This formula would add the constant 1 to the value in cell B2 and put the result in the cell that holds the formula.

*A cell address in a formula is a **variable** because its value will change if the contents of the cell change. An actual number value in a formula is a **constant**.*

Decimals and Fractions for the Half-Hearted

It's okay to use decimal values and fractions as constants in formulas. For example, there is no symbol in Excel for the arithmetic operation of extracting roots, but you can do this with an exponent that's a fraction. For example, taking the square root of 64 is the same as raising it to the power $1/2$. You will get the correct answer (8) if you enter

```
=64^0.5
```

Notice that the decimal in this formula is less than 1. You could enter it as .5 instead of 0.5, but preceding the decimal point with a 0 makes the formula easier for us humans to read. (Excel will add the 0 if you don't.)

Attempting the same thing using a fraction for the exponent seems to produce an incorrect result:

```
=64^1/2
```

This formula results in 32 instead of 8! The reason is that Excel prefers to do some kinds of arithmetic before it goes on to do other kinds—rather like always eating your green beans before getting dessert. In this case, Excel looks at the exponent first, then does the division, as though the formula said, "64^1 divided by 2."

Just as in algebra (sorry to bring it up), in Excel you can change the order of operations, the order of evaluation, or both by using parentheses to enclose anything that you want Excel to do first. You could get the right answer in the fractional exponent example by changing the formula to

```
=64^(1/2)
```

This formula says, "Divide 1 by 2, then raise 64 to that power."

This Order of Operations Doesn't Come from the Pentagon

The order in which Excel does different kinds of arithmetic is called the *order of operations*:

```
+ or -    Evaluating signed constants
^         Exponentiation (raising to powers or extracting
          roots)
*         Multiplication
/         Division
+         Addition
-         Subtraction
```

If there are two or more operations of the same kind in a formula, Excel will do them in left-to-right order. This is called the *order of evaluation*.

A Few More Parenthetical Remarks

Parentheses are like love birds: You have to pick them in pairs. Use as many as you want in one formula—one pair *nested* within another—but you'll really screw things up if you use one without the other! For example, you could nest the little love birds as follows:

```
=((B2+B3)*3)/2
```

The stuff within the innermost pair of parentheses will be done first, and so on proceeding outward. So the formula above says, "Add the value at B2 to the value at B3. Multiply that by 3. Then divide that by 2."

When you type a formula in the formula bar, Excel will thank you by flashing, or highlighting, any correctly matched pair of parentheses. If you omit one of the critters and then press ↵ or click ✓ to accept the formula, Excel will brusquely reject it with the warning "Error in formula" or "Parentheses do not match."

Name That Range and It's Yours Forever

The open range can be a scary place, until you give it a name and move right in. Range references like B2:B7 tend to clutter up your formulas. The cell addresses themselves don't tell you anything about the values they hold unless you look back at the sheet.

Excel has a much handier way of referring to ranges—you give them names. Of course, this is especially handy if the name you pick describes the stuff that's stored there. But Excel can make this easy by automatically picking up nearby labels as range names.

Here's how it works: In the bowling example, select the range C3:E3. These are Murf's game scores. Select Formula from the menu bar, then select Define Name (see Figure 2.8).

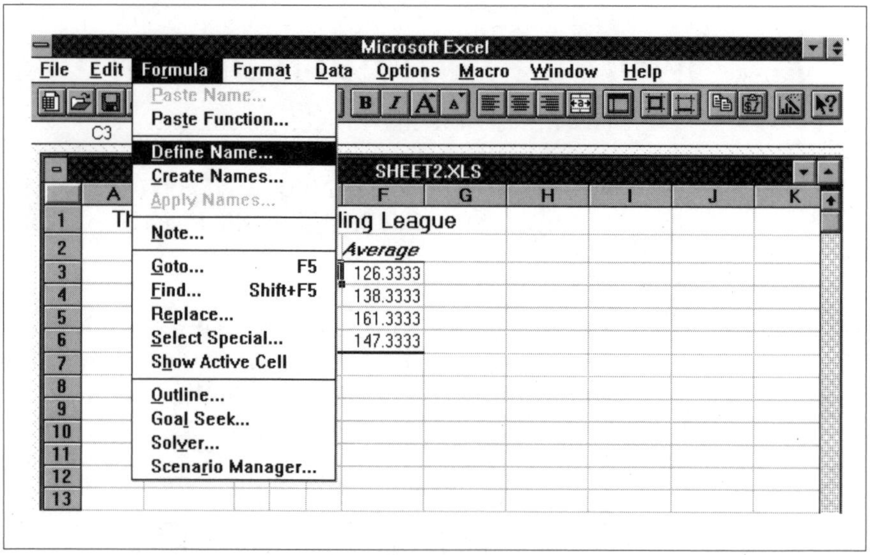

Figure 2.8:

The Formula menu with Define Name highlighted

The Define Name dialog box will open. Excel, in its helpfulness, has already proposed the nearby label—Murf—as a name for the range. It has also picked up the correct range reference, C3:E3.

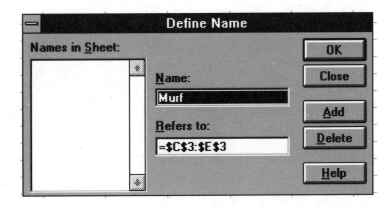

Basic Formulas

Ignore the $—Unless There's Money Involved

The range reference in the example is shown as $C$3:$E$3. The dollar signs just mean that the cell references will stay where you put them and will not be readjusted later by the program. Irresponsible as it may sound, you can ignore the dollar signs—at least in this case.

When you select OK to close the Define Name dialog box, the label Murf will be added to the range names in the sheet, and the name will appear in the cell reference box when you select the range.

Once you've assigned a range name, you can use that range name in formulas. For example, to get the average in cell F3, instead of

```
=AVERAGE(C3:E3)
```

you could enter

```
=AVERAGE(MURF)
```

Excel doesn't much care whether you use specific addresses or range names. But naming those ranges gives you a real advantage: When you go back to check your results, you'll more easily remember how you built the sheet—even long after you've forgotten that Murf didn't pay you for his beer that night.

There's Always a Catch

The catch to using range names in formulas is that you can't use AutoFill and expect Excel to match the names to the new ranges. If you copy =AVERAGE(MURF) by dragging the fill handle, you'll get an exact copy of that formula in each of the cells. Of course, you can edit the range names in each of the copies, provided that you used the Formula ➤ Define Name command to name the ranges first.

Water Won't Flow into a Range, but Data Will

When you're entering data into a range, there's a quick alternative to clicking each cell or moving from cell to cell with the arrow keys.

Before you type your entries, drag the range. That is, click on the upper-left corner of the range and keep holding the mouse button down as you move the cell pointer to the lower-right corner, then release the mouse button. The range you dragged across will be highlighted.

When you begin to type, your first entry will go into the top left cell of the highlighted range. To enter values quickly, press ↵ (instead of clicking ✓) and the selection will drop to the next cell down, ready to receive the next entry in that column.

When you press ↵ after typing the last entry in a column, the selection will move to the top of the next column to the right. And when that column is filled, entries will begin at the top of the next column over. So, if you drag the range first, data will flow into it as you type, as shown in Figure 2.9.

Figure 2.9:

If you highlight a range before typing in entries, Excel will fill a column at a time, advancing one cell each time you press ↵.

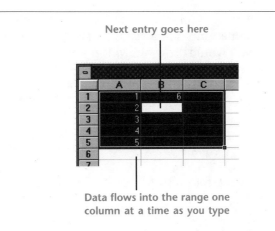

Next entry goes here

Data flows into the range one column at a time as you type

Basic Formulas

Watch That Overflow!

Quite another kind of flowing can happen in a single cell if the formula there produces a result that is too wide for the column. This is called *overflow*. Excel lets you know about overflow by displaying this indicator in the cell:

    #######

When you see such a string of pound signs (#), it does not mean that the formula has produced an error—the result is just too long to fit in the cell. As I explain in Chapter 1, you can adjust the width of a column in which ####### appears by dragging the right column border (up in the area of the column letters). Or, just double-click the right border and Excel will adjust the width to fit the longest entry in the column.

Watch Those Errors, Too!

The situation is much different if you see *one* pound sign in a cell followed by some kind of message. In this case, Excel is reporting an error that occurred when calculating the formula you entered in that cell. For example, you might see this:

    #DIV/0!

This is Excel's way of saying, "You can't make me divide by zero!"—something it has been strictly programmed not to do because otherwise you would grow old waiting for a result that never came. (The result of dividing any number by 0 is undefined, for practical purposes. Early computers without this prohibition had their little circuits fried in the process of dividing by 0.)

You might also see

#NAME?

This error message states, "I don't recognize that function or range name." This happens when you start an entry with an equal sign (telling Excel to expect a formula to follow) but provide an incorrect function name. Recovering Lotus users get this all the time because they enter foreign function names that Excel spits back out.

Here are some other error messages that might appear in cells that contain formulas:

EXCEL SHOWS	EXCEL MEANS
#N/A!	"Your formula refers to a cell that doesn't have a value in it yet, so how can you expect an answer?"
#NULL!	"Your formula said that these ranges overlap, but they don't."
#NUM!	"There's a problem with a number, but I'm not saying what it is."
#REF!	"Your formula refers to some cell I've never even heard of."
#VALUE!	"There's something wrong with the argument in your formula."

More about Overflow without Spillage

Another kind of overflow can happen when you're typing. If you type a text entry that's too long for the current width of the selected cell, one of two things will happen (neither with disastrous results).

In the first situation, if the cell to the right of your entry has nothing in it, the entry will extend into that cell. However, its address is still just the first cell:

In the second situation, if the cell to the right of your entry has stuff in it, the display in the first cell will appear cut off at its right edge. However, all of your stuff is in there; you just can't see it (see Figure 2.10).

Figure 2.10:
Here the entry in cell B5 is too long to fit in the column, and since the adjacent cell is filled, the long entry cannot extend into the next cell. The full entry, "Massachusetts," appears in the formula bar.

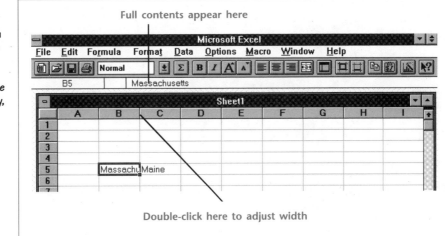

To display all of the entry, double-click the right border of the column heading, and Excel will adjust the column width to fit the overflow item.

If You Liked the Movie, Read the Book

This chapter is kind of a movie version of formulas—you get the story, but not many of the details. If you long to experience the thrills of statistical sampling or investment analysis, Chapter 4 is for you. But before we get to that, Chapter 3 will show you how to find your way around as you start building larger and more complex worksheets.

Chapter 3

NAVIGATION FOR LANDLUBBERS

Murphy's Guide to Navigation: Red sky at morning, sailors take warning. Red sky at night, sailors delight. Gray smoke anytime—everybody over the side!

NAVIGATION IN COMPUTERLAND means finding your way around—within worksheets as they grow larger than one screenful, and within collections of worksheets as they begin to accumulate in disk files. Here are some pointers so you don't find yourself all at sea.

You Mac users will find this chapter shamelessly slanted toward the world of windows. In particular, most of the keyboard stuff is strictly for PC's since Mac's and their mice have a solid relationship. Mac equivalents for some commands are given here in parentheses (like this) or in these little asides.

A Sheet as Big as a Bed Sheet

When you start Excel, the *document window* shows you nine columns (lettered A–I) and 18 rows (numbered 1–18). This is often enough work space for everyday problems. You could think of it as the top half of a printed letter-sized page.

Mac displays might look quite different depending on the size of the screen. On a standard, compact machine, such as the Macintosh SE, you will probably see columns A-F and rows 1-14.

The document window is like a camera viewfinder that shows you only a small part of a much larger area (see Figure 3.1). On a PC, if you press PgDn, you'll be looking at the bottom half of that letter-sized page. So the two screens (PgDn, PgUp) give you about the same amount of space as an accountant's workpaper. Some people might never have to explore beyond that.

Figure 3.1:
The document window is your viewfinder on a much bigger worksheet.

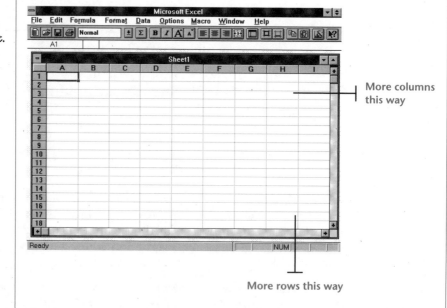

If you're the adventurous type, you'll want to know how far you can go. Well, if the biggest sheet you could make were the size of a bed sheet (king or queen), the part you could see through the window would be about *one tenth* the area of a postage stamp!

Yes, for Star Trek fans who long to go where no human has gone before, the worksheet universe is pretty big. But it's not limitless. One Excel sheet can have as many as 256 columns and 16,384 rows. (After column Z, the 26th column, double letters identify columns AA–IV.)

Jumping through Hyperspace

You need not trek across the expanse of the sheet to get to distant cells. Like Captain Kirk calling for warp drive, you can jump there with a single command.

Just because it's there, try going to the last cell in the sheet. From the Formula menu, select Goto (or you can press F5 on the PC or ⌘-G on the Mac). The Goto dialog box will open. Type the address of your destination cell in the Reference box, as shown in Figure 3.2.

Figure 3.2:
The *Goto* dialog box lets you jump to distant cells.

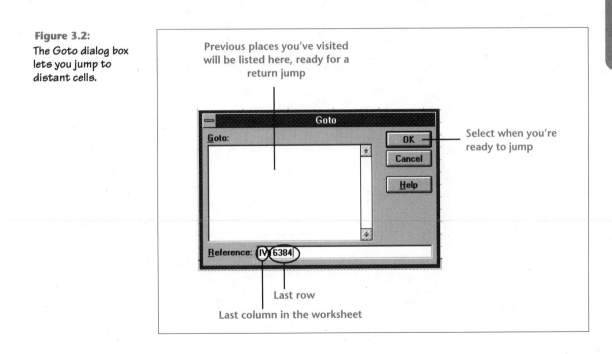

Previous places you've visited will be listed here, ready for a return jump

Select when you're ready to jump

Last row

Last column in the worksheet

Navigation

When you select OK, the cell pointer will jump through a magic wormhole in computer space and land you smack on the address you entered (Figure 3.3).

It's a cold, lonely place out there in that last empty cell. But never fear—you can tap your red shoes and be back in Kansas in a wink. Select Formula ➤ Goto again. This time, as if Excel had heard your wish, the address $A$1 (the top cell in the sheet— home!) is already entered in the Reference box. Select OK to jump back. (Sometimes, like now, you get to ignore those dollar signs. Selecting $A$1 just means, "Cell A1, and I *really mean* A1!")

Figure 3.3:
The last cell in an Excel worksheet is cell IV16384.

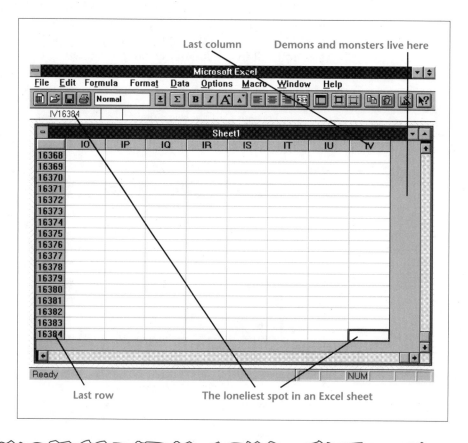

How to Scroll Even If Your Map Is Folded

Moving your window viewfinder around the sheet is called *scrolling*. There are ways of scrolling so that your mouse finger (not to mention your mouse) doesn't get tired.

Dragging the cell pointer

Drag the cell pointer off the screen in the direction of your destination in the sheet. The sheet will appear to move as it scrolls beneath your viewfinder. It will keep scrolling as long as you continue to hold the mouse button down. Release the mouse button when you get where you want to go.

As you drag, you are selecting a range, which grows and grows in reverse colors until the whole view of the sheet is black. Have no fear. Things are not as black as they look. Click anywhere within the sheet to release your range selection, and things will return to normal.

Using the scroll bars

The two gray bars at the bottom and right sides of the document window are the *scroll bars* (see Figure 3.4). (On the Mac, this control is called the *thumb*.)The bar at the bottom controls movement left and right; the bar on the side controls up and down movement. The square

Navigation

Figure 3.4:
The scroll bars let you move around a worksheet easily. You can gauge your position in the sheet by the two sliders in the scroll bars.

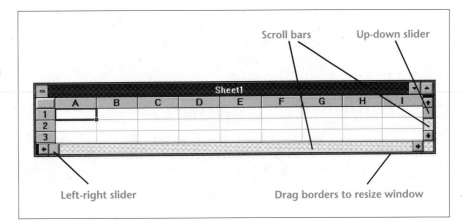

Scroll bars   Up-down slider

Left-right slider   Drag borders to resize window

slider indicates the current position of the viewfinder within the sheet. The view is at the end of the sheet when the slider has gone as far as it can go in either direction.

The scroll bars work like the tuning controls on some FM stereos: There's a coarse adjustment for covering a distance quickly, as well as a fine-tuning control for smaller increments (see Figure 3.5). Use the coarse, then the fine.

Figure 3.5:
The scroll bars give you fine control over your movements, as well as the ability to cover a lot of ground in a hurry.

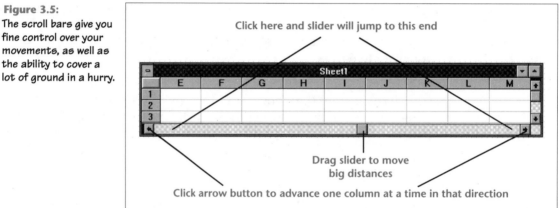

To be coarse about it, drag the slider. To advance even more quickly, click inside the bar at either of its ends and the slider will make a big jump in that direction.

After using the slider to get in the right neighborhood, you can go to a specific address by clicking one of the arrow buttons at either end of the scroll bar. Clicking an arrow button once advances the view one column or one row in the direction of the arrow.

Searching for Treasure

Sometimes, you don't know where you want to go. You just know what you want to find when you get there. Like most computer programs with *savoir faire*, Excel can conduct a search for specific stuff.

To make Excel go fetch, select Formula ➤ Find or press Shift-F5 (⌘-H on the Mac). The Find dialog box will open. Type the stuff you're looking for in the Find What box. Figure 3.6 explains the various options you can choose in the Find dialog box.

Figure 3.6:
The Find dialog box lets you search for stuff.

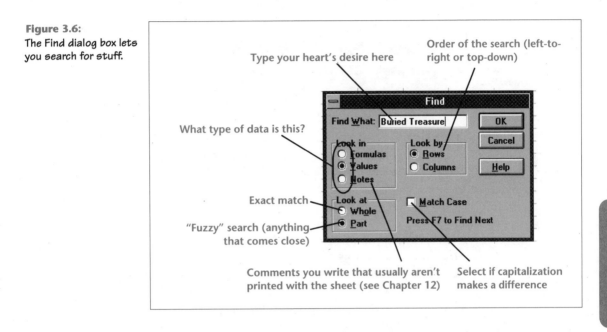

When it finds a match, Excel will move to the cell that holds the first match it finds. If you want to look at the next instance of the same stuff, you don't have to repeat the command. Just press F7 (⌘-H on the Mac), and Excel will jump to the next match. If there are no matches, Excel will politely clear its throat and say, "Could not find matching data."

Swapping Your Stash in a Cubbyhole

Often you search for something in order to replace it with something else. For example, soap opera writers who use word processors find the search-and-replace feature handy when they must change all instances of Carl to Carla after a character's sex-change operation.

Navigation

Not to be outdone, Excel for Windows will also do this trick. Just select Formula ➤ Replace to open the Replace dialog box. Replace works much like Find. Type the old stuff in the Find What box and the new stuff in the Replace With box, as shown in Figure 3.7.

Figure 3.7:
Use the Replace dialog box to search and replace. You can search and replace globally or selectively.

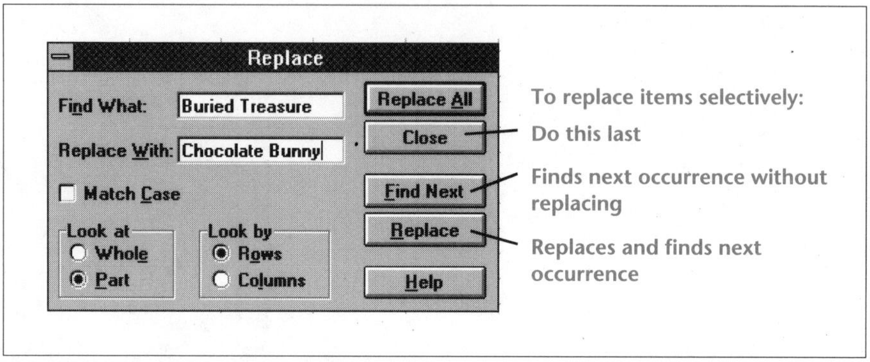

To start the process, select the Find Next button. If Excel finds a match for the old stuff, it will take you to the match. The dialog box will stay open. If you want to replace the old stuff, select Replace to replace the item and find its next occurrence. To continue without replacing, select Find Next. If you want to skip a replacement, select Find Next again. When you're done, select Close.

To replace all instances of the old stuff without having Excel ask you for confirmation each time, select Replace All. Excel will do all the replacements and then close the dialog box.

Navigation for Keyboard Maestros

Speed demons and people who just want to give their mouse a rest can navigate from the keyboard.

On some PC keyboards, you must use the navigation keys on the *numeric keypad*, which looks like a set of calculator keys. To use this keypad for navigation, press the Num Lock key to turn off its indicator light.

(When you want to resume entering numbers, press Num Lock again.) On other keyboards, there's a separate set of navigation keys so that you can leave Num Lock on all the time, if you want.

The status bar *at the bottom of the Excel screen also tells you when Scroll Lock, Caps Lock, and Num Lock are on.*

KEY COMMAND	MOVEMENT
PgUp	Up the height of one window (usually 18 rows)
PgDn	Down one window
Ctrl-PgDn	Right one window
↑	Up one row
↓	Down one row
←	Left one column
→	Right one column
Ctrl-Home	First cell in the same sheet (usually A1)
Ctrl-End	Last cell that contains data in the sheet
Home	Top left corner of the window (Scroll Lock must be on)
End	Bottom right corner of the window (Scroll Lock must be on)

These are just a few of Excel's navigation keys, which are of interest mostly to the PC folks. To make a real study of the rest of them, select Help ➤ Search ➤ Navigating ➤ Show Topics. Select the category of information you want from the list of topics, then select the Go To button. A Help screen with descriptions of all the navigation keys and commands for that category will appear.

Use Alternate Keys If You're Feeling Contrary

Excel is ever willing to accommodate and otherwise co-opt people who have stubborn, ingrained Lotus habits. If you're one of those people and you're using a PC, select Options ➤ Workspace and mark the Alternate Navigation Keys check box. Excel will then accept some of the navigation keystrokes you already know.

To view a table of the alternate navigation keys, select Help ➤ Search ➤ Navigating ➤ Show Topics ➤ Alternate Navigation Keys ➤ Go To.

Splitting Is No Headache

Dealing with a long sheet is often inconvenient, to say the least. All that scrolling up and down can make you downright dizzy. This is especially frustrating when you're trying to compare two parts of a sheet that are separated by some distance.

Consider a sheet that holds a check register. The sheet expands downward as each check is recorded. For ease of reference, the account balance and subtotals are shown at the top of the sheet, where they can stay put rather than continually moving downward at the bottom of the check entries. Excel makes it possible to *split* such a sheet so that you have two viewfinders. Each view can be adjusted independently of the other. Those clever people at Microsoft call these split sheets *window panes*.

Splitting *divides a document window into two or four* **panes.** *You can scroll the panes separately to view different portions of a sheet on the same screen.*

To split a sheet horizontally, place the cell pointer in the first cell of the row above which the split will appear. Then select Window ➤ Split. Here's the result for the check register example:

	A	B	C	D	E	F	G	H	I
				CHECKS.XLS					
1	Totals		$409.54	$500.00	$1,090.46				
2	Date	Reference	Checks	Deposits	Balance				
3				Balance forward >	$1,000.00				
4	1/3/95	721	$15.95		$984.05				
41	1/6/95	824	$21.50	$250.00	$965.56				
42	1/6/95	825	$40.00		$925.56				
43	1/6/95	826	$103.12		$822.44				

Notice that separate vertical scroll bars have appeared above and below the split. You can now adjust each view separately. To remove the split and restore the single document window, select Window ➤ Remove Split.

You can also split a sheet vertically so that the two halves scroll left and right independently. Place the cell pointer at the top of a column and select Window ➤ Split. A vertical split will appear to the left of the column you selected.

You can even do a four-way split—without hurting yourself. Select any cell that's not on an edge of the sheet, and two split lines will appear— one vertical and one horizontal. The result is four scrollable panes. Figure 3.8 shows a window split into four panes.

You can change the position of a split line by dragging it.

Figure 3.8:
A four-way split. Since the views overlap the cell E11, "Hi Mom!" appears in each of the four panes.

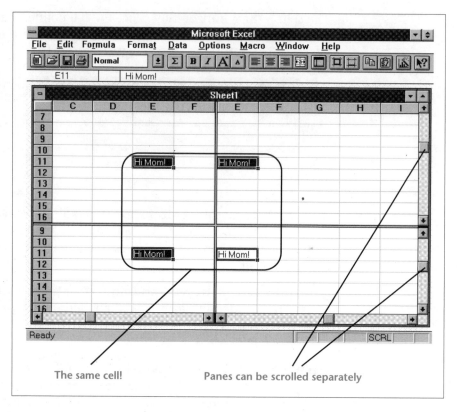

The same cell!   Panes can be scrolled separately

Iced-Up Windows and Freezing Panes

By splitting a sheet window into panes, you can create a pane with headings that don't change and another pane with entries that scroll. In the check register example, the top three rows should always be displayed. Therefore, that pane should be *frozen* so that it can't be scrolled.

You can freeze the view in a pane by selecting Window ➤ Freeze Panes. The split line will become thin and fixed in place, and you will not be able to scroll the pane closest to the top of the sheet. A single set of scroll bars will appear. Adjusting these scroll bars affects only the bottom portion of the sheet, while the top portion stays iced-up. Figure 3.9 shows a split window with the top pane frozen.

Figure 3.9:
The top three rows of the check register sheet have been frozen so that they won't scroll. The lower pane, below the split line, can still be scrolled.

Frozen pane   Frozen split line

	A	B	C	D	E	F	G	H	I
1	Totals		$409.54	$500.00	$1,090.46				
2	Date	Reference	Checks	Deposits	Balance				
3			Balance forward >		$1,000.00				
5	1/5/95	722	$64.35		$919.70				
6	1/6/95	723	$21.50	$250.00	1148.2				
7	1/6/95	724	$40.00		1108.2				
8	1/6/95	725	$103.12		$1,005.08				

CHECKS.XLS

This pane can scroll

Splitting and freezing can be permanent! *Actually, it's not as dangerous as it sounds. Just remember that splits and frozen panes will be saved in the worksheet file, so these features will reappear when you open the sheet again. (Come to think of it, that's not bad at all. You can always remove a split with Window ➤ Remove Split and unstick a pane with Window ➤ Unfreeze Panes.)*

When Splitting Just Won't Do, Open More Windows!

A convenient alternative to splitting a window—particularly if your sheets grow very large—is to open multiple views (or windows) of the same sheet.

Selecting New Window from the Window menu will open another viewfinder through which you can look at a different portion of the current sheet. At first, the new window will look like the original view. However, you will be able to scroll and size the new window separately. This makes it possible to compare and work with widely distant parts of the same sheet.

Figure 3.10 shows a big sheet my clever friend the financial analyst made. It has about 20 columns and more than 100 rows. A second window has been opened with the Window ➤ New Window command so that different parts of the sheet can be worked on at the same time.

Navigation

Figure 3.10:

Here a second window of the sheet MURPHY has been opened.

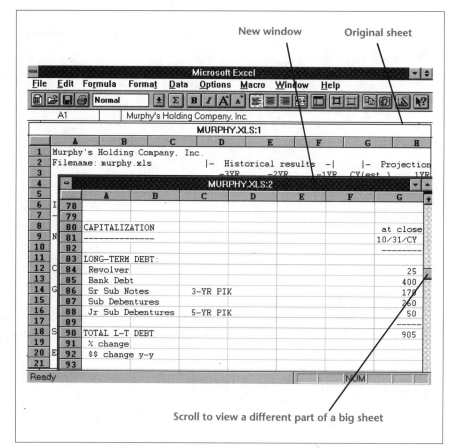

Scroll to view a different part of a big sheet

The new window in this case is entitled MURPHY.XLS:2 and the original view is MURPHY.XLS:1. (There's no .XLS extension on Mac files.) You can repeat the command to add as many windows as you like (limited only by the amount of memory in your computer). The program will add :3, :4, :5, and so on to the title of each new window.

Get Used to Your New Insect-Like Vision

No matter how many windows you open with the Window ➤ New Window command, each of the windows is a view of *the same sheet*. If you make a change in one of the windows, it will show up in all the others. You can also work with different sheets at the same time, but that's another story (called File ➤ New, described later in this chapter).

You don't need a decorator to arrange your windows

Having several windows open at the same time can be downright confusing unless you know how to nail them in place. New windows are normally shown *cascaded*, or layered on top of one another. You can drag the windows around the screen by their title bars, but this layering can be inconvenient— especially if you need to compare entries in different parts of the sheet.

To remedy this, whenever you have multiple windows open select Window ➤ Arrange. The Arrange Windows dialog box will open.

Navigation

Select one of the Arrange options to position the open windows. The *Tiled* option makes all windows visible, placed side-by-side in a best-fit for the screen. *Horizontal* shows full rows, as in Figure 3.11. *Vertical* displays full columns, side-by-side. You would select *None* to leave the current arrangement unchanged while you reset synchronization (this is described in the next section).

Figure 3.11:
Here the big-sheet investment example appears in two windows that are synchronized vertically.

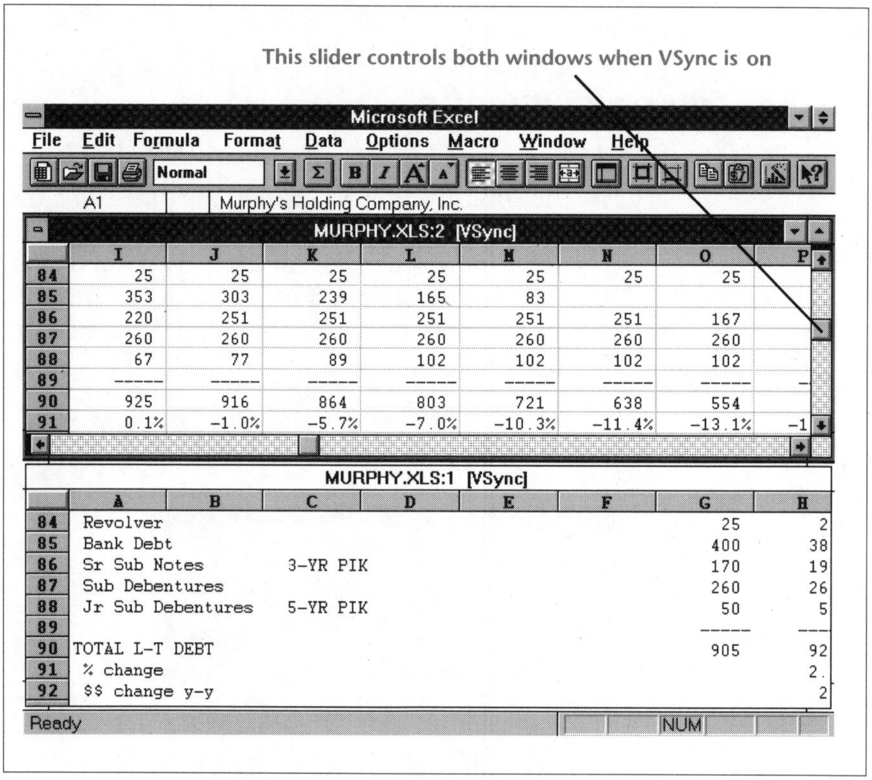

Get with it: synchronize your views

In the Arrange Windows dialog box, you can make the open windows scroll together, rather than separately. You can *synchronize* them horizontally so that the windows always show the same set of columns, or vertically so that they all show the same set of rows. You can also synchronize windows in *both* directions. But you can synchronize only windows that show *the same* sheet.

The synchronization options will be available only if the Windows Of Active Document box is checked. This option is important if you have several different sheets open, and each of those sheets is shown in multiple windows. To change synchronization without affecting the arrangement of windows, select None for the Arrange option.

Figure 3.11 shows that big-sheet investment example with two windows open on the same sheet, synchronized vertically (indicated by the [VSync] notation in the title bars). This is a handy way to read across a wide sheet. With vertical sync in Figure 3.11, you can view many columns on one screen. Both windows show the same set of rows as you adjust the vertical slider. However, you can adjust the columns separately.

Switching among open windows

The *active window*, or the window you're currently working in, is shown with the background of its title bar in color. (On a monochrome Mac, the active window has attractive *stripes* in its title bar.) To work in a different window that's visible on the screen, just click anywhere inside that window.

Figure 3.12 shows three tiled windows of the same sheet, with the first view active. When several windows are displayed, Excel hides the scroll bars of the inactive windows to conserve space. The scroll bars reappear when you activate the window.

For Switch Hitters: *There are two other ways to switch among open windows. These methods can be particularly handy when windows are cascaded, or overlapping:*

☞ *On a PC, you can press Ctrl-F6 to switch to the next active window in number sequence. You can press Ctrl-F6 repeatedly to cycle among the open windows until you've activated the one you want.*

☞ *Select the Window menu. The titles of all the open windows will be listed near the bottom of the menu. A check mark (✓) indicates which one is currently active. Select the title of the window you want to activate.*

Advice for Zoomers and Space Rookies

Another way to survey a sheet is to *zoom*, or adjust the magnification
of your viewfinder. Select a cell in an area you want to inspect and
choose Window ➤ Zoom. The Zoom dialog box will appear:

Select the magnification percentage you want. More than 100 percent moves in for a close-up; less than 100 percent pulls back for a broader view. (You can get magnifications greater than 200 percent by typing a value in the Custom text box.) If you want, you can select the Fit Selection option and Excel in its wisdom will size the view so that all of your sheet (or the selected range) just fits the window.

When you select OK in the Zoom dialog box, the magnified view appears on your screen. Figure 3.13 shows what 200 percent looks like. To restore the original view, select Window ➤ Zoom and pick 100 percent.

Figure 3.13:
A sheet displayed at 200 percent magnification

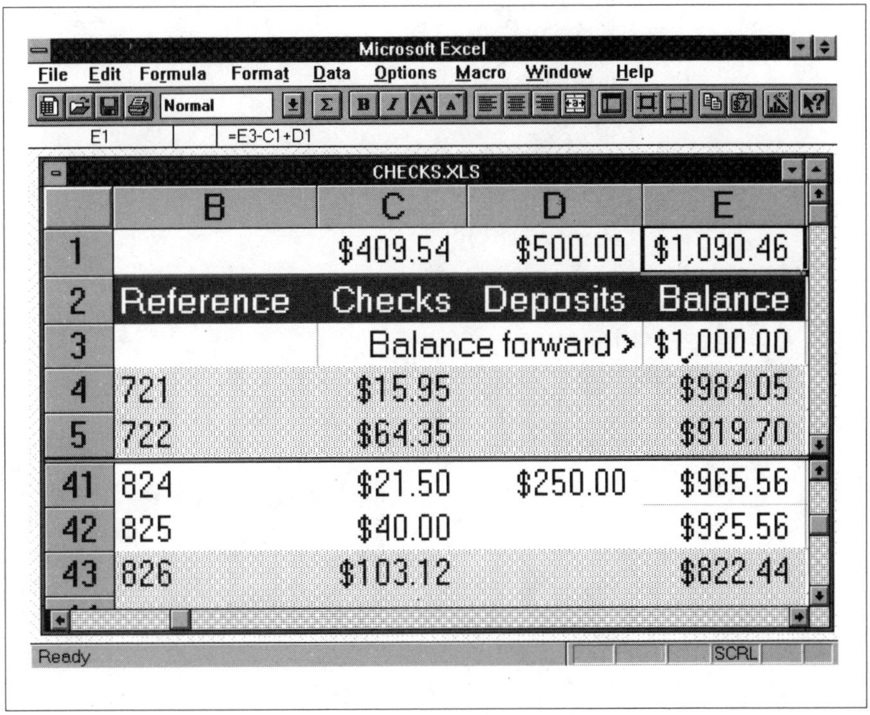

Nifty Zoom Buttons!

Excel offers would-be zoomers another quick way to select magnified views—involving the Zoom In and Zoom Out tools in the *Utility Toolbar*.

To display the tools, select Options ➤ Toolbars. The Toolbars dialog box will open. Select Utility from the Show Toolbars list:

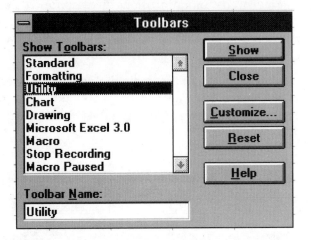

When you select the Show button, the Utility Toolbar (shown in Figure 3.14) appears on the screen.

Figure 3.14:
The Utility Toolbar

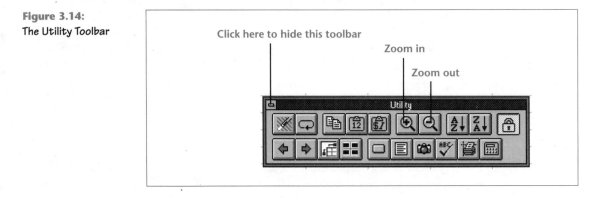

Starting from the full (100 percent) view, you can click the Zoom In tool once for 200 percent magnification. To restore the full view, click the Zoom Out tool. You can click Zoom Out as many as three more times to get a wider view of the sheet.

To get rid of the Utility Toolbar, click its *control box* (in the top left corner).

In Windows, the control box *is a small box with a hyphen in it, always located in the top left corner of any program or document window. The control box gives you control over the window itself, rather than the stuff inside it. For example, from selections in the control box, you can move or close the window. If the window is a toolbar, clicking the control box simply closes the window.*

On the Mac, the equivalent to the control box is called the close box, *and it doesn't have the little hyphen inside.*

Juggling Sheets

Rather than looking at multiple views of the same sheet, you can open multiple windows that hold *different* sheets. Each window will display a different Excel sheet file (.XLS extension on the PC).

Often, you will want to work with a set of sheets that have to do with the same thing. It can be convenient to work on the set of sheets as a group. Think of them as sheets of paper that you would clip together. If you had a check register, each sheet might hold the transactions for one month. Or, if a single sheet held bowling scores for one team, a stack of similar sheets could show the scores for the entire league—one sheet for each team. In Figure 3.15 three windows, each containing a different sheet, allow you to view the scores of three teams in the Thumbs Ballpeen Bowling League simultaneously.

You can open a new sheet by selecting New from the File menu. The New dialog box will appear. The Worksheet option is already picked, so just select OK.

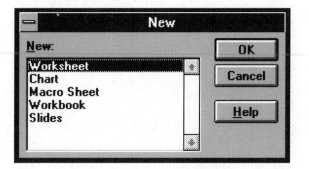

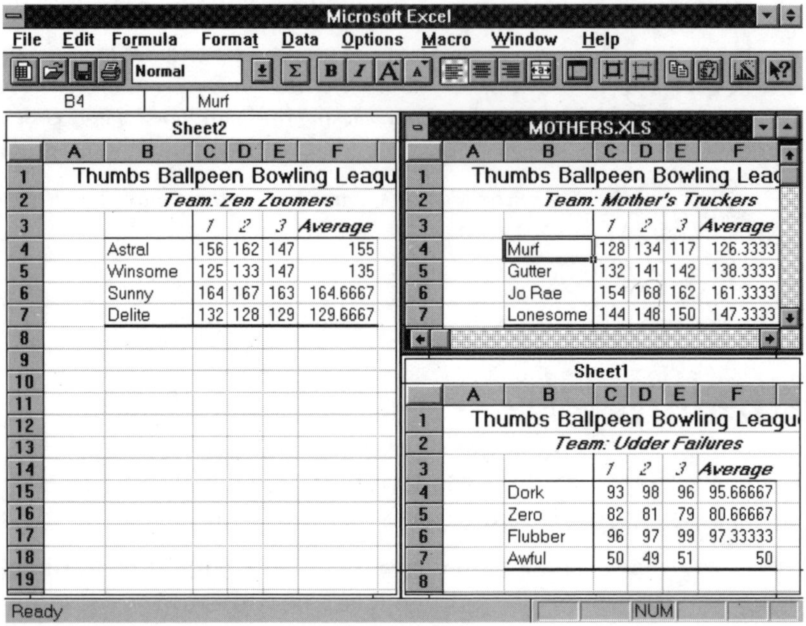

Figure 3.15:

Figure 3.15:

Three different sheets open in three separate windows allow you to compare information easily.

A new window will open, which Excel will call Sheet2 on the PC or Worksheet2 on the Mac (or the next available number). Unlike windows you open with the Window ➤ New Window command, this is a *separate document* and—initially, anyway—has no relation to other windows you may have open at the time.

You might need to work with two, perhaps as many as four, windows. You can choose File ➤ New repeatedly to open as many windows as your computer's memory will hold. After you open the ninth window (the sixth on the Mac), the selection More Windows will appear in the Window menu, allowing you to switch among windows by title. (Looking at more than six windows on a single screen is recommended only for insects.)

Each window can be saved to disk separately. Make the window active and then choose File ➤ Save. You can accept the program-assigned file name (Sheet2, Sheet3, etc.) or type your own file name.

Peek-a-Boo Windows: Now You See Them, Now You Don't

When you have several windows open at once (whether they are views of the same sheet or different sheets), you might want to reduce the clutter on your screen.

You can get rid of a window temporarily by making it active (selecting it so that its title bar appears solid on the PC, striped on the Mac) and then selecting Window ➤ Hide. The window will vanish, and its name will no longer appear among the open titles on the Window menu.

You can make the sheet reappear by selecting Window ➤ Unhide, picking the name of the sheet, and selecting OK. (If there are no windows left showing, choose File ➤ Unhide instead.)

Shrinking Sheets without Hot Water (PC Version)

On a PC, an alternative to hiding a window is to shrink it to an icon. To shrink a sheet, press Ctrl-F9 or click its Minimize button (found in the top right corner of its window):

The window will shrink to an icon, identified by its title:

Sheet2

Depending on the positions of other open sheets, the shrunken sheets may lurk beneath the others. You can find them by selecting their titles from the Window menu or by pressing Ctrl-F6. To restore a shrunken sheet, double-click its icon or select its title from the Window menu.

Navigation

Shrinkage Can Be a Good Thing

Shrinking a sheet window to an icon has two benefits. First, it gets the thing out of your way temporarily. Second, and perhaps more important, it reduces the amount of memory Excel can give to it and puts it last in line for its turn in the computer processor. So, if you're doing heavy calculations in an open sheet and memory is limited, things might move along faster if you reduce the other sheets to icons.

Maximized Windows Hog Everything (More PC Stuff)

Just as shrinking a window belittles it in both size and importance, maximizing a window will make it bigger on the screen and give it the most importance in processing and the greatest share of memory. To let a window hog everything this way, press Ctrl-F10 or select its Maximize button:

To put a maximized window back in its place, press Ctrl-F5 or click its Restore button:

You Don't Need Special Glasses to See in 3D

Excel lets you share data among open sheets. You might want to do this to carry totals from several sheets to a sheet that summarizes them. Sheets that have values or formulas in common are *linked* so that updating the shared value or formula in one sheet will also change it in the other sheets.

To pick up the contents of a cell in another sheet, select the cell in the sheet that will receive the linked data. Then type the reference to the cell in the other sheet, as shown in Figure 3.16.

Figure 3.16:
Use this format to link the contents of a cell to another sheet.

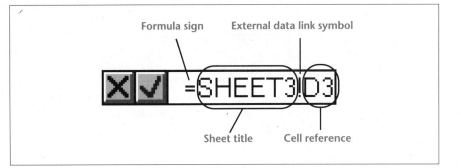

The equal sign (=) indicates that this is a formula. It is followed by the name of the other sheet (SHEET3, in this case). Then there's the external data-link symbol, the exclamation point (!), followed by the address of the cell that holds the data you want to insert in the current sheet.

If both sheets are open, you don't have to type the link reference. Excel will do the work for you. Just select the cell that holds the data and choose Edit ➤ Copy. Friendly crawling ants will march around the data, indicating that this is the stuff you want. Next select the cell in the sheet that will receive the data. Choose Edit ➤ Paste Link. Excel will insert the link formula in the second cell, and the data will appear in both places. (There's much more about data linking in Chapters 4 and 13.)

For data links to work properly, the references must be to sheets that are already saved on disk.

Navigation

If They Asked Me, I Could Write a (Work)Book

You can save a collection of Excel sheets (.XLS files on the PC) together so that you can grab them with a single swipe later. It's rather like clipping the sheets together in the same file folder. In Excel-speak, such a collection of sheets is a separate kind of file, called a *workbook* (with the file extension .XLW on a PC).

If all the sheets are currently open, it's easy to save them in a workbook. Just select File ➤ Save Workbook. The titles of the sheets will be listed as Workbook Contents, and a proposed file name (BOOK1.XLW in this PC example, WORKBOOK1 on the Mac) will appear in the Save As dialog box (see Figure 3.17).

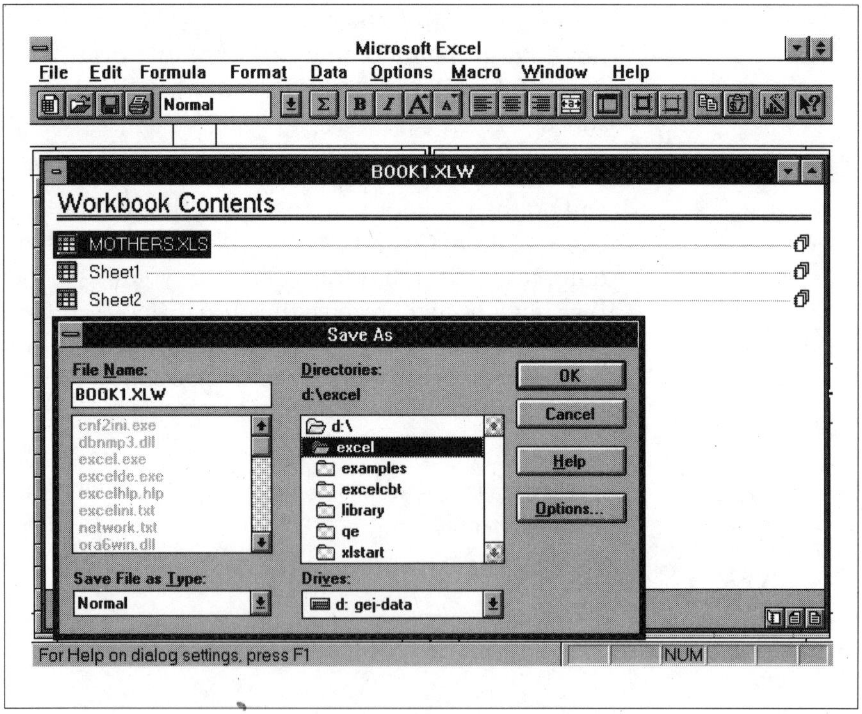

Figure 3.17:
When you select File ➤ Save Workbook, Excel lists the sheets currently open under Workbook Contents and proposes a file name in the Save As dialog box.

Murphy's Rules for Neat Workbooks (PC Stuff)

On the Workbook Contents page in the Windows version of Excel, sheets that are listed without extensions (such as Sheet2) have not yet been saved as .XLS files. If you save a workbook as an .XLW file without first saving its sheets, you will be able to reopen the sheets only by opening the workbook. However, if you first save the sheets individually (producing SHEET2.XLS, etc.) then bind them into a workbook, you will have the option of opening either the sheets themselves or the workbook. In any case, changes you make to the sheets individually will also appear in the workbook that contains them.

You can do all your file saving from the Workbook Contents screen. To save a sheet to an individual file, select its title from the Workbook Contents list, then select the Options button. Pick the Separate File (Unbound) option and choose OK. Sheet files that are unbound are not only included in the current workbook but can be stored in other workbooks as well.

Climbing the Perilous Directory Tree

Another kind of navigation is required when you get a file from disk (File ➤ Open) or save a sheet or workbook to a file (File ➤ Save or File ➤ Save As).

To provide an orderly way of storing files, computer disks are subdivided into directories. A *directory* is a category for grouping files. (On the Mac, a directory is called a *folder*.) Each directory can have other directories, called *subdirectories*, under it. You can think of the arrangement of directories as an upside-down tree. On a PC, the top directory—or starting point—is called the *root*. In some lists of files, the root is marked by the backslash symbol (\). (The \ symbol is also used as a separator between directory names.) Directories "grow" downward from the root, branching to form subdirectories. Figure 3.18 shows an example of how directories and subdirectories are organized.

A subdirectory is a branch, or subcategory, of a disk directory. The directory from which the subdirectory branches is called its parent. *The mother of all directories, or the starting point of the directory tree, is called the* root, *and its name is* \.

Navigation

Figure 3.18:
Files can be stored at the root or under any directory or subdirectory.

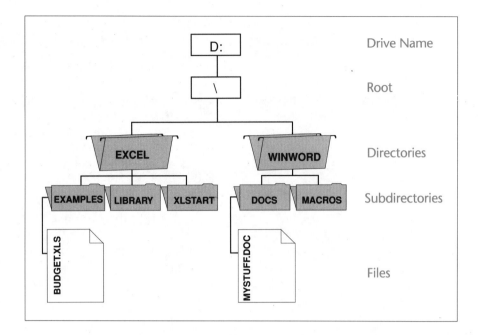

Finding the file or storage location you want involves navigating the directory tree. For example, look what happens when you choose File ➤ Open in Excel for Windows or File ➤ Open Document on the Mac. The Open dialog box appears. (Notice that it is almost identical to the dialog box for saving files.) The File ➤ Open command is preset to look at the directory EXCEL, where Excel expects to find sheet and workbook files. However, you can store files anywhere you want. You can even set up other directories for different clients or for different projects.

Let's say you wanted to open the ready-made sheet BUDGET, which is stored in the subdirectory EXAMPLES. Since you know the *path* through the directory tree, on a PC you could type your request in the File Name text box, like this:

```
D:\EXCEL\EXAMPLES\BUDGET.XLS
```

In PC talk, this request says, "Starting at the root of drive D (D:\), go to the EXCEL directory, then the EXAMPLES subdirectory, and get the file BUDGET.XLS."

It can be more convenient to navigate the Open dialog box, though, especially if you don't know the file name in advance. Fortunately for navigators, all file-access dialog boxes work the same way—even in different applications. Here are the steps in Windows (refer to Figure 3.19):

1. Select the file type. In most cases, you just want to double-check that Excel sheets and workbooks (.XL* on the PC) are preselected. However, you can click the ↓ button to select from a list of other file types, including Lotus (.WK*—the * in the PC file extension is a "wildcard," meaning that any character can go in that spot.)

2. Select the disk drive. In the Drives box, select the name of the disk drive where the files are, or will be, stored. Drives A and B are usually floppy disk drives. The main hard disk is usually drive C, possibly with an auxiliary drive D. A network server might be designated S.

Figure 3.19:
The Open dialog box. The numbered steps show how you can navigate the dialog box to locate and open a file.

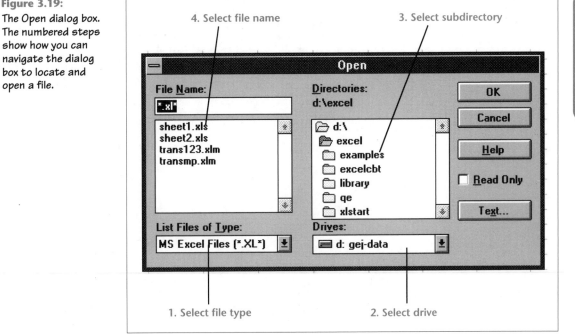

3. Select the subdirectory. In the Directories box, double-click the name of the subdirectory you want. If the subdirectory belongs to a different directory, double-click the root (\), then double-click the directory, double-click the subdirectory, and so on down the tree until you arrive at the subdirectory you want. After you have selected a subdirectory, the files *having the extension type you specified* will be listed beneath the File Name box.

4. Select the file name you want from the list by double-clicking it. Or, just type the name of the file you want in the File Name box and select OK.

Murphy's Guide to Tree Climbing

Many people have difficulty visualizing the directory tree at first. (Do Mac people have nightmares about stacks of folders?) Many more wonder, "Why bother?" Here's Murphy's reply to those people.

Would you throw everything you own into the same closet? It gets to be a mess, and, what's worse, stuff can get lost in there! The directory tree (or folder system) is a method of organization, and picky as that sounds, it's the single most useful thing you can learn about your computer.

Here, in three mercifully brief chapters, is fine dining for discriminating number-crunchers. If your worksheet does anything more complicated than addition, you should spend some time in this part of the book. You'll learn how to mix nutritious formulas, how to care for and feed those powerful but potentially dangerous Excel functions, and—most important—how to check Excel's math so that you can truly believe in your numbers.

GIVING ORDERS TO YOUR MATH SLAVE

Chapter 4

THIS FORMULA ISN'T FOR BABIES

Murphy's Rule Number 1: The computer is always right.

Murphy's Rule Number 2: If you suspect that the computer is wrong, refer to Rule Number 1.

CHAPTER 2 INTRODUCED the idea of formulas as math problems that Excel will cheerfully do for you. There I gave you some examples using the ready-made formulas, or functions, SUM and AVERAGE. In this chapter I'll get you started doing serious math with formulas and functions.

Excel has so many built-in functions that it would be impossible to include them all here. So instead I'll tell you how to construct formulas—especially how to refer correctly to cells and ranges in the sheet. Then, in Chapter 5, I'll point out some pitfalls of particular formulas and explain how to test your sheet to make sure that its results are reliable.

TECHNO NOTE

You Don't Have to Know It if You Know Where to Find It

Microsoft includes the *Excel Function Reference* with the Excel software. This booklet describes all of Excel's built-in functions and their required syntax.

If you know the name of the function you want to use but (like any normal person) can't remember the syntax, Excel will look it up for you. From the menu bar, select Help ➤ Contents (Window ➤ Help on the Mac). A list of topics will appear. Scroll down the list until you see Worksheet Functions (in the Reference section), and select it. From the next list you see, select All Worksheet Functions. An alphabetical list of function names will appear. Click the name of the function you want (scroll through the list, if necessary). Excel will display a full description of the function's purpose and syntax.

To get a quick reminder of the syntax, press Ctrl-A after you have typed the function name in the formula bar.

Building Formulas without a Permit

The syntax of (rules for writing) the SUM function is

=SUM(*number1* , *number2* , ...)

Remember that contrary mathematicians call stuff like **number1** an *argument*. An argument is just data that you feed to the hungry function. Excel is picky about this: If you don't feed a function the things it likes to eat, you will either get a message saying that you goofed or—and this is much worse—an answer that looks okay but is just downright wrong.

If you feed more than one argument (number1,number2) to a formula, you must separate them with commas.

In this book, formula stuff shown in **bold** is required any time you use that function. If you don't include it, Excel will flatly refuse to do the work and will tell you so with a terse, cryptic error message. (See Chapter 2 for a list of these error messages with their translations.) The other stuff (not bold) is optional.

Italics indicate that the stuff is a placeholder for values. You can put anything in its place that results in a data value (more about this presently). Stuff shown in Roman (not italic), including function names and special characters, should be typed literally—just as it appears.

The dots (...) mean, "and so on." In the case of most functions, you can include as many as 30 arguments without upsetting Excel in the least.

Murphy's Guide to Computer Errors

To the complaint "My computer must be wrong!" Murphy says, "GIGO—garbage in, garbage out!"

Computers can indeed produce incorrect results. But as your faithful math slave, Excel will do exactly what you tell it to do—no more and no less. Things can go seriously wrong when you feed Excel stuff that looks okay but really isn't. This is where computers are dumb as the nuts they're made of: *Excel does not know the difference between right and wrong answers!* Usually you can trace the errors in a sheet to incorrect references in the formulas.

Arguments can be about different stuff

In Chapter 2 the arguments used in the example functions SUM and AVERAGE are simply range references, such as a column (B1:B5) or row (B2:E2) of number values to be summed or averaged. But arguments can actually be all kinds of stuff, as long as Excel interprets that stuff as data. In fact, arguments that refer to values in a formula can be any of the following:

☞ An address of a cell that contains a value: C3

Formula Syntax

☞ A range that contains a series of values: C3:J3

☞ The name of a range that contains a series of values: TOTALS

☞ A specific number value (a constant): 9.356

☞ For arguments that are labels, specific text characters, *enclosed in quotation marks*: "Murphy's Stuff"

☞ A reference to a cell or range in another open sheet: SHEET3!D3

☞ A formula for a calculation that produces a value or a series of values: C3*(B2+4)

☞ A function that produces a value or a series of values: sum (C3:J3)

Formulas that are used as arguments are not preceded by equal signs. As with any formula, use parentheses to control the order in which Excel performs the calculations.

If you specify a range using a range name (such as TOTALS) instead of addresses, remember that you have to define the range name with the command Formula ➤ Define Name before you can use it in a formula.

Don't Space Out!

Like file names in DOS, range names in Excel cannot contain blank spaces. If you want to invent nifty names that contain two or more words, separate the words with the underscore character (_). (Don't use a hyphen; Excel might think it's a minus sign.) Use any combination of upper- and lowercase letters (Excel ignores the difference, except in labels), and keep it to no more than 255 characters in all. For example, you could type **home_runs_I_hit** for a range name.

Some arguments are very specific

Some particularly picky functions require special kinds of arguments called *keywords*, or *reserved words*. Placeholders (in italics) often represent these words in formula syntax, but the words themselves must be typed literally as text and enclosed in quotation marks ("").

For example, one of the functions that uses keywords is INFO, which sends reports back from the battle raging inside your computer. The syntax for INFO is

    =INFO(*type_text*)

In this formula syntax, *type_text* is a placeholder for any of ten specific keywords. One of these keywords is "memavail", which can be fed to INFO to make it report on the amount of computer memory that is currently available. To put the amount of memory (number of bytes) into the cell that holds the formula, the syntax would be

    =INFO("memavail")

This kind of function is handy for people who are writing *macros,* or precooked and canned packages of Excel commands and formulas. You can read about macros in Chapter 9.

Some happy functions don't have arguments

Some functions—and they are rare—don't have arguments. But for reasons known only to Excel, you need to supply an empty pair of parentheses to hold the stuff that's not there, for example,

    =RAND()

This function generates a random (unpredictable, but not temperamental) decimal value between 0 and 1. If you make sheets for playing games or simulating business scenarios, you might use this function to get things off to a wild start.

Most functions can have lots of arguments

Most functions in Excel can have as many as 30 arguments. That means you can include up to 30 sets of values in a single formula. And the cells that hold the values need not be adjacent to one another. In fact, you can pick them up from anywhere in the sheet—and even from other sheets.

For example, here's a SUM function that calculates the grand total of three nonadjacent columns of numbers:

    =SUM(B2:B5,D2:D5,F2:F5)

And here's an AVERAGE function that averages those same values:

=AVERAGE(B2:B5,D2:D5,F2:F5)

To calculate an average, Excel counts the number of data values in all the arguments, adds the values, then divides the result by the count. But here's a possible source of error: In doing the count, Excel skips cells that contain blanks but counts those that contain zeros. To include the skipped cells in the count, you must insert zeros in them.

Clicking Your Way to Higher Math

Excel hates for you to type if you don't have to. Therefore, it provides a handy way for you to enter formulas without ever touching the keyboard.

The do-it-yourself Formula Toolbar

To click and drag your way to higher math, you must first create a toolbar that contains the *formula tools*. (Most of these tools don't appear in any of the ready-made toolbars.) Select Options ➤ Toolbars. The Toolbars dialog box will open. Type a name for the new toolbar in the Toolbar Name box:

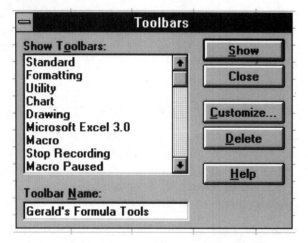

Select the Customize button to open the Customize dialog box (see Figure 4.1). From its list of categories, select Formula. The formula tools will appear. Now, drag each of the tools out of the dialog box and into the waiting toolbar. (Unless you're using Windows for Pen Computing, you can omit the tool with the picture of the pen on it.) When you're finished building the new toolbar, select the Close button in the Customize dialog box.

Figure 4.1:
The Customize dialog box allows you to create your own custom toolbar. (You might have to look hard to spot the empty toolbar when you first try this.)

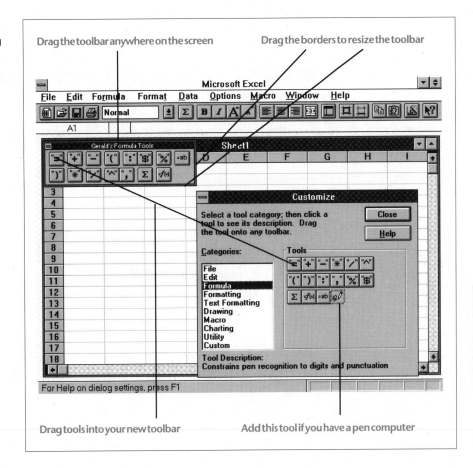

Drag the toolbar anywhere on the screen

Drag the borders to resize the toolbar

Drag tools into your new toolbar

Add this tool if you have a pen computer

Formula Syntax

You now have a customized toolbar for building formulas by way of mouse clicks. To hide your new toolbar, just click its control box (the close box on the Mac). To make it reappear, choose Options ➤ Toolbars, select the name you gave it, and click the Show button.

Working out on the Formula Toolbar

Think of the Formula Toolbar as a handy set of push buttons for entering functions and calculations. Here's how to use it:

1. Select the cell that will hold the result of the calculation. If you're inserting a function, skip Step 2 and go straight to Step 3.

2. Click the Equal Sign tool. The formula bar will open, and Excel will enter an equal sign (=) into it (see Figure 4.2).

Figure 4.2:
When you click the Equal Sign tool in the Formula Toolbar, Excel opens the formula bar and enters an equal sign.

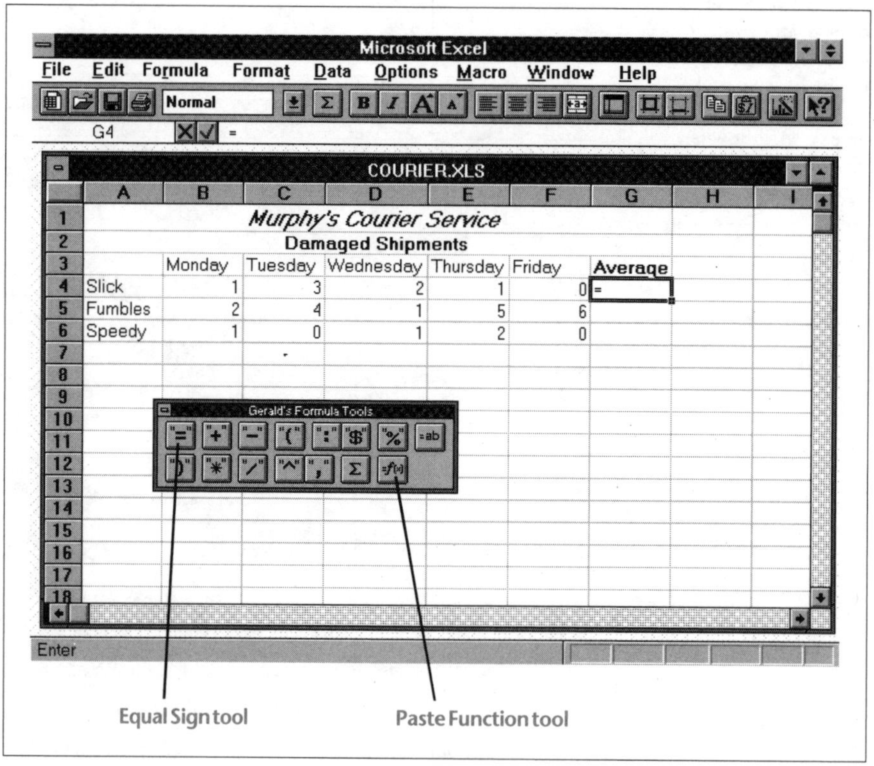

3. To enter the equal sign and a function name, click the Paste Function tool (the Paste Function tool is identified in Figure 4.2). The Paste Function dialog box, shown in Figure 4.3, will open. If you know the name of the function you want, select it from the

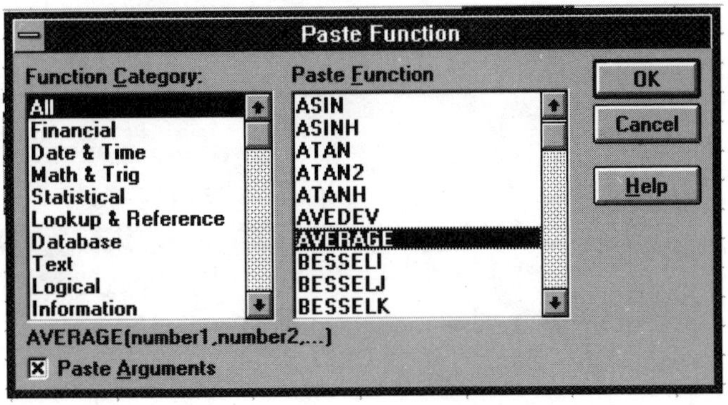

Figure 4.3:
The Paste Function
dialog box. If the Paste
Arguments box is
checked, Excel will
remind you what to
feed the formula.

list on the right. To pick by category, select a category on the left, then select the function name on the right. To have Excel insert placeholders for the required arguments, leave the Paste Arguments box checked.

4. When you select OK, Excel will enter the function into the formula bar, along with placeholders for its arguments. The first argument will be highlighted, or shown in reverse color.

5. Click the cell that holds the value for the first argument (*number1* here). Or, drag a range that holds a series of values. The crawling ants will march around your selection, and its reference will appear in the formula bar (see Figure 4.4).

6. Drag the I-beam cursor over the next argument in the formula bar so that it appears in reverse color.

7. Click the cell or drag the range you want to insert for the argument. You'll see the ants again, and the reference will appear in the formula bar.

8. Repeat steps 6 and 7 to select portions of the sheet for each argument that requires values. If necessary, click the Comma tool to insert commas between the arguments.

Formula Syntax

Figure 4.4:
Drag across a range of
cells to enter it into
the formula bar. The
"crawling ants" identify
your selection.

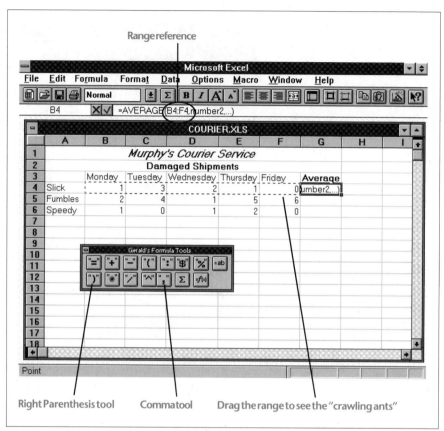

9. When you're finished inserting arguments, drag the I-beam cursor over everything that you don't need to the right of the ready-made formula. The text you drag over will be highlighted:

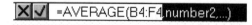

10. To replace the highlighted part of the formula, click the Right Parenthesis tool (identified in Figure 4.4).

11. To accept the completed formula, click the Confirm (✓) button to the left of the equal sign:

In the case of this simple formula, it would probably be just as easy to type it in the formula bar as it would be to use the Formula Toolbar. But as you begin to enter more complex formulas, clicking your way to higher math becomes really tempting—especially if you let Excel provide you with placeholders for the required arguments (see step 3 above).

Most of the other tools in the Formula Toolbar insert the symbol shown on them into the formula bar. Exceptions are the AutoSum tool, which inserts the SUM function and a nearby column or row reference, and the Paste Names tool, which inserts the name of a range. (You must have defined the range name previously using the Formula ➤ Define Name command.) The AutoSum tool and the Paste Names tool are labeled in Figure 4.5

Remember that range names in formulas, unlike keywords and text values, are not enclosed in quotation marks.

Figure 4.5:
The customized
Formula Toolbar

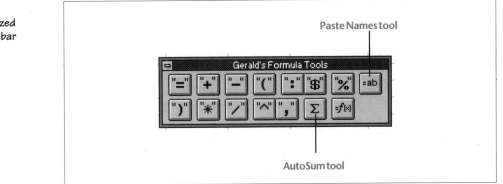

The Formula ➤ Paste Function and Formula ➤ Paste Name commands do the same things as the Paste Function and Paste Name tools. This means that keyboard maestros can get pasted, too.

Formula Syntax

Absolute and Relative References: The Untold Story

Many people have trouble with absolute and relative cell references in formulas. In the sections below I'll do my best to clear up this potentially confusing aspect of worksheet arcana.

Definitions are the easy part

An *absolute address* is part of a cell reference that will not change, even if you copy or move the formula that contains it elsewhere in the sheet. You can make a column letter ($A1), a row number (A$1), or both ($A$1) absolute so that Excel can't mess with it.

A *relative address* is part of a cell reference (with no $ in front of it) that can be reset by the program if you copy or move the formula that contains it.

Copying a formula almost always requires changing its cell references. Moving a formula might require changing its cell references, especially if the cells it refers to are moved along with it. (See "Moving Means Changing Addresses," in Chapter 6.)

You can make a reference absolute by inserting a dollar sign ($) in front of the column letter or row number when you are typing a formula. In the cell reference $A$1, the locations of both the column and the row are absolute and can't be changed. But in the reference A$1, only the row is absolute; the column letter is relative and can be reset by the program. In the reference $A1, the column is absolute and the row is relative. In the address A1, both the column and the row are relative.

When and when not to use your relatives

If you're like me, these definitions aren't much help about when to use the pesky $, so here are some guidelines.

In general, use relative cell references in formulas (no $). This gives you the convenience of being able to copy and move things around. Let Excel worry about the addresses.

Relative addresses are particularly handy when you use AutoFill to copy one formula into several adjacent cells, as demonstrated in Chapter 1. Because Excel is free to change the relative addresses, it seems to know how to reset each copy of the formula so that the calculation refers to the correct row or column.

Murphy's Guide to Addressing for Success: *Make an address absolute only if the program's changing it would produce an incorrect answer. Except for whizzes who develop a sixth sense about this stuff, the rest of us have to work this out on a case-by-case, trial-and-error basis.*

So try using relative addresses, check the result, and edit your formula, if necessary. In making your edits, it's usually easier to change the addresses in the original formula, then recopy it. (Copying formulas by methods other than AutoFill is covered in Chapter 6.)

Often, if Excel provides a reference for you, it takes the safe road and makes the addresses absolute. This happens, for example, when you select a range and choose Formula ➤ Define Name. You don't have to put up with this if you don't want to. Just edit the address to get rid of the $.

Remember that readjusting addresses may be necessary when a formula is copied or moved to a different cell. However, that's not the only kind of change that can cause Excel to reset the references in a formula. For example, all the addresses in all the formulas in a sheet might be affected if you delete or insert entire columns or rows with Edit ➤ Delete or Edit ➤ Insert.

An absolutely relevant example

Figure 4.6 shows an example in which readjustment of a relative address screws things up and produces an error.

Formula Syntax

Figure 4.6:
In this example, resetting a relative address produces an error.

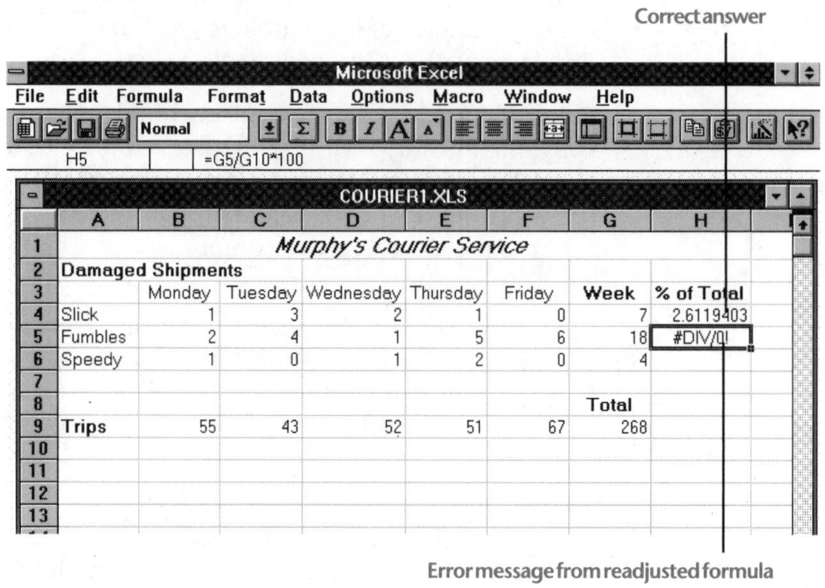

The formula in cell H4 calculates the percentage of Slick's damaged shipments to the total number of delivery trips Murphy's Courier Service made that week. The formula in cell H4 is

=G4/G9*100

This means "personal screw-ups divided by total company deliveries, multiplied by 100."

When AutoFill is used to copy this formula into the cell below it (to find out how much Fumbles screwed up), the result is an error. The program, in its misguided helpfulness, changes G4 to G5 and G9 to G10. G5 is the right stuff, but there is literally nothing in G10. In this case, Excel interprets the blank as zero and returns an error message stating that it refuses to divide something by nothing.

The formula will be copied correctly if the divisor (the total number of deliveries) is made absolute ($G$9). The number of damaged shipments for each courier (G4 in the original formula) remains relative so that it can be adjusted as it is copied into each new cell.

The formula in cell H4 should read

```
=G4/$G$9*100
```

To fix the sheet, you would need to edit the formula in cell H4, then recopy it by dragging the fill handle downward into cells H5 and H6.

Defying Relativity—Absolutely!

Excel has a way for you to convert relative addresses to absolute addresses quickly so you don't have to retype the address. This saves you time and also helps prevent errors caused by *mis*typing an address.

Highlight the address in the formula bar by dragging the I-beam cursor over it:

Then, from the menu bar select Formula ➤ Reference. (Keyboard maestros can press F4 instead; Mac users can press ⌘-T.) The highlighted address will change from all relative to all absolute:

Notice that Excel has added the $ character in front of both the column letter and the row number, making both absolute. If you repeat the command with the address still highlighted, just the row number will be made absolute (G$9). If you do the command again, just the column will be absolute ($G9). And if you do it a fourth time, the address will be all relative again (G9). You can choose Formula ➤ Reference (or press F4) repeatedly to cycle among all the combinations of absolute and relative columns and rows.

An Even Deeper Mystery: R1C1 Addressing

Just when I thought I had all this address stuff down pat, they come up with a completely different way of referring to columns and rows—called *R1C1*.

R1C1 addressing is totally optional. Do it if it feels good. In R1C1 addressing, each cell is referenced not by letter of column and number of row, but by *two numbers*: the number of its *row first* (R1), followed by the number of its column (C1). (They should have called it "bassackwards.")

You can enter the exotic world of R1C1 at any time by selecting Options ➤ Workspace. The Workspace dialog box will appear. Mark the R1C1 check box and select OK. When the sheet reappears, column letters will be changed to numbers, and all addresses will be in R1C1 notation. Figure 4.7 shows a sheet with cell addresses in R1C1 notation.

R1C1 has advantages that some people just love.

☞ All numbered addresses are absolute. Relative references are specified by just R or C—meaning the current row or column—and a bracketed number adding to or subtracting from that position. *Negative* numbers in brackets [-1] mean *left* or *up* from the current row or column. *Positive* numbers in brackets [1] mean *right* or *down*. In Figure 4.7, G4 has been converted to RC[-1]. This address means, "the current row and one cell to the left (minus one) from the current column." Notice that the absolute address

Figure 4.7:
In this sheet, column letters have been replaced with numbers, and cell addresses are in R1C1 notation.

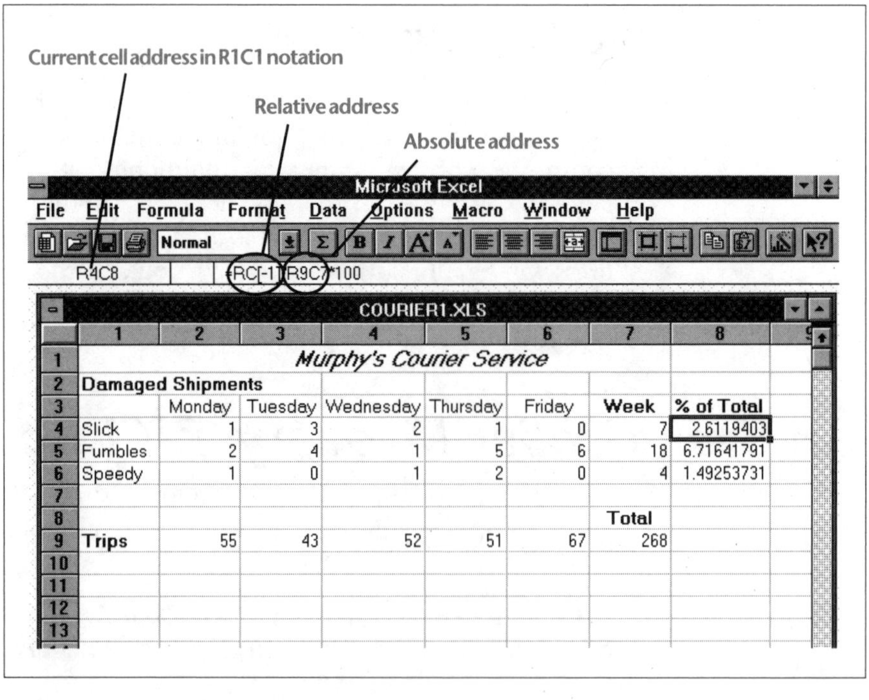

appears as a set of row and column numbers (R9C7). If this appeals to you, have at it.

☞ R1C1 can be really convenient when used with formulas (particularly macros) that must calculate row and column positions. It's just simpler to calculate and keep track of column 256 than to puzzle over column IV. For example, you might use this notation if you were writing formulas that fetch stuff from a large table (quite naturally called a *lookup* table).

☞ Obviously, R1C1 is more compatible with other people, data files, and software that also use R1C1 (whoever or whatever they are).

In short, if you ever need R1C1, you'll probably know it.

Formula Syntax

Chapter 5

BECOMING A MORE CALCULATING PERSON

Murphy's Guide to Pitfalls: If the left one doesn't get you, the right one will. She was last seen trying desperately to divide by zero. As for him, the poor devil got caught in a circular reference. Not a pretty sight.

This chapter ventures fearlessly, ever deeper, into the dark wood of formulas. Readers with a lust for adventure will have begun the journey in Chapters 2 and 4.

There's a reason for this obsessive exploration of formulas. If you want Excel to be your math slave, you must be able to describe the problems you want it to solve. You do that with formulas. Also, remember that *functions* are the ready-made formulas that Excel knows by heart. So, why reinvent the wheel? To do trigonometry problems just like a rocket scientist, all you have to know is the name of the function you need. Let Excel sweat the details.

First, I'll describe some of the more commonly used functions (besides the now-familiar SUM and AVERAGE). And I promise to pay close attention to crucial differences between functions that seem to work alike but actually don't.

Murphy Alert! Using the wrong function for a task is probably the number-one cause of Murphy-assisted worksheet death.

Second—and here's the super-secret information the Excel gurus keep to themselves—I'll suggest ways you can test your formulas and worksheets to make sure that the results will be reliable. I call these tips "Murphy's Eight Great Steps to Success beneath the Sheets." (Well, to some of us it's sexy!)

If you start to type a function into the formula bar but can't remember its required argument syntax, press Ctrl-A after typing the function name and Excel will give you a hint.

This Is SUM Review

Recall from Chapter 2 that the SUM function adds a series of values, which you feed to it as arguments (stuff inside parentheses, separated by commas). This formula, for example, adds the stuff stored in cells C2, C4, and C6:

    =SUM(C2,C4,C6)

Remember also that the following formula, which does not use the name of the ready-made SUM function, does exactly the same thing:

    =C2+C4+C6

Minus is cool

There is no separate ready-made formula for subtraction. If you want to subtract a value, put a minus sign (–) in front of its argument in the SUM formula. (Remember to keep the comma!) For example, if you wanted to subtract the value C6 from the sum of C2 and C4, you could enter this formula:

=SUM(C2,C4,–C6)

Or, you could use this formula:

=C2+C4–C6

*Beware the subtraction pitfall! Rookie formula writers often specify subtraction in a formula when the value in the sheet is already negative (preceded by a minus sign or enclosed in parentheses). Two negatives make a positive, so the resulting calculation will be addition, not subtraction. For example, suppose you entered debits in a checking account as negative numbers. In that case, you would **add** the debit values to the prior balance to get the current balance.*

Don't get parenthetical here

In formulas that do addition and subtraction only, you don't have to worry about using extra sets of parentheses to control the order of calculation. The reason is simple: The order in which values are added or subtracted has no effect on the result. (However, the order of calculation will be *very* important if the formula also involves multiplication or division.)

More Help for Recovering Lotus Users

If you're used to 1-2-3, and you're using a PC, Excel can accommodate your old Lotus habits. Select Options ➤ Calculation and mark the Alternate Expression Evaluation and Alternate Formula Entry check boxes. You can then enter formulas in Lotus syntax and even work with Lotus sheets directly, and Excel will translate the formulas. If you don't mark the check boxes, you can still type in formulas using the Lotus syntax (for example, using @ instead of =), but you must use the names of Excel functions only.

Sheet Logic

Oh Great, More Arithmetic

If you liked SUM for doing addition and subtraction, you'll love PRODUCT for multiplication and division. If you have a thing for integers and want whole-number answers, you can use QUOTIENT and MOD for division instead.

Here's a PRODUCT you'll love

PRODUCT works just like SUM. You feed it a series of arguments, and it multiplies them by one another to generate a single value as the product. For example,

```
=PRODUCT(B3:D3,6)
```

gives the same result as

```
=B3*C3*D3*6
```

So, if the cells in the range B3:D3 contain the values 4, 10, and 5, both formulas will calculate $4 \times 10 \times 5$, which is 200, then multiply by the constant 6, producing a result of 1200.

*Many math functions can take as many as **30** arguments. (Usually, all arguments must refer to the same type of data.) This is not to say that you are limited to **30** values, though. Any of those arguments can be a range reference (for example, A1:C1) or a range name (MYSTUFF). In that case, any one of the arguments might contain many values.*

Divide and conquer

Division is simply the inverse of multiplication. This means that you can do division as an inverse multiplication calculation using the PRODUCT function. For example, to make the argument C3 a *divisor* instead of a multiplier, enter the argument in the formula as its inverse, or reciprocal:

```
1/C3
```

This means, "the constant 1 divided by the value in C3."

To get *just the remainder* of a division problem, you use a different function:

```
MOD(D2,D3)
```

Supposing again that D2 is 10 and D3 is 3, the result of this formula would be the remainder of 10 divided by 3, or 1. Remember that you can have only one formula in a cell. So, if you wanted to use both QUOTIENT and MOD to get an integer result and a remainder, you would have to put the two formulas in different cells.

Don't Get Caught in an Argument

Don't use arithmetic signs (the arithmetic operators +, −, *, /, or ^) *between* arguments in formulas that use function names. The function name takes care of the arithmetic for you. You must separate the arguments with commas instead.

However, *within* a single argument, there can be good reasons to use arithmetic operators such as +, −, *, / or. For example, within arguments that refer to values, you can change the sign of a value by inserting a leading minus sign, or you can specify its inverse (1/A1). If you want to, you can ask for arithmetic calculations within an argument (A1+1).

An argument can even contain another function, as long as the function results in a single value. If you put one function inside another, use only *one* equal sign—in front of the whole formula:

```
=SUM(AVERAGE(A1:C1), AVERAGE(F2:F9))
```

Get to the root of the problem

Recall from Chapter 2 that you can get the square root of a number by raising it to the power of $1/2$, or 0.5. The calculation for the square root of the value in cell A1 would be

```
=A1^0.5
```

Let's say you wanted to multiply A1 by B1, then divide
The PRODUCT formula for this calculation is

```
=PRODUCT(A1,B1,1/C3)
```

Remember that not all numbers can be divided evenly.
there's a little something left over, called a *remainder*. F
divided by 3 equals 3, with a remainder of 1. A remain
either as a fractional part ($\frac{1}{3}$) or as a decimal value (.33
Excel will show a remainder as a decimal. So if the valu
and C3 were 5.1, 10, and 2, Excel would calculate 5.1 ×
produce 25.5.

The QUOTIENT can be a surprise

The hasty function explorer might think that QUOTIEN
thing for division that PRODUCT does for multiplicatio
QUOTIENT does divide one value (the dividend) by anc
divisor):

```
=QUOTIENT(D2,D3)
```

However, the result will be *only the whole number* (or inte
answer. If the answer includes a remainder, the remain

So in the formula above, if D2 and D3 contain the valu
result of the calculation will be 3, and the leftovers (a re
or the decimal part 0.33333...) will evaporate.

Can't Find QUOTIENT?

The QUOTIENT function is not in the standard set of ready
mulas, but is a selection in the Analysis ToolPak—a bonus
made formulas. If you installed this option with Excel, yo
function as described above and Excel will do the rest. For
one of these tools, have a look at the AutoSave section in C

As an alternative, you can use the SQRT function. SQRT takes one argument only—the number you want the square root of. The argument can be a constant (such as 64) or a reference to a cell that holds a number value (such as A1). The following formula gives the same result as the calculation above:

```
=SQRT(A1)
```

It's Not Nice to Be Negative

When you're using the SQRT function to extract a square root, you will insult Excel if the argument turns out to be negative. In mathematics, the square root of any negative value is an *imaginary number*—not something Excel is equipped to handle with this particular function.

Rather than entering into the realm of the imaginary, Excel will give the result #NUM!. This is Excel's way of saying that you had better change the sign of the argument to make it positive if you want to get an answer.

Extend and foot in one easy step

A common accounting calculation is to *extend*, or multiply, one column of values by the values in another column, then *foot*, or total, the extended values. For this neat trick, Excel offers the ready-made function SUMPRODUCT.

Figure 5.1 shows an order form for replacement parts for the Bionic Person. Notice that the SUMPRODUCT function multiplies the Quantity in column A by the Unit Price in column C, then foots the extended amount to give an Order Total.

Notice in this example that cell A9 has no value in it; evidently the customer did not wish to order the optional belly button. The blank cell is okay here because SUMPRODUCT treats cells that don't contain numbers as if they held zeros. However, if you used a simple multiplication formula (A9*C9) instead of SUMPRODUCT, you would have to enter a zero in cell A9 in order for the calculation to work.

Sheet Logic

Figure 5.1:

In this order form, the SUMPRODUCT function multiplies the Quantity values in column A by the Unit Price values in column C, then totals the results.

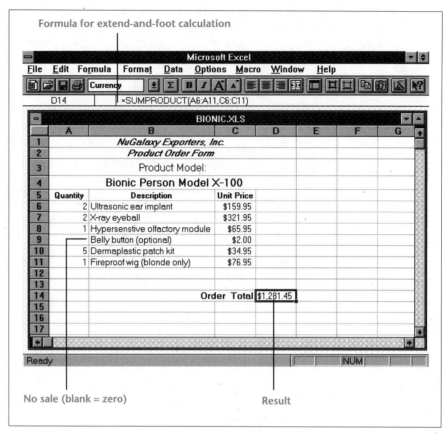

Formula for extend-and-foot calculation

No sale (blank = zero)

Result

SUMPRODUCT returns the answer #VALUE!, Murphy has struck again. This will happen if there are more cells in one column than in the other. SUMPRODUCT will only work if each argument (each column, in this case) holds the same number of cells.

The two-column example is probably the most common type of extend-and-foot calculation, but SUMPRODUCT will work with anywhere from two to thirty arguments. Each argument is an *array*. An array can be a column, a row, or a block of adjacent cells. Each array used as an argument in the same SUMPRODUCT function must be the same size and shape, or have the same *dimensions* (columns × rows).

An array *is a block of cells having* m *columns* × n *rows, or dimensions of* m × n.

In an array that contains more than one column or row, SUMPRODUCT will multiply the values in the cells in columnwise order. For example, if one of the arguments was the range A1:C5, the program would use the values from A1–A5, then from B1–B5, then from C1–C5 (see Figure 5.2). A second argument in the formula could be D1:F5, which has the same dimensions as A1:C5. SUMPRODUCT would process this second array in the same columnwise order. Keep this in mind when you're checking the logic of your sheet (this is strongly recommended later in this chapter).

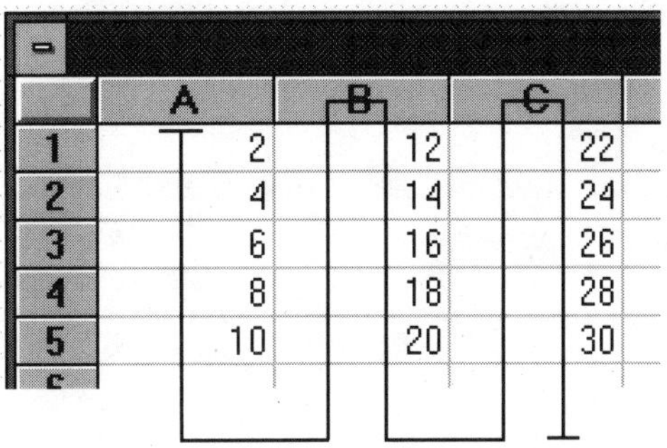

Figure 5.2:
Excel reads an array in this columnwise order.

	A	B	C
1	2	12	22
2	4	14	24
3	6	16	26
4	8	18	28
5	10	20	30

When is array like a beam of inspiration?

As an alternative to SUMPRODUCT, you can use an *array formula*. An array formula in Excel can be one of two things:

☞ A single formula that produces multiple results

☞ A single result from multiple-valued arguments (arrays of values)

Single formula, multiple results

The first kind of array formula has the same effect as copying a single formula into a block of cells using AutoFill, as described in Chapter 1.

Sheet Logic

The only difference is that the arguments are arrays rather than single cells. You use only one array formula for an entire block of cells that will hold its results.

To see how this works, look back at the Bionic Person order form. In Figure 5.3 I've added a fourth column, Extension, to hold the results of the Quantity values multiplied by the Unit Price values. To enter an array formula for this calculation, first you must select the array that will hold the formula. In this case, the array is the Extension column, or D6:D11.

Once you've selected the array, type the following formula:

```
=A6:A11*C6:C11
```

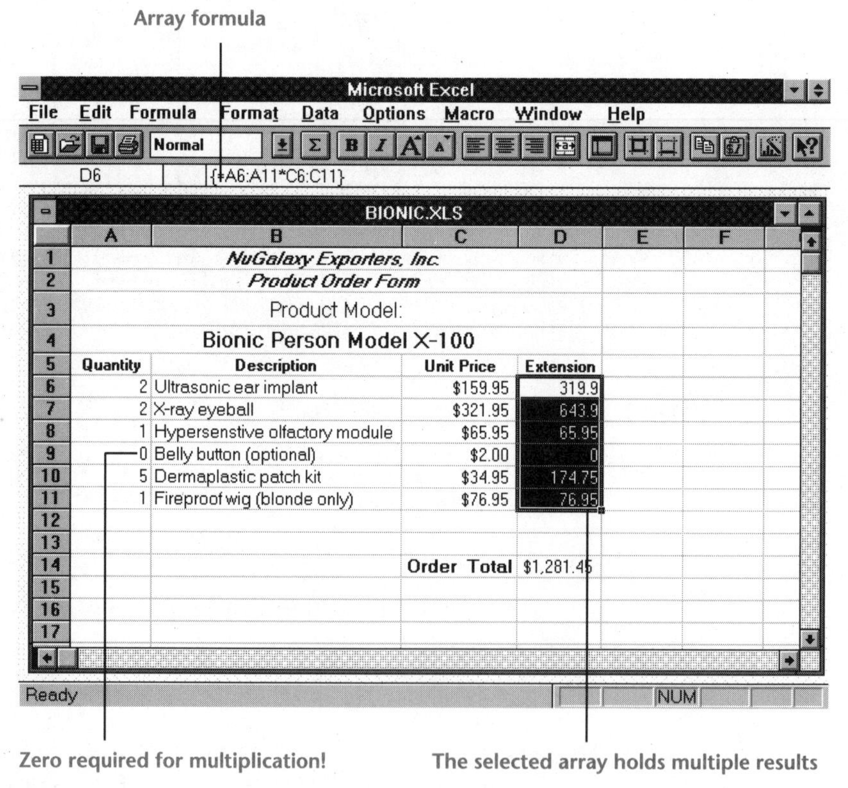

Figure 5.3:
In this example, an array formula calculates each of the Quantity values by the corresponding Unit Price value and enters the results in the Extension column.

Now, rather than pressing ↵ or clicking ✓ to accept this formula, press Ctrl-Shift-↵ (press the three keys at the same time). (If you're using a Mac, press Control-Shift-Return or ⌘-Return.) Excel calculates each of the separate products and places one result in each cell of the selected array.

Notice that Excel puts curly brackets around the formula syntax when you press Ctrl-Shift-↵. These brackets indicate that the formula is an array formula. However, you cannot enter an array formula simply by typing the brackets. If you do, Excel will think the formula is text.

Excel treats an array formula and its block of cells as a single thing: You can't edit the cells separately. To edit an array formula, select the entire array and edit the formula in the formula bar. When you're done, press Ctrl-Shift-↵, to reenter the edited syntax as an array formula.

Multiple-valued arguments, single result

You can replace the SUMPRODUCT formula in the order form with an array formula that multiplies two column-array arguments within a SUM formula. This is an example of multiple-valued arguments that produce a single result. The formula would be entered in cell D14 as

```
=SUM(A6:A11*C6:C11)
```

When you press Ctrl-Shift-↵, the formula multiplies the arrays in columns A and C, then feeds the products to the SUM function, which adds them and places the result in cell D14.

These Arrays Can Be Both Beneficial and Harmful

Array formulas are convenient, and they save computer memory that would be tied up if you entered multiple copies of single-value formulas. Plus, they're versatile. Although the example above uses an array formula that can be an alternative to SUMPRODUCT, Excel can do any combination of arithmetic operations on arrays.

A drawback of array formulas is that they are not as easy to understand at a glance. The individual values are hidden within the array references. This can make it harder to check the logic of your worksheet.

Sheet Logic

Counting without using your fingers

Excel will happily count how many number values are in a set of ranges. Or, it will count all data entries, including text and numbers.

The sheet in Figure 5.4 contains numbers indicating inches of rainfall at various sites. Values have been entered only for the rainy days; the rest of the cells are blank. The formula in cell B8 counts the nonblank number entries in row 3:

=COUNT(B3:H3)

In this example, I used AutoFill to copy the formula in cell B8 into cells B9 and B10 to show the rainy-day count for the other two cities.

The COUNT function counts valid number entries, as well as any other values that can be interpreted as numbers, such as dates. A similar function, COUNTA, counts almost anything except blanks—including text, numbers, even error messages.

Figure 5.4:

The formula in cell B8 gives a count of the cells holding number values in row 3.

	Microsoft Excel							
File	Edit	Formula	Format	Data	Options	Macro	Window	Help

B8 =COUNT(B3:H3)

RAIN.XLS

	A	B	C	D	E	F	G	H
1	Precipitation in Inches of Rainfall							
2		Sunday	Monday	Tuesday	Wednesday	Thursday	Friday	Saturday
3	Possum Hollow	0.5	1.5			0.4		
4	Varmint Creek		1.2	0.6				
5	Ugly City	0.4	1.3				0.1	
6								
7		Rainy Days						
8	Possum Hollow	3						
9	Varmint Creek	2						
10	Ugly City	3						
11								
12								
13								

Go for the MAX—or not!

Excel provides other handy functions that report on the high (MAX), low (MIN), and median (MEDIAN) of a series of values. For example, using the data from Figure 5.4, the formula below returns the peak rainfall for the week in Possum Hollow:

    =MAX(B3:H3)

The formula =MIN(B3:H3) would give an answer of 0.4, not 0, because the formula only looks at nonblank cells. Therefore, the result is the minimum amount of rainfall *on the days that had rain*. To include all the days in the MIN calculation, you would have to place zeros in the blank cells. (Then, of course, you couldn't use COUNT to calculate the number of days it rained.)

The next formula calculates median rainfall for the same place:

    =MEDIAN(B3:H3)

Figure 5.5 shows the results of this formula.

Figure 5.5:
The formula in cell E8 calculates median rainfall for Possum Hollow. Note that MEDIAN looks only at nonblank cells.

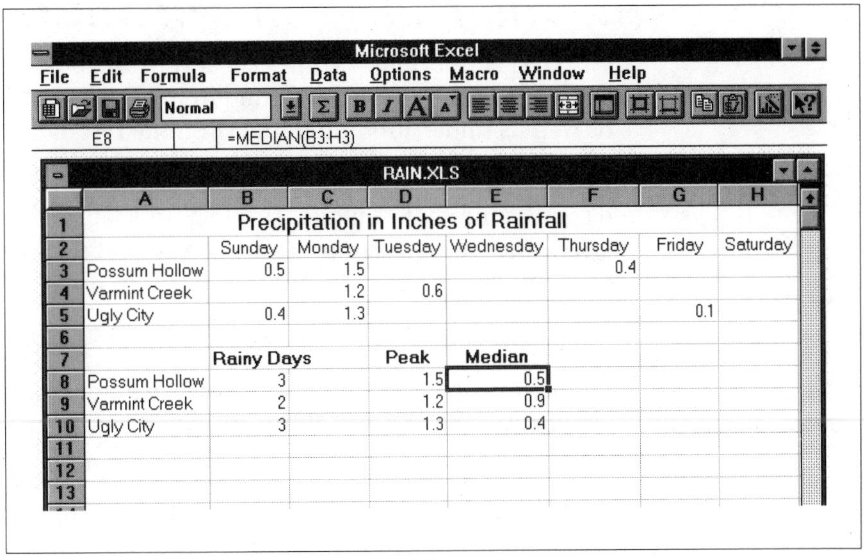

Just as with MIN, the MEDIAN function looks only at the rainy days, ignoring the blank cells. If you wanted MEDIAN to include the dry days as well, you would have to fill the blank cells with zeros.

What Do You Median by That?

Here's another example of similar formulas that do significantly different things: AVERAGE sums a series of numbers and then divides by the count. MEDIAN finds the number value that is smack in the middle of a series: Half the values in the series are above it, half below. (If there is an even number of values, MEDIAN will average the two values in the center.)

In many cases, AVERAGE and MEDIAN produce different results when used with the same data series.

In fact, the two functions can produce nearly the same result *only* if the data series has a lot of items that are evenly distributed in value.

Converting the Heathen Decimals

Working with decimal values is perhaps the biggest gaping pitfall in the worksheet jungle. Not falling in involves picking the right function as well as understanding its effect on the rest of the math in your sheet.

Decimal values are problematic because a worksheet cell can only hold a specific number of digits. This fact, in itself, is a potential source of error, since some decimals could go on forever. For example, 10 divided by 3 equals

`3.333333333333333333333333333333333333333333333333...`

That ellipsis (...) means "and so on," so what you see is just an approximation, despite all those digits.

Excel provides a wide variety of ready-made functions you can use to hack decimals down to size. These functions all work differently, and woe unto you if you use one and mean another.

ROUND up the usual suspects

The ROUND function does the seemingly simple job of rounding off a long decimal value to a shorter, more manageable one. In so doing, ROUND can adjust the last digit of the result so that it better approximates the original, longer number. (In other words, ROUND fudges the result.)

ROUND takes two arguments—the decimal value you want rounded and the number of decimal places you want in the result. If you wanted to round off the value in cell B2 to two decimal places, the formula would be

```
=ROUND(B2,2)
```

In this example, if cell B2 held the value 1654.9876, the result would be 1654.99 (with the last digit rounded up).

Okay, fine. Close enough for government work. Indeed, ROUND can be the most accurate way of dealing with unruly decimals—provided that the result can also be a decimal.

The second argument you feed to ROUND can also be zero or a negative number. If the second argument is zero, Excel will round the result up or down to the nearest integer. If the second argument is negative (less than zero), Excel will round the number to the left of the decimal point at the position indicated by the number. For example, an argument of –1 would round 34.9 to 30.

Just chop off its TRUNC

A function that works very much like ROUND is TRUNC. TRUNC wantonly chops off some or all of the decimal stuff. Like ROUND, TRUNC takes two arguments—the number you want to truncate and the number of decimal places you want in the result:

```
=TRUNC(B2,1)
```

In the formula above, if B2 held the value 1654.9876, the result would be 1654.9. If you omit the second argument, TRUNC will assume it's zero, in which case it will throw away all the decimal stuff, leaving you with a naked integer.

Meet TRUNC's cousin INT

Copy-cat INT works exactly the same as TRUNC when TRUNC has only one argument—unless the value is a negative number. INT rounds a decimal value *down* to the nearest integer. So =TRUNC(–5.6) is –5, but =INT(–5.6) is –6. If the argument were positive (5.6), TRUNC and INT would produce the same result (5).

And now the rest of the Decimal-Eaters

Excel offers a host of other functions that digest decimals. Each of these Decimal-Eaters works differently:

CEILING Rounds a decimal value up (away from zero) to the nearest multiple of a constant that you enter as a second argument.

FLOOR Works like CEILING, but rounds a number towards zero.

MROUND Rounds to the nearest multiple (be it smaller or larger) of a constant that you enter as a second argument.

EVEN Rounds a value up to the nearest even integer.

ODD Rounds up to the nearest odd integer.

Take the Logical Alternative

Every worksheet explorer's tool kit should include the six *logical functions*: IF, AND, OR, NOT, TRUE, and FALSE. You can use these logical functions to test the depth of the waters without getting wet. For example, the IF function tests the stuff in a distant cell without your having to go there to select it. And it reports back in a secret code that you invent.

TECHNO NOTE

Historical Marker

This logical path was first trekked by nineteenth-century British mathematician George Boole. His method of using mathematical statements to perform logical tests is known as *Boolean algebra*.

Consider the set of test scores in Figure 5.6. The logical IF formulas in column D test the scores in column C and report whether the student passed or failed. The IF function has three arguments: the logical test (C5>60), meaning "Is the score greater than 60?"; the report if the test is true (the text value "Pass"); and the report if the test is false ("Fail"). (Recall that you must enclose text values in formulas in quotation marks.) Here's the formula:

```
=IF(C5>60,"Pass","Fail")
```

The first and second arguments are required; the third is optional. If you omit the third argument, Excel will put FALSE in the cell if the test is false.

Figure 5.6:
The IF formula in the formula bar tests whether the score in column C is greater than 60.

	A	B	C	D	E	F	G	H	I	J
1	A Course in Boolean Miracles									
2		Student Test Scores								
3										
4		Ernestine	92	Pass						
5		Spark	59	Fail						
6		Ahab	72	Pass						
7		Farfel	83	Pass						
8										
9										
10										
11										
12										
13										

Microsoft Excel — File Edit Formula Format Data Options Macro Window Help — Normal — D5 `=IF(C5>60,"Pass","Fail")` — BOOLE.XLS

Sheet Logic

The greater-than sign (>) in the first argument is a *logical operator.* Logical tests in Excel can use any of the following operators:

>   greater than

<   less than

=   equal to

>=   greater than or equal to

<=   less than or equal to

<>   not equal to

These are the other logical functions:

☞ AND   reports the logical value TRUE if all its arguments are true.

☞ OR   reports TRUE if *any* of its arguments is true.

☞ NOT   reverses the logic of its argument so that a TRUE result becomes FALSE, and vice versa.

☞ TRUE() and FALSE()   return the values TRUE and FALSE. TRUE() and FALSE() take no arguments.

Logical functions are the basic means of processing sequence control in macros (automated sequences of Excel commands), just as they are in computer programming languages such as BASIC, Pascal, and C.

A few mathematical functions are also useful for testing cell values:

☞ DELTA   takes two arguments and reports 1 if the arguments are equal, 0 if they are not equal.

☞ GESTEP   which takes two arguments and reports 1 if the first argument is greater than or equal to the second argument, 0 otherwise.

Nested Functions Can Be Cozy

Sometimes it's okay to put one function inside another. This is often done inside IF formulas. The nested function must be enclosed in parentheses, and it must result in a single value that can be used as a valid argument. Here's an example:

```
=IF((MOD(B2,3)=0),"No remainder",MOD(B2,3))
```

This formula uses the MOD function to test whether the result of dividing the value in B2 by 3 leaves no remainder. If this is true, Excel returns the text "No remainder" to the cell. If it's not true, Excel places the remainder produced by the MOD function in the cell. Notice the matched, nested pairs of parentheses and the fact that only the formula itself is preceded by the equal sign (=).

Excel for the Wizards of Wall Street

As you might expect from a program that has become wildly popular with the captains of industry, Excel has memorized all kinds of financial calculations.

There is scarcely room in this modest book to open up those financial functions and peer at their intricate inner workings. Here are some basic guidelines for picking the right function for the task at hand.

If you save your bucks, you'll need this function:

```
=EFFECT(nominal_rate,npery)
```

EFFECT gives you the effective annual interest rate on an investment such as a bank certificate of deposit. The effective rate is often advertised as the APR, or annual percentage rate. EFFECT takes two arguments—the *nominal_rate* (the published simple-interest rate with no compounding taken into account) and *npery*, the number of compounding periods each year. (Compounding reinvests the interest earnings. If you don't understand compounding, watch out for former S & L officers who have swamp land to sell.)

Sheet Logic

If somebody quoted you the APR and you wanted to calculate the simple interest, you would use this function:

```
=NOMINAL(effect_rate,npery)
```

NOMINAL works like EFFECT, but in reverse. The first argument is the *effective_rate* (net percent returned with compounding), and the second argument is *npery*, the number of compounding periods per year. The result is the simple interest rate.

Don't use bank interest formulas on other types of investments. Excel offers these specialized financial functions:

INTRATE	rate of return on a fully invested security
YIELD	return on a bond
TBILLYIELD	return on a Treasury bill

When Is NOW Not TODAY?

Excel will time-stamp your worksheet for free. In any cell, just enter the formula

```
=NOW()
```

This function—which never has an argument—reports the current date and time from the system clock of your computer. If the current date were February 23, 1999 and the time were 2:29 P.M., the result would be

```
2/23/99 14:59
```

Excel usually displays time according to the 24-hour clock used by the military and other people who presumably never sleep.

To get just the date (no time for anything else), enter

```
=TODAY()
```

Formulas that use NOW or TODAY are updated each time the sheet is recalculated. Normally, Excel recalculates the sheet whenever you enter new stuff into a cell. To force recalculation, press F9 or Ctrl-= on the PC (⌘-= on the Mac).

If you want, you can freeze the result of NOW or TODAY so that it is not updated. Select the cell that holds the NOW or TODAY formula, click the formula bar (or press F2 on a PC) to open the formula for editing, recalculate the formula as described above, then press ↵ to enter the result into the cell.

You Must Try Dates in Your Serial

Calculations with dates and times can be a real pain. Ask anybody who has tried to add times of day or figure out the aging of accounts receivable (or, "How old are our outstanding bills?").

Excel has a way to do calculations with dates that reduces the problem to simple decimal arithmetic. The program first converts the date (or date and time) to a *serial date*. In a serial date system, every second of every day starting from the year 1900 (on a PC) is assigned a sequential decimal number. Days are expressed as the integer part. Hours, minutes, and seconds are represented as fractions of a whole day.

Mixing Dates with Apples and PC(an)s

The Macintosh version of Excel starts the serial date system with the year 1904, so the serial-date values are different. But if you open a sheet created on the Mac in Excel for Windows, you won't have to worry. The program will convert the values automatically. (If you are working on a PC and want to be compatible with your friends in the Apple world while working in Big Blue, select Options ➤ Calculation and mark the 1904 Date System check box.)

You never have to worry about figuring out serial dates on your own. Excel has ready-made functions to handle the conversion for you. However, you should be aware of how Excel does date and time calculations, and you should know how to convert dates and times displayed as text into serial dates that other formulas can use.

To get the serial date for February 23, 1999, you could use this formula:

```
=DATEVALUE("February 23, 1999")
```

Sheet Logic

The argument of DATEVALUE can be text enclosed in quotation marks, as shown above, or the address of a cell that holds a text label.

Or, you can feed the year, month, and day to the DATE function:

`=DATE(1999,2,23)`

The result in either case is 36214, a number that is easily used in arithmetic. (How this date is displayed in the cell that holds the formula depends on the *number formatting* of the cell. See Chapter 6.)

To calculate a date 90 days hence (the day to call the collection agency if your invoice hasn't been paid), you might use this formula:

`=DATEVALUE("February 23, 1999")+90`

Ninety days from this date would be 36214+90, or 36304. Excel can convert this serial date back into something people can understand by using these three formulas (each contained in a different cell):

`=MONTH(36304)`
`=DAY(36304)`
`=YEAR(36304)`

In this case, MONTH returns 5, DAY returns 24, and YEAR returns 1999. So 90 days from February 23, 1999, will be May 24, 1999.

In practice, you do not have to use MONTH, DAY, and YEAR to convert a serial date back into something you can understand. Just select Format ➤ Number ➤ Date. Excel will give you several date formats to choose from. Select the date display style (Format Code), and select OK. This changes the display format of the cell. (There's more about this in Chapter 6.)

Clock time can also be part of a serial date. It is the part of the date appearing to the right of the decimal point. For example, if the current date is February 23, 1999, and the time is 14:59:00 (hours, minutes, and seconds) the equivalent serial date and time value would be

`36214.624305555555556`

Just as with dates, you can format a cell to display serial time values in more conventional notation. Just choose Format ➤ Number ➤ Time, or use the functions HOUR, MINUTE, and SECOND to extract the hours, minutes, and seconds from the serial time.

> ### Who Says Accountants Are Weird?
>
> The accounting systems of some businesses are based on twelve 30-day months, or a 360-day year instead of the usual 365.25 days. (The 0.25 gets corrected every fourth, or leap, year.) Normally, you could add and subtract serial dates to your heart's content to calculate forward or backward. But if your year is based on 360 days, you must use the special DAYS360 function to calculate the difference between two dates:
>
> ```
> =DAYS360(start_date,end_date)
> ```

Circular References Are Worksheet Quicksand

One of the more exotic pitfalls for the unwary Excel user is the dreaded *circular reference*. A circular reference is the result of a formula that refers to itself.

Direct circular references are easy to spot

A circular reference can be *direct*. This happens when you enter the address of the current cell in the formula that it holds. For example, try entering this formula in cell A1:

```
=A1+1
```

At my urging, you have created a logical impossibility. When you enter this formula, Excel replies, "Cannot resolve circular references."

Indirect circular references can be insidious

The *indirect* kind of circular reference looks less like a stupid mistake, and therefore is both easier to make and much more difficult to trace. For example, cell A1 might hold the formula

```
=B1+1
```

Sheet Logic

This, in itself, looks perfectly fine. No circular reference here. But look what's in B1:

=A1*2

As you can see, A1 has a formula that refers to B1, which has a formula referring back to A1. Rather roundabout, or indirect, and most certainly circular. Once again, Excel replies, "Cannot resolve circular references."

Some Math Freaks Do It Anyway

Circular references are not necessarily wrong. For some kinds of problems, it can be productive to keep Excel running in circles—as long as you tell it when to stop. The trick is to limit the number of circular calculation passes, or *iterations*.

Normally, Excel will refuse to run in circles. But—*if you're sure you need to do this*—you can make it whirl. Select Options ➤ Calculation and mark the Iteration check box. Two settings here control when the circular calculations will stop: Maximum Iterations (normally 100 passes) and Maximum Change, whichever occurs first. The maximum change value becomes important if repeating the calculation causes the result to come closer and closer to some value that it never quite reaches. Normally, calculation will stop when the next pass produces a difference smaller than 0.001.

Murphy's Eight Great
Steps to Success beneath the Sheets

As promised, here are some basic steps you can follow to ensure that your worksheet produces reliable results:

1. Pick the right function for the job.

   ☞ For calculations with dates or times, convert the dates or times to serial date and time values, use arithmetic functions, then convert the answer back to the original date or time format. (Usually you do this by formatting the cell that holds the formula.)

☞ Beware of differences between functions that have similar purposes: INTRATE for securities, YIELD for bonds; ROUND for rounding, TRUNC for truncation; AVERAGE for arithmetic averages, but MEDIAN for the mid-point value.

2. Watch for common sources of error.

☞ Avoid division by zero, or by any reference that might result in zero.

☞ Beware of any rounded or truncated value that is used in other calculations, particularly multiplication calculations. In many cases, inaccuracy will get worse each time a rounded value is multiplied.

☞ Avoid circular references unless you're ready for trouble.

3. Make sure to feed a function everything it wants.

☞ If you don't enter the arguments as required, Excel will protest when you press ↵ or click ✓ to enter the formula. For example, it may reply, "Too few arguments" or "Too many arguments." When you select OK in one of these warning boxes, Excel will highlight the location of what it suspects is the offending syntax item in the formula bar.

☞ Be sure to supply the correct keywords for the functions that require them (such as INFO). Enclose keywords in quotation marks (""), and spell them correctly.

☞ Enclose text values used as arguments in quotation marks. If you omit the quotation marks, Excel will think that the item is a range name and will try to find its value.

☞ Use parentheses in matching pairs. Excel will thank you for this courtesy by flashing the pair in the formula bar as you type the matching parenthesis. If you get lost among nested pairs of parens, count them. If you have an odd number, you're definitely in trouble. If you have an even number, you're not necessarily out of the woods.

Sheet Logic

☞ TRUE and FALSE are logical values, not text. Do not enclose them in quotation marks when you use them in formulas or when you type them as explicit values in cells.

4. Use the right stuff.

☞ Make sure that arguments refer to cells or ranges that hold the values needed by the function. This is probably the most common source of errors from formulas—especially from formulas that *appear* to work because they produce values instead of error messages.

☞ Use range names for clarity, but don't assume that the name refers to the correct range until you recheck it: Select the range you think is named and look in the cell reference box (top left of the screen) to see if the name appears there.

☞ Use absolute and relative addressing correctly to prevent errors that might creep in if you edit the sheet later—perhaps long after you've forgotten how you built it.

☞ You can use array formulas for convenience and to conserve memory, but be sure that the range references within them refer to the individual values you need. Also, remember that arrays used as arguments in the same formula must be the same shape and size.

5. Test each formula.

☞ When you're done building a worksheet, make a copy of it for testing purposes. (Testing might corrupt the sheet, so always test a *copy*.) Enter sample data and note the results. First, use stuff that produces answers you already know or can calculate manually. Then, use data at extremes (high and low anticipated values), and even try data that's out of bounds. Use data of incorrect types, such as a date entered as text where a date value is expected, as well as of correct types.

☞ Watch for error messages (there's a list in Chapter 2) and incorrect results. Revise your formulas until the sheet works as expected.

6. Test the sheet.

☞ Generating graphs from ranges in the sheet can be a quick visual check to see whether your results are in the ballpark. See Chapter 11 for details.

7. If you make changes to the sheet, recheck and retest it.

☞ Excel may reset formulas if you copy or move ranges or if you delete or add columns or rows. Be alert to the difference between absolute and relative cell addresses, and use them correctly in your formulas to prevent errors from such readjustments.

8. If you think Excel goofed, think again.

☞ It's not that Excel is smart. Quite the contrary. It just does what you tell it to do.

Chapter 6

WHEN DESIGNING WOMEN MEET CALCULATING MEN

The Henry Higgins Rule: The French don't care what you do, as long as you pronounce it correctly.

It's all very fine for you to make Excel slave over your math problems, but you also need to display the results so that people—including you—can understand them. To be a calculating person in polite company, you need to pay attention to the *design* of your worksheet as well as to its content. You might call this "information etiquette."

This chapter is about arranging and rearranging worksheets. Here you'll learn to make the stuff in your sheets look the way you (and your boss) expect it to look. For example, as I mention in the last chapter, Excel likes to work with dates and times as serial numbers. These are nearly impossible for humans to understand at a glance. But by controlling the *number formatting* of a cell that holds a serial date or time value, you can display the date or time in a variety of easy-to-read combinations of month, day, year, hours, minutes, and seconds.

Number formatting is a set of options for displaying the stuff in a cell. For example, number format controls whether the value 1000 appears as 1,000, $1,000.00, or 100000%. Number formatting does not affect the actual value that Excel holds in memory. It just controls the way Excel displays the value on the screen and in printouts.

Which format do you use if your stuff isn't numbers? Well, the data format of text is text, and that's that. To Excel, anything that isn't in a number format or doesn't have an equal sign in front of it (a formula) is *text*. (The logical values TRUE and FALSE are an exception.) Text is whatever you type. It's free-form data. That's why if you make a mistake typing a number or a formula, Excel usually permits the entry and assumes it's text.

Another way of changing the look of information is to use *appearance formatting*. While number formatting is *muy importante* to the way a result is interpreted (as a date or as money, for example), appearance formatting is cosmetic. (I discuss appearance formatting in Chapter 7, where you'll find out how to dress up your sheet to meet the boss.)

Don't Let Relocation Upset You

Let's face it, moving can be stressful. But in Excel it doesn't have to be. Use the Cave Man method to move a cell or a block of cells—just drag your stuff to a new location.

Recall that you can select a cell by clicking it, or you can press the arrow keys to move the cell highlight to it. To select a block of cells, drag the cell pointer from one corner of the block to the opposite corner, as shown in Figure 6.1, or move the highlight by holding down the Shift key while pressing the arrow keys.

Number Formats

Figure 6.1:
You can select a block of cells by dragging it with your mouse.

$1,000,000
$5,200,000
$12,500,000
$100
$100
$1

Drag from here...

to here

To move your selection, position the cell pointer at the border of the cell highlight (anywhere but on the little square in the lower-right corner). The pointer will change to an arrow tip:

Click the mouse button (the left one for PC users) and keep holding it down as you drag the arrow and the border to another location in the sheet (see Figure 6.2). When you release the mouse button, the cell contents will pop into the new location, as shown in Figure 6.3. The cell highlight will move, too, so that your stuff remains selected, awaiting your next imperial command.

Figure 6.2:
To move the stuff in selected cells, position the mouse pointer over the border of the selection and drag the stuff to a new location

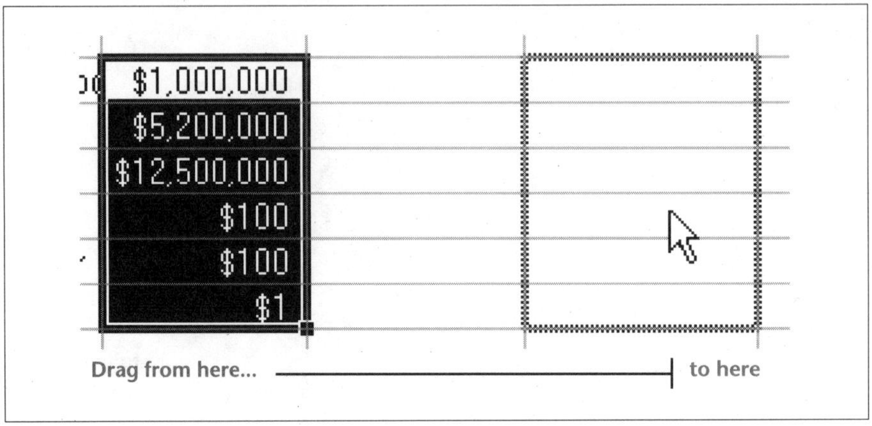

| $1,000,000 |
| $5,200,000 |
| $12,500,000 |
| $100 |
| $100 |
| $1 |

Drag from here... ⸻⸻⸻⸻⸻⸻ to here

Figure 6.3:
The block of stuff, still highlighted, in the new location

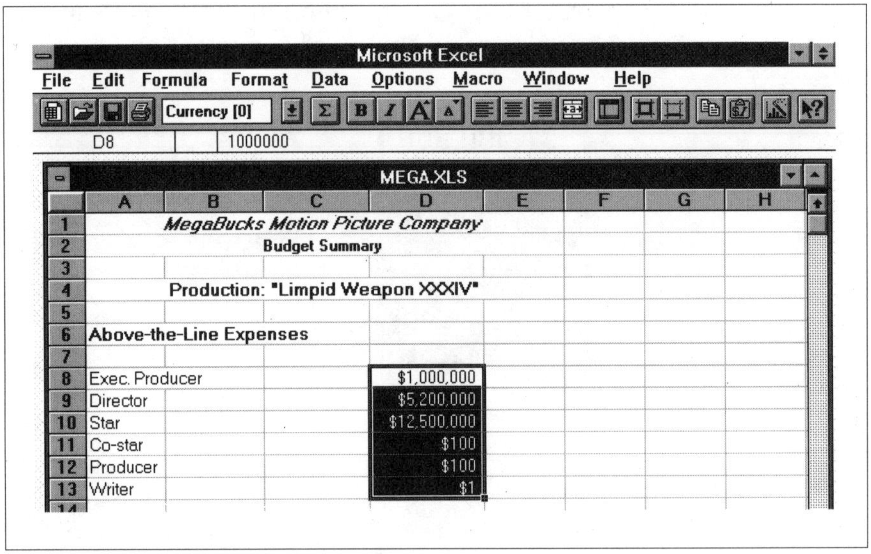

Microsoft Excel

File   Edit   Formula   Format   Data   Options   Macro   Window   Help

Currency [0]

D8   1000000

MEGA.XLS

	A	B	C	D	E	F	G	H
1		*MegaBucks Motion Picture Company*						
2			Budget Summary					
3								
4			Production: "Limpid Weapon XXXIV"					
5								
6	Above-the-Line Expenses							
7								
8	Exec. Producer			$1,000,000				
9	Director			$5,200,000				
10	Star			$12,500,000				
11	Co-star			$100				
12	Producer			$100				
13	Writer			$1				

When you move the stuff in a cell or a block of cells, normally everything in those cells goes along for the ride—data, formulas, and formatting. It's a mover's dream. When the stuff is in its new place, it will be arranged just as it was in the old place!

Moving into a Smaller Space

If you try to move stuff into columns or rows that are smaller in width or height than the old place, you'll get that cramped feeling. If the data that you moved is a number and the new column is too narrow, Excel will complain by displaying ######. Data that's text will overlap adjacent empty cells. If the adjacent cells aren't empty, the right-hand part of the text will appear cut off (Excel doesn't lose that text; it's just hidden).

To make Excel adjust the column width or the row height to accommodate your stuff, double-click the right edge of the column heading or the bottom edge of the row heading. If you want to adjust it yourself, drag the border in a heading to any width or height, as shown in Figure 6.4.

Figure 6.4:

To adjust the height or width of a cell that's too small to fit its contents, double-click or drag the edge of the column or row heading.

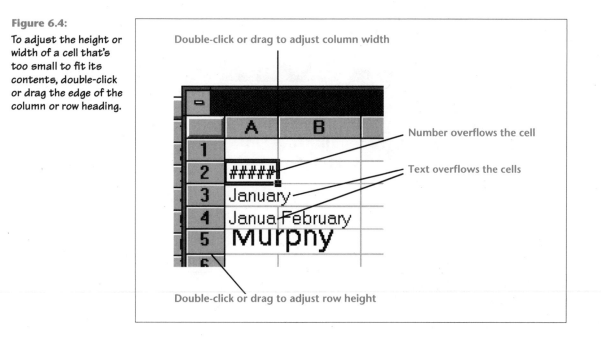

Double-click or drag to adjust column width

Number overflows the cell

Text overflows the cells

Double-click or drag to adjust row height

It's Not a Drag to Cut and Paste

If dragging doesn't appeal to you, you can use the Kindergarten method to move stuff—cutting and pasting. This way is handy if you're moving stuff from one open sheet (document window) to another.

When you cut and paste, your stuff invisibly passes through the Windows Clipboard, a kind of electronic scratch pad. On its way through, it blows away any other stuff that you put there previously. Just thought you should know.

To do the cut-and-paste thing, first select the stuff you want to move. Then, if you're using a PC, click the *right* mouse button and keep holding it down. A menu will pop up on your screen. (On the Mac, press ⌘ - Option as you click the stuff.) Move the pointer to the top of this menu to highlight the Cut command:

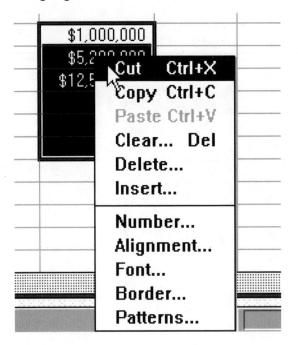

Or, PC-users can click the right button and release, then click and release on the command. After you do the Cut command, the infamous crawling ants will surround your stuff. Move the cell pointer to the first cell (top left) of the new location. Click the right mouse button again (⌘-Option on the Mac.) When the pop-up menu reappears, select Paste (Figure 6.5).

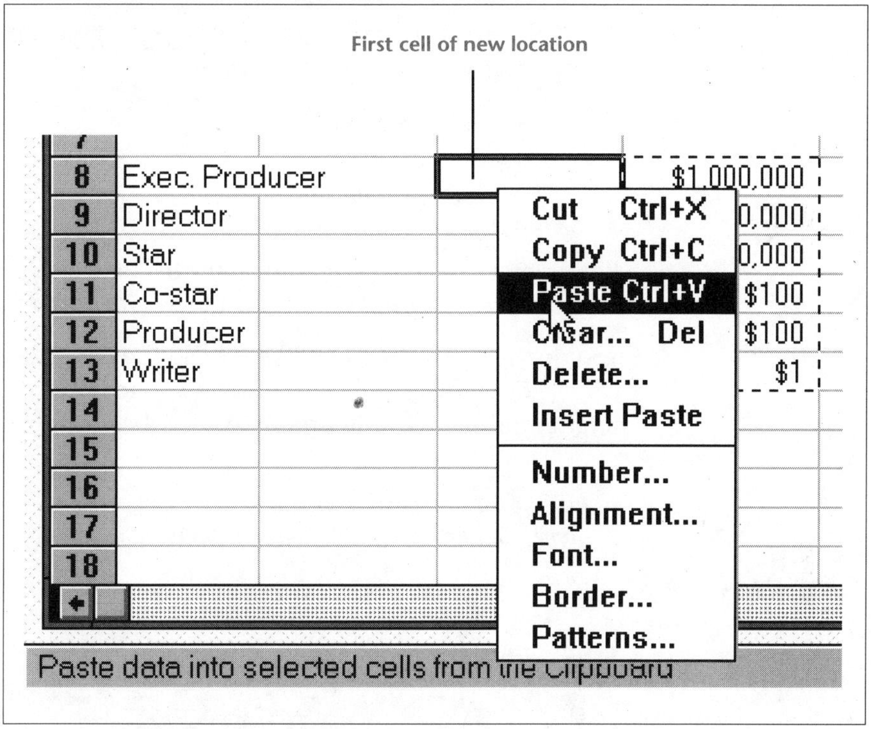

Figure 6.5:
The Paste command moves the stuff from the Clipboard (placed there with the Cut or Copy command) to a new location. You only need to select the first cell in the new location.

When you do the Paste thing, the cell contents pop into the new location, still selected so you can do something else with that stuff right away.

Number Formats

Copy-Cats Can't Cut It

Rather than moving your data, you can clone it so that the stuff stays at home *and* gets trucked to the new place. (Try doing that, Captain Kirk!)

You do the copy thing just like you do the cut-and-paste thing, but choose Copy instead of Cut. If you need to bone up on cut-and-paste, refer to the Kindergarten method described in the last section.

Just like cut-and-paste, copy-and-paste passes your stuff through the Clipboard. Same warning: Any old stuff in the Clipboard evaporates.

If you hold down the Ctrl key while dragging a selection as if to move it, Excel will copy the contents to the new location. So you might say copying can be a drag (and a drop!)

If You Can't Move, You Can Always Add On

Sometimes you need more elbow room, but it's just downright inconvenient to move. Fortunately, adding a column or a row is no big deal.

Let's suppose I've been making Excel slave over the budget for the latest Hollywood catastrophe *Limpid Weapon XXXIV*. Now the kid who's producing this movie fiasco informs me that a co-producer has been hired. Naturally, the co-producer won't put up with being listed after the writer, so a new row must be inserted into the budget sheet.

I swallow my pride, and the rest is easy. To add a row, select any cell in the row just *below* where you want the new row to appear. Then click the right mouse button (⌘-Option on the Mac) and select Insert from the pop-up menu (see Figure 6.6).

Figure 6.6:

To add a row, select the cell immediately below where you want the new row to appear, click the right mouse button (⌘-Option on the Mac) and select Insert from the pop-up menu.

8	Exec. Producer	$1,000,000
9	Director	$5,200,000
10	Star	12,500,000
11	Co-star	$100
12	Producer	$100
13	Writer	$1
14		
15		
16		
17		
18		

Pop-up menu:
- Cut   Ctrl+X
- Copy   Ctrl+C
- Paste Ctrl+V
- Clear... Del
- Delete...
- Insert...
- Number...
- Alignment...
- Font...
- Border...
- Patterns...

Insert row, col... lls   NUM

Number Formats

The Insert dialog box appears. In this case, you would select the Entire Row option:

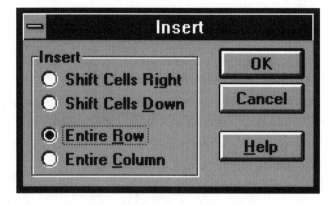

When you select OK to close the Insert dialog box, Excel inserts a new, blank row, as shown in Figure 6.7. In this case, row 13 was selected to begin with. After the insertion, the old row has moved down to become row 14, and the new row is row 13.

Figure 6.7:
The budget sheet after inserting a new row. Notice that the first cell of the new row is selected, ready for you to type stuff into it.

	A	B	C	D	E	F	G	H
1		*MegaBucks Motion Picture Company*						
2		Budget Summary						
3								
4		Production: "Limpid Weapon XXXIV"						
5								
6	Above-the-Line Expenses							
7								
8	Exec. Producer		$1,000,000					
9	Director		$5,200,000					
10	Star		$12,500,000					
11	Co-star		$100					
12	Producer		$100					
13								
14	Writer		$1					
15								
16								
17								
18								

To insert a column, select a cell in the column to the right of the insertion point. Then follow the procedure for inserting a row, but select Entire Column in the Insert dialog box.

The first two options in the Insert dialog box are for inserting a cell or a block of cells. To do this, you must select the cell or block of cells in the sheet before issuing the Insert command. Excel will insert blank cells exactly where the highlighted cells are currently. The original cells and their contents will be displaced according to your selection—Shift Cells Right or Shift Cells Down.

Close Up Those Ranks!

It's just as easy to delete an entire column, an entire row, or a selected cell or block of cells. Select a cell in the column or row you want to delete, or select a block of cells you want to remove. Then do the procedure described in the previous section (click the right mouse button—or press ⌘-Option on the Mac—to display the pop-up menu), but select Delete instead of Insert. The Delete dialog box will appear. Tell Excel what you're doing by picking an option, then select OK.

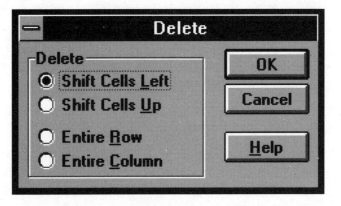

Maybe this seems obvious, but if you delete a column, a row, a cell, or a block of cells, the contents will disappear. Sorry. (If the loss is devastating, read the forthcoming section headed "Okay, Just Forget It!")

That pop-up menu is pretty nifty, but there's another way to insert or remove cells (or entire columns or rows). From the menu bar, select Edit ➤ Insert or Edit ➤ Delete.

Deleting Is Not Clearing

When you use Delete to remove a selection from a sheet, you are removing both the contents of your selection *and a chunk of the sheet*. Excel closes the wound, so to speak, by relettering the columns and renumbering the rows.

To delete *just the contents* of a selection—as you might erase pencil entries on a sheet of grid paper—you use one of the Clear procedures described below.

Clearing your field with a fill handle

One method of deleting the contents of a selection without deleting the actual cells in the selection is to drag the fill handle (the little square in the bottom right corner of the selection) upward, as if wiping the cells clean. I describe this nifty feature of Excel in Chapter 1.

Unlike other methods of clearing and deleting, dragging the fill handle upwards clears only the numbers, text, or formulas stored in the cell. Number and appearance formatting are retained.

Clearing on command

There are three other ways to go about clearing the contents of a selection: Select Clear from the pop-up menu, choose Edit ➤ Clear from the menu bar, or press Del. (The Delete Key won't work on the Mac.) However you choose to do it, the Clear dialog box will open.

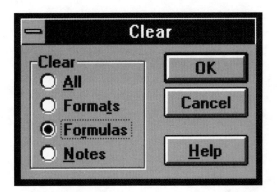

Number Formats

In this dialog box, select whatever you want to get rid of. The All option clears data (numbers, text, and formulas), number and appearance formats, formulas, and notes (comments you hide in your sheet). The other options specify just one of these. (The Formulas option clears both data values and formulas.) When you select OK to close the dialog box, the selected stuff gets blown away.

Moving Means Changing Addresses

Whenever you move, copy, insert, or delete stuff, the addresses of cells in the sheet can change. For example, if you select a cell in column B and then insert a new column, the new column will become column B, and the column that now holds what was the selected cell will become column C. All of the columns to the right of the new column will be relettered. The same thing happens with rows, only everything moves downward and Excel renumbers the rows.

This means, of course, that the address of the cell you selected before you inserted the column will change. If it was B2 originally, it will become C2 after a new column B is inserted.

If you move or copy a formula, Excel will attempt to change the cell references in it so that the math still works. However, the program can't always guess what you had in mind.

You can take control of the situation by specifying addresses as *relative* (subject to change) or *absolute* (can't change). To get the full scoop, read the best-selling exposé "Absolute and Relative References: The Untold Story" in Chapter 4.

Okay, Just Forget It! (Undo and Redo)

Moving can be especially traumatic if you get to the new place and find that you don't like it there. Other changes to your worksheet, such as copying, insertion, or deletion, can have unexpected results. Perhaps you don't like the way the revised sheet looks, or you find that cell addresses or formula references got so screwed up that you don't want to bother straightening them out.

No problem.

After a move or other disruptive adjustment that you don't like after all, just select Edit ➤ Undo or press Ctrl-Z.

Some Excel commands and operations can't be undone. That's life.

Provided that you don't sneak in another change first, Excel will put things back the way they were—no questions asked—and you will have the luxury, so rare in life, of rethinking your next move.

Murphy's Law of Undo: To undo a change, you must undo what you did before doing anything else. If you do something else first, Undo will undo the something else instead.

What, change your mind again?

If you decide that the new way was better after all, just choose Edit ➤ Redo or press Ctrl-Z (⌘-Z on the Mac. Like a patient friend waiting for you to decide where to hang the picture she's holding, Excel will restore what you did the first time, with no hard feelings.

You can flip-flop indecisively between Undo and Redo to your heart's content—unless you screw things up by doing something else between doing Undo and doing Redo.

Murphy's Law of Redo: *To redo an undo, you must redo what you undid before you do and undo anything else. If you do and undo something else first, Redo will redo (undo the undoing of) the something else instead.*

Pete and Re-Pete Were Sitting on a Fence...

Perhaps you're so tickled with the last change you made that you want to do another one just like it. No need to go through the motions again. Excel has an excellent short-term memory for such things.

Suppose you inserted a new row, and now you want to add yet another new row to your sheet. Just select Edit ➤ Repeat, (or press ⌘-Y on the Mac) and you'll get more of the same.

Like Undo and Redo, Repeat only works on the last command you gave Excel. If you do something else first, it's the something else that will get repeated.

Number Formats: The Short Version

Excel offers a quick way to apply the most commonly used *styles*, or number and appearance formats, to selected cells.

Start by selecting the cell or cells to be formatted. Then click the arrow button just beneath the word Format in the menu bar. (On the Mac it's just beneath Formula.) This button activates the *Style Box*, which will open to display a list of styles, as shown on the next page.

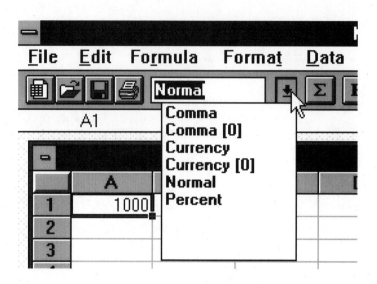

Click the style you want. (On the Mac, you have to drag the Style Box to make a selection.) The Style Box will close, and Excel will display the value in the selected cells in the number format of the style you chose.

Normally, all cells in a new sheet are Normal in style. Here's what the number value 1000 looks like in the preselected number formats of each style:

```
Normal(General) 1000
Comma           1,000.00
Comma [0]          1,000
Currency      $1,000.00
Currency [0]    $1,000
Percent          100000%
```

Notice that Excel thinks a number entry of 1000 means 100000 percent. That's because it expects percentages to be values less than 1. For example, an entry of 0.5 formatted in Percent would appear as 50%.

Normal style produces different results if your entry looks like a date or a time. If you type **September 6, 1999**, Excel will display it in the cell as 6-Sep-99. But if you type **9/6/1999**, Excel will display 9/6/99. If you type **2 PM**, Excel will display 2:00 PM. If you type **14:00**, Excel will interpret it as a time of day and display 14:00 in the cell.

You can format cells that are empty as well as cells that contain data. Of course, you will only see the effect on the cells that have stuff in them. If you later type data into a formatted empty cell, the stuff will be displayed in the format you chose.

Number Formats: The Unabridged Version

If you don't see a format you like in the Style Box, you can go shopping for other formats. Select the cell or cells you want to format, then click the right mouse button. In the pop-up menu that appears, select Number (see Figure 6.8). (Alternatively, you can select Format ➤ Number from the menu bar.)

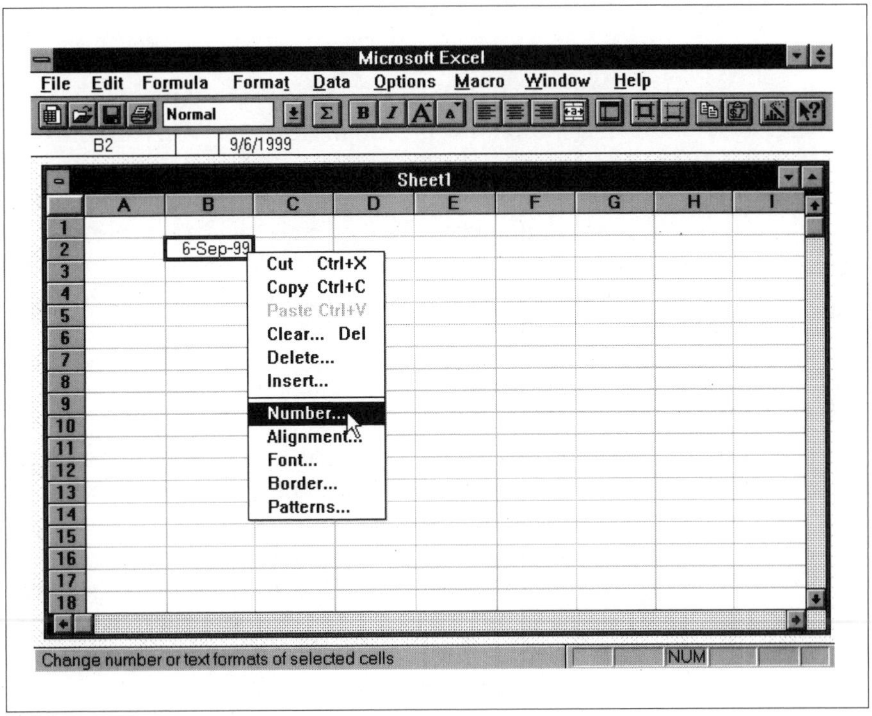

Figure 6.8:
Select Number from the shortcut menu to view the entire range of number formatting options.

```
                      Microsoft Excel
File  Edit  Formula  Format  Data  Options  Macro  Window  Help

      Normal        Σ  B I A A

      B2              9/6/1999

                          Sheet1
     A     B      C      D     E     F     G     H     I
 1
 2        6-Sep-99  Cut      Ctrl+X
 3                  Copy    Ctrl+C
 4                  Paste Ctrl+V
 5                  Clear...  Del
 6                  Delete...
 7                  Insert...
 8
 9                  Number...
10                  Alignment...
11                  Font...
12                  Border...
13                  Patterns...
14
15
16
17
18

Change number or text formats of selected cells          NUM
```

When you let go of the mouse button, the Number Format dialog box appears. Select a Category of number formats from the list on the left. (Or, if you have time on your hands, select All to browse through them all.) The options for the category you picked will appear in the Format Codes list on the right:

Select the format code for the type of number display you want. The first number in the stuff you selected in the sheet will appear formatted this way in the Sample entry in the lower-left corner of the Number Format dialog box. You can preview another format simply by choosing something else from the list. When you've found a format you're happy with, select OK to close the dialog box.

Normal Is Whatever You Say It Is

Suppose you've chosen one of the more exotic number formats for a cell in the sheet, and you want to make that formatting part of your normal style. Excel will allow you to make it the Normal setting in the Style Box. All cells in the sheet—including the empties—are normally Normal, so you will be changing the style Excel will use for any new stuff you enter into the sheet, unless you pick a different style.

To redefine Normal, reset the number format of a cell in the sheet as described in the previous section. With that cell selected, click the Style Box button and reselect Normal. You'll see this:

```
┌──────────────────────────────────────────────────────┐
│ ▬              Microsoft Excel                         │
├──────────────────────────────────────────────────────┤
│                                                        │
│    ❓    Redefine 'Normal' based on selected cells?    │
│                                                        │
│    ┌─────┐   ┌─────┐   ┌────────┐   ┌──────┐          │
│    │ Yes │   │ No  │   │ Cancel │   │ Help │          │
│    └─────┘   └─────┘   └────────┘   └──────┘          │
└──────────────────────────────────────────────────────┘
```

Select OK to accept the new number-format definition. Excel will think this is Normal until such time as you redefine Normal. However, your changes will apply *only to the current sheet*. If you open another sheet or restart the program, Excel will revert to its old ways.

3

Don't read this part unless you care about making a good impression. In other words, this stuff is for everybody except sole proprietors with no customers. Learn how to dress it up (Chapter 7) and how to get it all on paper (Chapter 8).

MAKING A PUBLIC APPEARANCE

Chapter 7

NEED TO DRESS UP TO PLEASE THE BOSS?

Murphy's Wisdom: Dress for success. If you fail, you'll end up in a classier bar.

WORKING WITH EXCEL is a lot like dating: If you never go out, you don't have to worry about your looks. But as soon as there's someone else involved—especially an influential someone else—cosmetics become a real concern.

This chapter is all about dressing up your sheet. This involves *appearance* formatting, as opposed to *number* formatting, which is a big topic in Chapter 6. Formatting of any kind affects the way your stuff is displayed—whether on the screen or in printouts. Number formatting controls the way your stuff will be interpreted—for example, whether the value 35792 appears as a date (12/28/97) or as money ($35,792.00). Appearance formatting is less crucial to the understanding of the information in your sheet. It just makes your stuff look good.

Sometimes Excel doesn't know the difference between number formatting and appearance formatting. If you choose Edit ➤ Clear to get rid of the contents of a cell and then select Formats, Excel will remove both the number formatting and the appearance formatting, leaving just the naked data. Also, copying formats from one cell into another can affect both the number style and the appearance formatting of data.

You Really AutoFormat Your Stuff

As you might have noticed in Chapter 1, Excel has a magic button that will dress up an entire sheet with a single click. If you like the results you get with this AutoFormat feature, you can skip the rest of this chapter and return to it only when you want more frills.

The sheet in Figure 7.1 is pretty raw. Not much has been done to make it presentable, except that some of the column headings have been dragged to adjust the widths of the columns.

To apply AutoFormat, you must first select the part of the sheet that you want it to affect. In the case of Figure 7.1, you would select the entire sheet by dragging the range A1:E14. Then, click the AutoFormat tool. (The AutoFormat tool is labeled in Figure 7.1.)

When you use AutoFormat, your initial selection must look like a table, with headings and data. Otherwise, when you click the AutoFormat tool, Excel will complain, "AutoFormat could not detect a table around the active cell." If this happens, select OK and reselect the table before trying AutoFormat again.

When you click AutoFormat, Excel applies a ready-made appearance format to the sheet (see Figure 7.2).

I never promised the result would be perfect. In this example, the titles aren't centered over the columns. The subtitle (the second line) should be smaller than the title (the first line). And the Disposition heading

Figure 7.1:
A plain-vanilla sheet
with no special
formatting

AutoFormat tool

Microsoft Excel

File   Edit   Formula   Format   Data   Options   Macro   Window   Help

Normal

A1 | Worksheet Horror Stories

HOTLINE.XLS

	A	B	C	D	E	F	G
1	Worksheet Horror Stories						
2	Summary of Calls to the Support Hot-Line						
3							
4		Disposition					
5	Problem	Resolved	Needed	Needed	Stumped		
6		on First Call	Tech Reply	Field Call			
7	Memory overflow	12	3				
8	Circular reference	20	6				
9	Divide by zero	18	2				
10	Relative/absolute confusion	36					
11	Loose cables	128		3			
12	Dead computer				1		
13							
14	Totals	214	11	3	1		
15							
16							
17							
18							

Ready

Appearance Formats

should be centered over the four columns beneath it. It would also be a
nice touch if Disposition were in the same font as Problem, since the
table refers primarily to those two things.

The reason for these imperfections is that the ready-made format is
designed for a "typical" sheet, and this one is just a little odd. For one
thing, its column widths aren't uniform, and this affects the centering
of the titles. Also, the layout of the column headings differs from the
ready-made format. But, on balance, you get a lot with that single click.

*When you try AutoFormat, the results you get may be different from the example
in Figure 7.2. The AutoFormat tool applies the **last** ready-made format used. If
no one has ever used ready-made formats with your copy of the program, Excel
will pick something. Read on to find out how you can control which of many
ready-made layouts Excel will use.*

Figure 7.2:
The HOTLINE work-
sheet in Figure 7.1 after
applying AutoFormat

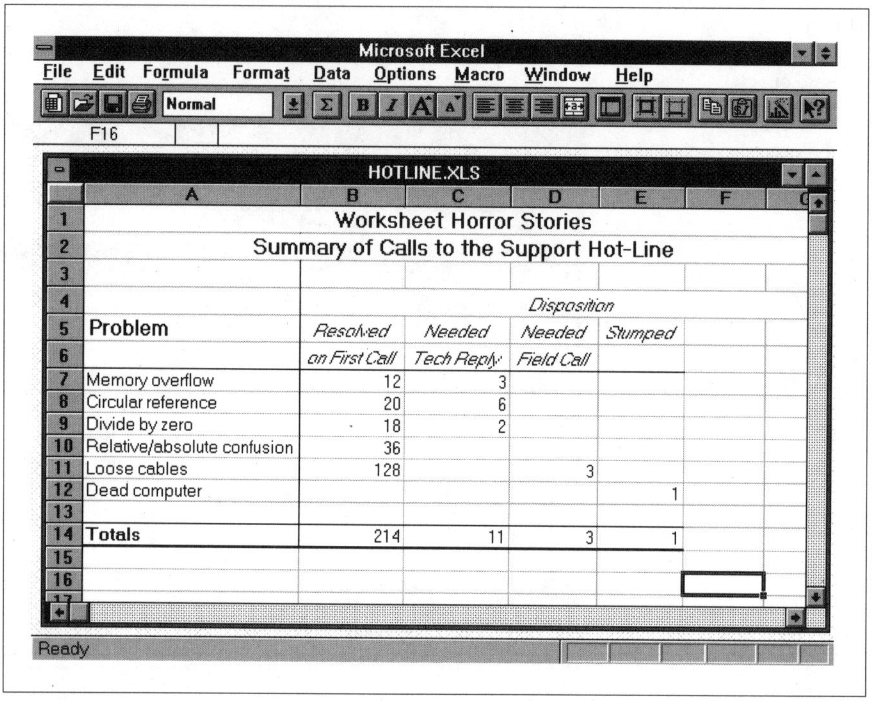

Get Picky about AutoFormats

You might be able to improve the appearance of a particular sheet simply by selecting a different ready-made format for AutoFormat to use.

With the sheet selected, choose Format ➤ AutoFormat from the menu bar. The AutoFormat dialog box, shown in Figure 7.3, will appear. Select one of the ready-made appearance formats from the Table Format list on the left. Excel will give you a preview in the Sample box on the right. If you want to get picky about exactly which options Excel will use, select the Options button and the formatting options will appear as check boxes at the bottom of the dialog box. To turn off one of these options, clear (unmark) its check box.

When you find something you like, select OK. Excel will transform your sheet in a wink (see Figure 7.4).

Figure 7.3:
The AutoFormat dialog box. When you select the Options button, the Formats To Apply check boxes appear at the bottom of the dialog box.

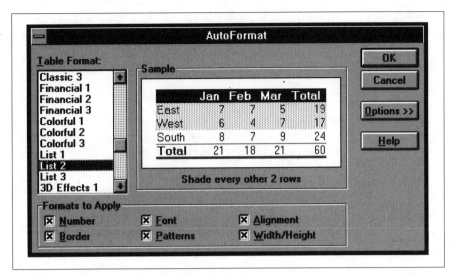

Figure 7.4:
The HOTLINE sheet after applying another one of AutoFormat's ready-made formats

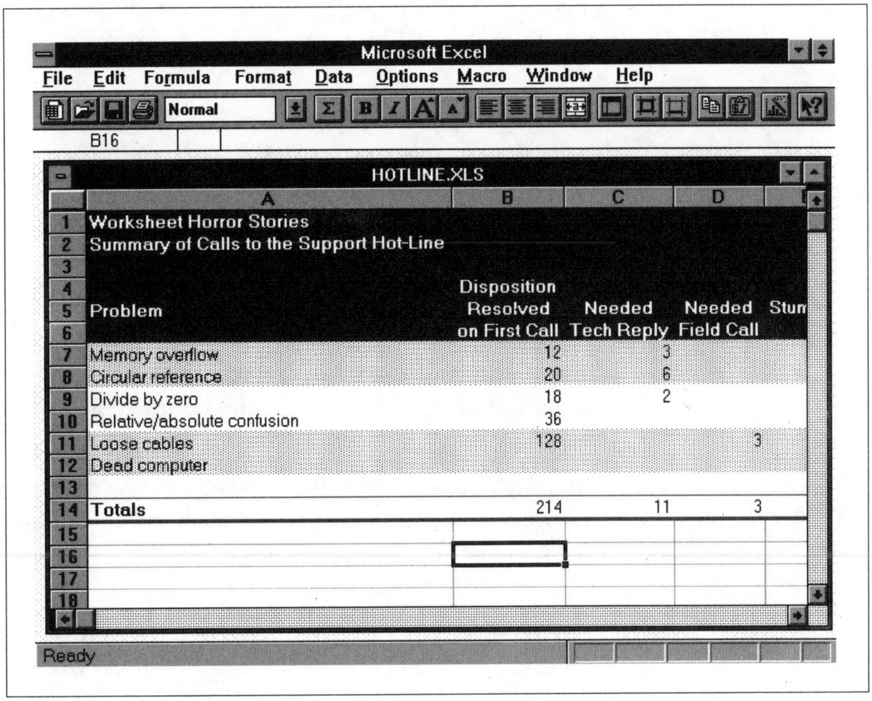

If you see something in your sheet that's formatted the way you want, you can copy its appearance to other cells. Select the good-looking stuff, then click the Copy tool:

Crawling ants will surround your selection. Move the pointer to the bad-looking stuff, and click the Paste Formats tool:

Keyboard maestros of the PC can choose Edit ➤ Copy and Edit ➤ Paste Special ➤ Formats instead.

The rest of this chapter describes how to do what AutoFormat does—but cell by cell or block by block. This way you can customize a ready-made layout or build your own layout from scratch.

From the standpoint of appearance formatting, Excel treats text and numbers the same. For example, you can change the typeface, color, or alignment of a number just as if it were text.

Write a Line, Right Align

In Excel, the position of stuff in relation to the edges of the cell that holds it is called *alignment*. (Some people call this *justification*.)

Murphy's Rule of Alignment: *There's a simple rule for the way Excel normally puts stuff into a cell. Text goes left, numbers go right. (Error messages and the logical values TRUE and FALSE are centered.)*

You can change the alignment of a cell or block of cells by selecting it, then clicking one of the Alignment tools shown in Figure 7.5.

Alignment usually refers to the position of data within individual cells. If you select a block of cells and then select the Align Center tool, Excel will center each value in the block within the cell that holds it.

Figure 7.5:
The Alignment tools

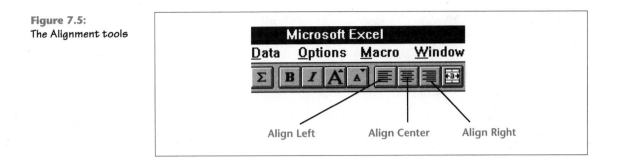

Alignment Can Be Fine-Tuned

For the truly fastidious, Excel offers many more choices and degrees of alignment.

Instead of clicking an Alignment tool, click the right mouse button (⌘-Option on the Mac) and select Alignment from the pop-up menu that appears (you can choose Format ➤ Alignment from the menu bar if you prefer). The Alignment dialog box will appear, as shown in Figure 7.6.

The Horizontal box in the Alignment dialog box includes the options Left, Center, and Right. These are the same options available with the

Figure 7.6:
The Alignment
dialog box

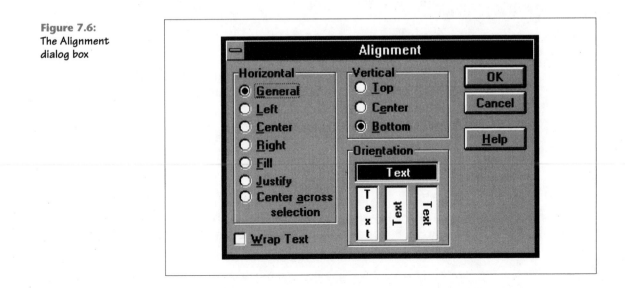

Appearance Formats

Alignment tools. The General option is Excel's usual way of doing things—text on the left, numbers on the right. The other options are

- ☞ Fill
- ☞ Justify
- ☞ Center Across Selection
- ☞ Wrap Text
- ☞ Vertical Option Buttons
- ☞ Orientation

The sections below explain each of these alignment options.

Fill a cell with stuff

The Fill option copies the stuff in the selected cell or block so that it completely fills all the available character positions in that cell or block. For example, if a cell holds the value 0, and the cell is eight characters wide, the Fill option will fill that cell with eight zeros:

00000000

If the selection were a block of cells, Excel would fill each cell in the top row with multiple copies of the value in the first cell.

Justify your righteous stuff

The Justify option aligns stuff both left and right. The effect is noticeable only when there are several words of text in a cell that is wider and taller than normal:

```
┌─────────────────┐
│Friday   Morning │
│Meeting          │
└─────────────────┘
```

Excel offers two other ways to justify stuff both right and left: Choose Format ➤ Justify, or open the Formatting Toolbar by selecting Options ➤ Toolbars ➤ Formatting, then click the Justify Align tool, shown in Figure 7.7.

Figure 7.7:
The Justify Align tool in the Formatting Toolbar

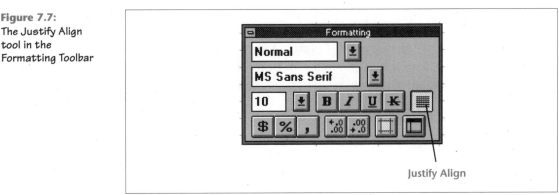

Justify Align

Appearance Formats

Self-centered stuff

The Center Across Selection option puts your stuff horizontally smack in the middle of a selected row of cells. For this to work properly, your stuff should be in the first, or far-left, cell of the row you select, like this:

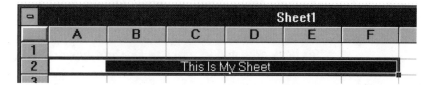

When you select OK in the Alignment dialog box, the stuff will move to the middle of the selected row:

When you can do the same thing by selecting the entire row that holds the title and then clicking the Center Across Columns tool in the toolbar:

Wrap the text without bruising your knuckles

The Wrap Text option stacks text, usually several words, as multiple lines within a single cell. In most cases, you will have to adjust the row height to display all of the text, as in Figure 7.8. If individual words are long, you'll also have to adjust the column width to avoid breaking words.

Figure 7.8:
The Wrap Text option allows you to wrap words onto several lines. In this example, I adjusted the row height to accommodate the wrapped text.

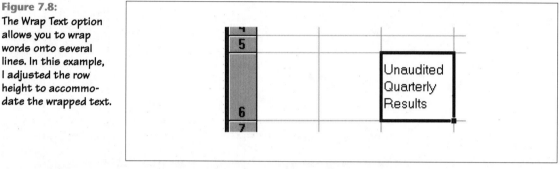

There are two reasons Excel won't let you wrap numbers: First, you can't have more than one number in a cell, and second, a number must be displayed on a single line.

Get vertical in the morning

The three Vertical options in the Alignment dialog box refer to the position of stuff in relation to the top and bottom edges of a cell. The differences in vertical alignment will be apparent only if the row height has been adjusted to make taller-than-normal cells:

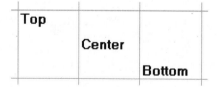

Vertical alignment is independent of the Horizontal setting. For example, you can align text both to the left and to the top, as shown in the first cell of this example.

This orientation won't make you dizzy

You can use the Orientation options to rotate text in a cell. The top option, which reads horizontally, is normal. You don't have to choose this unless you're trying to restore rotated text to the normal position. The other three options make text run up and down:

The option on the left stacks the letters vertically from top to bottom. The middle option rotates the text counterclockwise so that it runs uphill. The option on the right rotates the text clockwise so that it runs downhill. You can use any of these selections in combination with the Vertical options. You can also use them with all of the Horizontal options *except* Fill, Justify, Center Across Selection, and Wrap Text.

Put on a Pretty Face

Most of the things you'll want to do with the typeface of text or numbers can be controlled with the four type style buttons shown in Figure 7.9. The following sections explain how to use those buttons.

A Typographical Aside

People who design and set type for a living use the term *font* to refer to a typeface in a specific point size. In Excel (and in the world of Windows, in general), the Font option usually means *typeface*. However, the Font options include all the appearance selections for text: typeface, style, size, effects, and color.

Appearance Formats

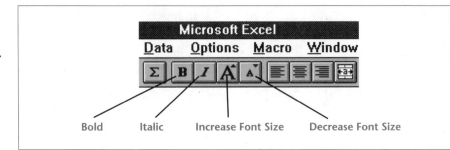

Figure 7.9:
The Standard Toolbar includes four of the Text Formatting tools.

Be bold, be italic, or be both

Select a cell or block of cells and click the Bold tool or the Italic tool. The Bold and Italic tools are on-off switches: Click B once, the text is bold. Click B again, the text is back to normal. If you want, you can make text and numbers bold *and* italic.

Size up, size down

To change the size of text, select the text you want to change. Then click the Increase Font Size tool to make the text bigger, or click the Decrease Font Size tool to make it smaller. The number of times you can click up or down depends on the current size of the text and the range of sizes available for that font.

Get fancy with fonts

If you want to get fancy, you can use any font that you have installed in Windows or in System 7. Here's how.

Select the text (or numbers) you want to change. Then, click the right mouse button (⌘-Option on the Mac) and select Font from the pop-up menu. Or, choose Format ➤ Font from the menu bar. The Font dialog box, shown in Figure 7.10, will open. This is where you'll find all the bells and whistles for every Windows font known to your computer.

Figure 7.10:
The Font dialog box

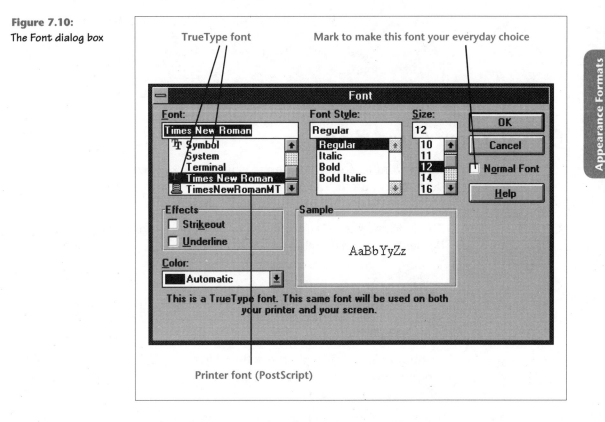

TrueType font   Mark to make this font your everyday choice

Printer font (PostScript)

Appearance Formats

Pick a set of options: Font (typeface), Font Style, Size (in points—12 is typewriter pica size, 10 is elite), Effects (strikeout, underline, or both—Mac users have an outline option as well), and Color (this option affects screen displays and color printers). A preview of your selections will appear in the Sample box. Select OK to accept your changes.

There Are Fonts and Then There Are Fonts...

Many of the fonts that come with Windows are TrueType fonts, preceded by the TT symbol in font lists. These fonts can be adjusted up or down in size continuously (scaled), and they look the same on the screen as they do in printouts.

Another kind of scalable font is designed to be used with PostScript-compatible software and printers. These include the fonts supplied with Adobe Type Manager (ATM). Such printer fonts are preceded by a printer symbol in Excel's font lists.

Draw Your Own Borders

If you want to draw attention to cells or blocks of cells, you can put borders around them. As with most of the appearance formats, there's a quick way to do this, and there's a fancy way.

The quick way is to select the cell or block of cells and click one of the Border tools in the toolbar:

The button on the left is the Outline Border tool. The button on the right is the Bottom Border tool.

Normally, the borders are fairly thin, so it can be difficult to see them among the grid lines on the screen. The borders will be more obvious when you print the sheet.

The fancy way to add borders gives you more choices and more control. Select the cell or block of cells that you want to border. Click the right mouse button (⌘-Option on the Mac) to display the pop-up menu, and select Border from the menu. (If you prefer, you can choose Format ➤ Border from the menu bar.) The Border dialog box will appear, as shown in Figure 7.11.

Figure 7.11:

The Border dialog box

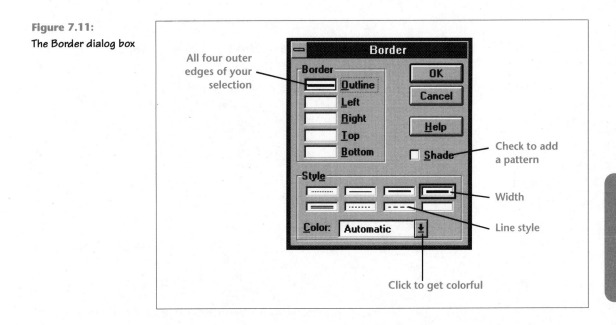

The Border options, in the upper-left corner of the Border dialog box, control which edges of the selected cell or block of cells will get a border. The Outline option surrounds all the edges of the selected block of cells, giving the same effect as the Outline Border tool. The Left, Right, Top, and Bottom options put borders on *each cell* in a selected block of cells.

The Style selections control the appearance of the border. The options in the top row control the width, and the options in the bottom row control line style: double-ruled, dotted, dashed, or no border (use this last option to remove a border).

If the Shade box is checked, a pattern will fill the cell or block. (You can select the pattern by choosing Format ➤ Patterns, as described in the next section.) You can pick one of the Color options, or leave the setting at Automatic to make Excel do the choosing.

When you're done selecting options, select OK to close the Border dialog box and see the border you picked.

Keyboard Maestros Can Run for the Border!

With Excel you can even make a border from the keyboard—and *pronto*. If you're using Excel for Windows, press Ctrl-Shift-& to add an outline border, and press Ctrl-Shift-<minus sign> to remove all borders. Mac users can press ⌘-Option-0 to add an outline border and ⌘-Option-<minus sign> to remove all borders.

The Mice Strike Back!

Not to be outdone by a few keystrokes, the mice make this offer: You can add a variety of borders and shading effects to your sheet by clicking special tools in the Formatting Toolbar (select Options ➤ Toolbars ➤ Customize ➤ Formatting). These are Excel's special Border tools: Outline Border, Bottom Border, Bottom Double Border, Left Border, Right Border, Top Border, Light Shading, Dark Shading. (To use these tools, you must add them to a toolbar. See the example of the Formula Toolbar in Chapter 4.)

Choose a Nice Pattern for Your Sheet

Another fancy trick is using a pattern, or shading, within a cell or block of cells. This is particularly stunning when you set it off with a nice border. Once again, there's quick and there's fancy. Take your pick.

To add a pattern quickly, click either the Light Shading tool or the Dark Shading tool. You can find these tools in the Formatting tools category (see the sidebar above, "The Mice Strike Back"). You can also select the Shading check box when you're picking Border options, as described in the previous section. This will put a ready-made pattern inside the border of the selected cells.

To pick a fancier pattern (without going to bridal registry), click the right mouse button (⌘-Option on the Mac) and select Patterns from the pop-up menu, or choose Format ➤ Patterns from the menu bar. The Patterns dialog box will appear, as shown in Figure 7.12.

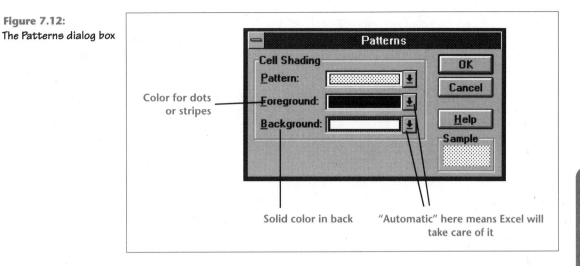

Figure 7.12:
The Patterns dialog box

The Pattern option in the Patterns dialog box includes a combination of dots or stripes of one color (the Foreground option) over a second, solid color (the Background). When you've made your selections, Excel will give you a preview in the Sample box in the lower-right corner of the dialog box. (Or, after you pick a pattern, select Automatic for the colors, and Excel will do the rest.) When you're done, select OK and Excel will put your new pattern in place.

Get Colorful

If you pick any of the Color options for text, borders, or patterns, the colors will show up on the screen and in printouts if you have a color printer or film recorder. (Plotters can also do color, but in a very limited way.)

Excel uses 16 colors in all, including black, white, and two shades of gray. Unless your computer has a 256-color (or more) video display, these 16 are the only solid colors you've got.

However, you can mix colors to your heart's content. Select Options ➤ Color Palette. The Color Palette dialog box will appear, displaying the 16 colors currently available. Select a color, then click the Edit button. The Color Picker dialog box will open, and you can pick from an entire rainbow of colors. Select OK when you've chosen a color to mix with the color you picked from the Color Palette.

Appearance Formats

On 16-color displays, some colors will be *dithered*, appearing as fuzzy, multicolored patches. More of the colors will appear solid on 256-color displays. It's anybody's guess what will happen on your printer, since color capabilities vary considerably from one model of printer to another.

More commonly, printers of the dot-matrix, bubble-jet, or laser ilks can render only black, white, and grays. The exact grays you get won't have much to do with Excel. It's up to the driver software for your printer, which translates colors into patterns. (The driver's boss is Windows or System 7, not Excel.)

Adjusting the Color Palette in Excel won't make much of a difference with gray-scale printers. The main reason to mess with colors is to make sheets look sexy on the screen. (Read about electronic slide shows in Chapter 11.)

Be a Style Setter

In Excel, *styles* are collections of format settings. You can think of a style as a mini-AutoFormat selection (although a style doesn't have to be that fancy). Excel lets you apply all of the format options in a style with a single, masterful stroke. As you might expect, this feature is a real time-saver.

Excel's ready-made styles are right where you would expect to find them—in the Style Box at the top of the screen. For example, the Normal style usually includes the following settings:

Number Format	General
Font	MS Sans Serif
Font Size	10 points
Alignment	General, bottom
Borders	None
Shading	None
Cell Protection	Locked

Locked or Hidden in a Dark Cell?

There are two Cell Protection options: Locked and Hidden. The Locked setting doesn't mean you can't change your stuff. It just means that stuff formatted with this style (Normal, in this case) will *become* locked—protected from changes—*if* you ever choose Options ➤ Protect Document to prevent changes to the sheet. The Hidden option prevents any formula stored in the cell from being displayed—again, *if* the sheet is protected.

To create a style of your very own, choose Format ➤ Style and select the Define button in the Style dialog box. The categories of options covered in this chapter appear as buttons at the bottom of the Style dialog box (see Figure 7.13).

Type a new name for the style in the Style Name box. Select the options that define the new style, first by selecting any button in the Change section, then by resetting the dialog box that appears and selecting OK.

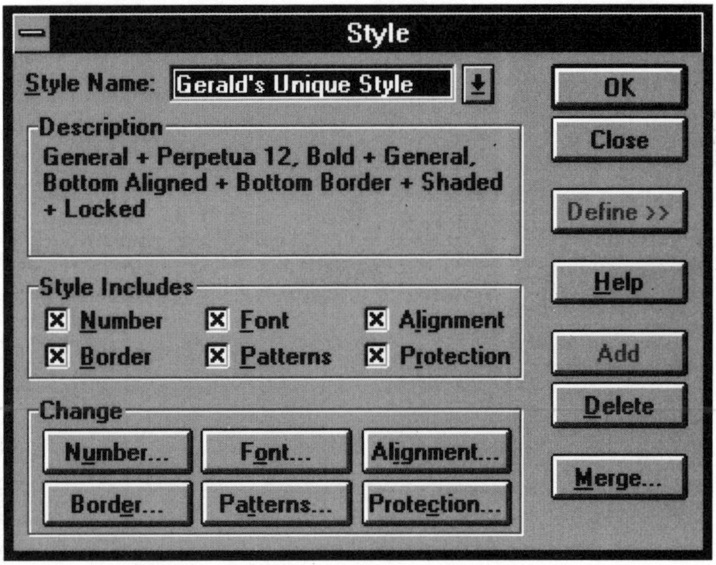

Figure 7.13:
The Style dialog box. The style name you enter will appear when you open the Style drop-down box at the top of the screen.

When you're finished defining the new style, select the Add button to add the entry to the Style Box. Then select Close or OK to close the Style dialog box.

Pick Up Your Formatting Tools

I've dropped several hints throughout this chapter about the Formatting Toolbar. It's easy to display, a snap to use, and it has most of the formatting options that you'll ever need. (You can add additional tools from any tool category, including Formatting, as explained in Chapter 4.)

To get at the formatting tools quickly, move the pointer up to the toolbar at the top of the screen and click the *right* mouse button (⌘-Option on the Mac). A pop-up menu will appear, with the names of ready-made toolbars (see Figure 7.14).

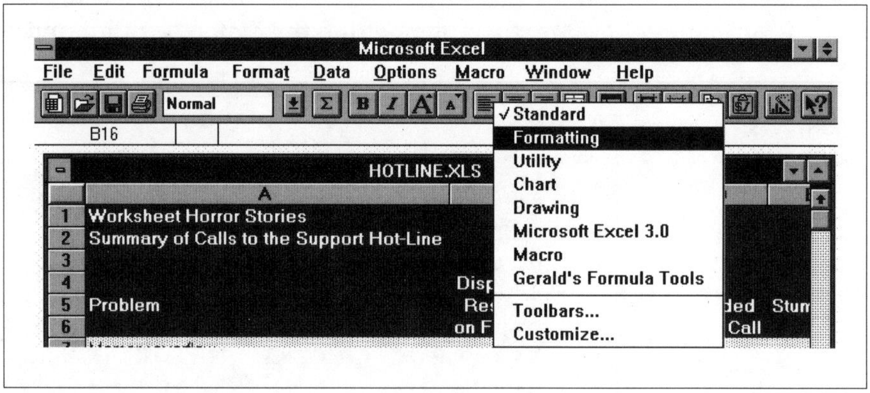

Figure 7.14:
Position the mouse pointer in the toolbar at the top of the screen, then click the right mouse button (⌘-Option on the Mac) to display a pop-up menu of available toolbars.

Select Formatting from the pop-up menu, and—presto!—you'll have the appearance- and number-formatting tools shown in Figure 7.15 at your mouse-finger tips.

Figure 7.15:
The Formatting Toolbar

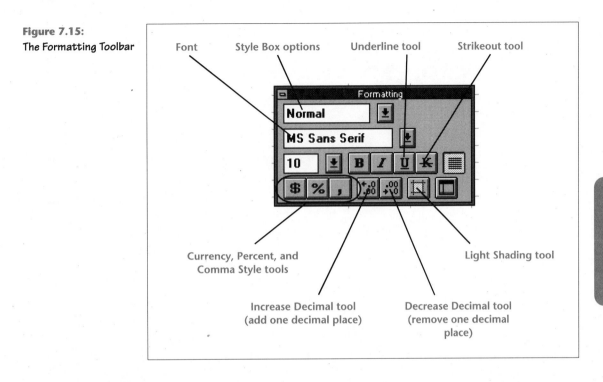

Font   Style Box options   Underline tool   Strikeout tool

Currency, Percent, and
Comma Style tools

Light Shading tool

Increase Decimal tool
(add one decimal place)

Decrease Decimal tool
(remove one decimal
place)

Appearance Formats

Chapter 8

GET IT ON PAPER
(before Murphy Strikes Again!)

Murphy's Law of Electronic Storage: A computer file can only be corrupted beyond retrieval if you haven't printed it yet.

DESPITE THE FACT that technology gurus have long been predicting the glorious advent of the paperless office, it hasn't happened yet. Business continues to use paper like a toddler in toilet training.

So, it's all very well that you can bury those intricate calculations in an Excel worksheet and dress them up prettily on the screen. But, when decision time comes, you'd better get it on paper.

Click a Button and Skip This Chapter!

For moving stuff out quickly, Excel has a Print tool:

When you're happy with the way your sheet looks on the screen, make sure your printer is turned on, then click this tool. If you like what comes out of your printer, you can ignore the rest of this chapter. But feel free to come back anytime to get the Big Picture.

It Was a Setup, Boss

If your boss doesn't like the results of your reckless clicking of the Print tool, you might recall one of Murphy's more famous laws:

Murphy's Law of Printing: *To do anything, you must do something else first. To print a worksheet, you must first set up your printer. Before you set up your printer in Excel, you must install it. And just before you click the Print tool, you should make sure the contraption is cabled up and loaded with paper, fresh ribbon, toner, font cartridges, memory modules, bubbles, or whatever else it needs or greedily consumes.*

The setup option that usually hits you smack in the face when you print a sheet is the *orientation* of the printing on the page. Having the printer set up for the wrong orientation is the number-one cause of dissatisfaction when you click the Print tool without forethought.

In *portrait* orientation, the long dimension of the paper is vertical—the way you'd print a letter. In *landscape* orientation, the long dimension is horizontal—the way Van Gogh would paint a cow and a barn (and the way most big-sheet wizards print their stuff). Figure 8.1 illustrates the difference between portrait and landscape orientation.

Figure 8.1:
Portrait vs. landscape orientation

Landscape

Portrait

Setting Up a Page to Take the Hit

You can fix most printing problems without ever leaving the cozy environment of Excel, *provided you have installed and set up your printer properly.*

As you may know, all printing requests from applications are handled by the printer driver (a software chauffeur), not by the application. Excel refuses to take a back seat, though. It can give orders to the driver, overriding the printing instructions that apply to other, less pushy, applications.

Herein lies the solution to a common dilemma. If you're like most computer users, you work with word processing applications as well as spreadsheets. Letters must be printed in portrait orientation, but most worksheets look better in landscape. Since Excel can override the default, or routine, setup instructions to the printer driver, you can reset the page orientation to landscape *inside Excel*, leaving portrait as the default system setup for word processing and other applications.

Use the File ➤ Page Setup command to switch between portrait and landscape printing in Excel. The Page Setup dialog box, shown in Figure 8.2, will appear.

Printing

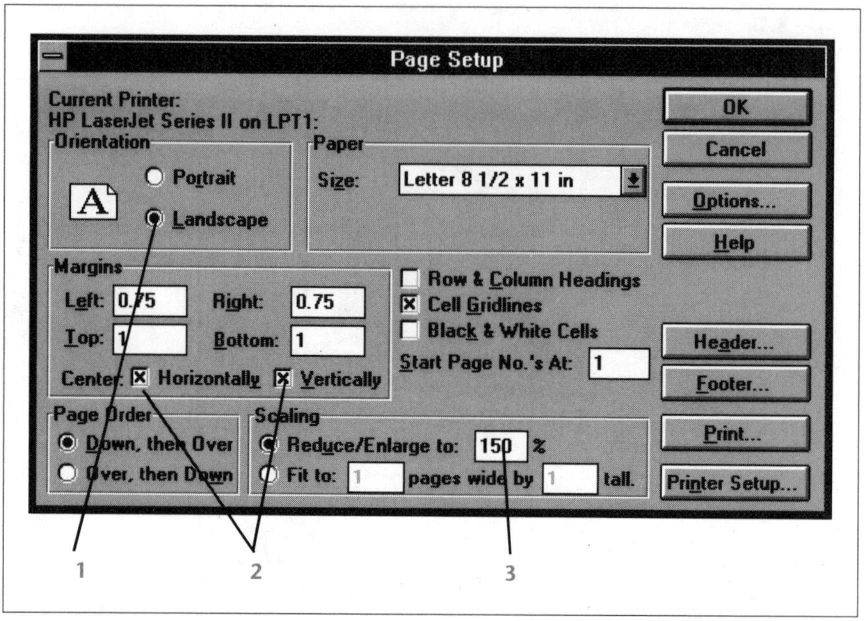

Figure 8.2:

Three things you can do to make a sheet pretty

There are quite a few settings in the Page Setup dialog box, but usually you'll only have to worry about three of them:

☞ Orientation

☞ Centering

☞ Scaling

Pay attention to these three things (discussed in the sections below), and you'll be able to fix most of the common complaints that result from using the Print tool hastily.

When you're working in the Page Setup dialog box, once you have changed the settings (as described below), you're ready to print. Select the Print button.

If you want to be picky about what's printed, select File ➤ Print instead. In the Print dialog box that appears, you can select multiple copies or specific pages to print. To start printing, select OK.

Orientation: tall or wide?

In general, choose Landscape orientation for worksheets, unless the sheet has no more than six or so columns.

Get centered

I don't know why Excel doesn't center sheets on the page automatically, but it doesn't. To make sure Excel composes the page nicely, mark both of the Center check boxes: Horizontally and Vertically.

Scale it up (down not recommended)

Your everyday worksheet—if it's a screenful of information or a little more—won't fill a letter-sized page. The Reduce/Enlarge setting in the Page Setup dialog box is usually 100 percent. If your sheet is modest in size, try typing 150 in this box to enlarge your sheet $1\frac{1}{2}$ times.

You can reduce a bigger sheet to fit a page by entering a number less than 100. However, if you do this, you'll need to get out your magnifying glass.

Read This If You Have a Big Sheet

If your worksheet is so big that it can't fit on a single printed page, you need to pay attention to some other Page Setup options.

The Page Order setting (located in the bottom left corner of the Page Setup dialog box) is normally Down Then Over—meaning that pages will be filled by going down the sheet first, then by moving over one page width to the top of the sheet, and going down again (see Figure 8.3).

When this option is set to Over Then Down, printing proceeds from left to right across the sheet until the tops of all the columns are printed, then moves the height of one page downward and, starting at the left border of the sheet, moves left to right again (see Figure 8.4).

Printing

Figure 8.3:
When Page Order is set to Down Then Over, pages print in this order.

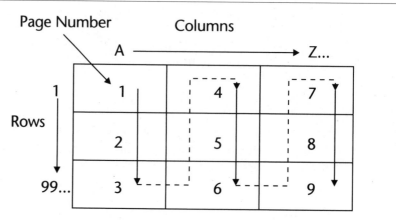

Figure 8.4:
With the Page Order option set to Over Then Down, Excel prints pages in this order.

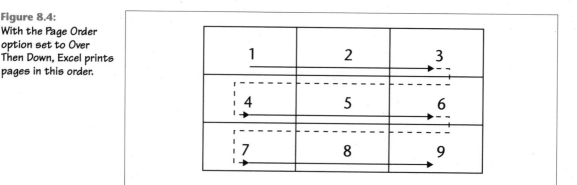

The choice of Down Then Over or Over Then Down depends mostly on the way your sheet is constructed. If the sheets were bound together in a report, which sequence of presentation would be easier for the reader to follow?

If your sheet runs to several pages, you might also reset the Scaling option to Fit To x Pages Wide By y Tall. (The Scaling option can be found at the bottom of the Page Setup dialog box.) By entering whole numbers for x and y, you can control how many sheets are used in the down-then-over or over-then-down sequence. Excel will adjust the reduction or enlargement so that the sheet fits the number of pages you specify.

Printing a big sheet on multiple pages attractively involves some trial and error. Futz with these settings and print until you're satisfied (or preview your work, as described later in this chapter).

Break it, it's yours

To select a place in the sheet where you want the page to break (forcing a page break at a spot where it wouldn't otherwise be), select a cell just below or to the right of the breaking point and choose Options ➤ Set Page Break. (To put a break at the top of a new sheet, select the first cell in the first row. To make both a horizontal break and a vertical break, select a cell inside the sheet.) A dashed line will appear at the break. This line will be darker than the dashed lines that indicate page breaks the program has set.

To get rid of a page break that you set, place the pointer in the cell below and to the right of the break and select Options ➤ Remove Page Break.

Titles for the truly lazy

Some big sheets have one set of column and row headings and then tables of numbers that go on for pages. You can create such pages without having to enter the repeating column and row titles on each page of the worksheet. Select Options ➤ Set Print Titles. The Set Print Titles dialog box will appear.

The Set Print Titles dialog box contains two text boxes. Type a range reference for a row (A1:Z1) that contains titles to be used for column headings. Type another range reference (A1:A46) for a column that contains row titles. Select OK, and the titles that you've specified will appear on each printed page.

Crying at the Font of Your PC Troubles

Sometimes fonts don't look the same when they're printed as they do on the screen. This is more likely to happen in Windows than on a Macintosh. Fortunately, there's a quick fix to that problem that works most of the time.

Excel is a Microsoft product. So is Windows. Windows comes with True-Type fonts. As you might expect, Excel works nicely with TrueType. Fonts that you installed with other Windows applications may or may not be printed as they appear on screen.

The quickest way to resolve font problems on the PC is simply to use only TrueType fonts with Excel. (This might not work for other applications, though.) In the Windows Program Manager, open the Main program group and select Control Panel ➤ Fonts. The Fonts dialog box will open. Select the TrueType button. Mark both check boxes in the dialog box that appears:

```
┌─────────────────────────────────────────────────────────┐
│ ▬                      TrueType                           │
├─────────────────────────────────────────────────────────┤
│  ┌─TrueType Options──────────────────────┐  ┌──────────┐ │
│  │                                        │  │    OK    │ │
│  │  ☒ Enable TrueType Fonts               │  └──────────┘ │
│  │                                        │  ┌──────────┐ │
│  │  ☒ Show Only TrueType Fonts in Applications│ Cancel │ │
│  │                                        │  └──────────┘ │
│  │                                        │  ┌──────────┐ │
│  │                                        │  │   Help   │ │
│  └────────────────────────────────────────┘  └──────────┘ │
└─────────────────────────────────────────────────────────┘
```

Select OK to close the TrueType dialog box, then choose Cancel to close the Fonts window. Next, select Close in each of the control boxes of the Control Panel and the Main program group. (If you are using a font management program, you may have to turn it off and restart Windows.) When you restart Excel, only the TrueType fonts will appear in menu selections. (Remember that changes you make in the Control Panel will affect all other Windows applications.)

Get a Sneak Preview

If you're still in doubt, perplexed, or otherwise bamboozled about how your sheet will look when you print it, Excel will gladly paint you a picture.

With your sheet on the screen (in the active document window), hold down the Shift key as you click the Print tool (see Figure 8.5). When you do this, the button changes into the Preview tool:

Figure 8.5:

To preview an active document, hold down the Shift key and click the Print tool.

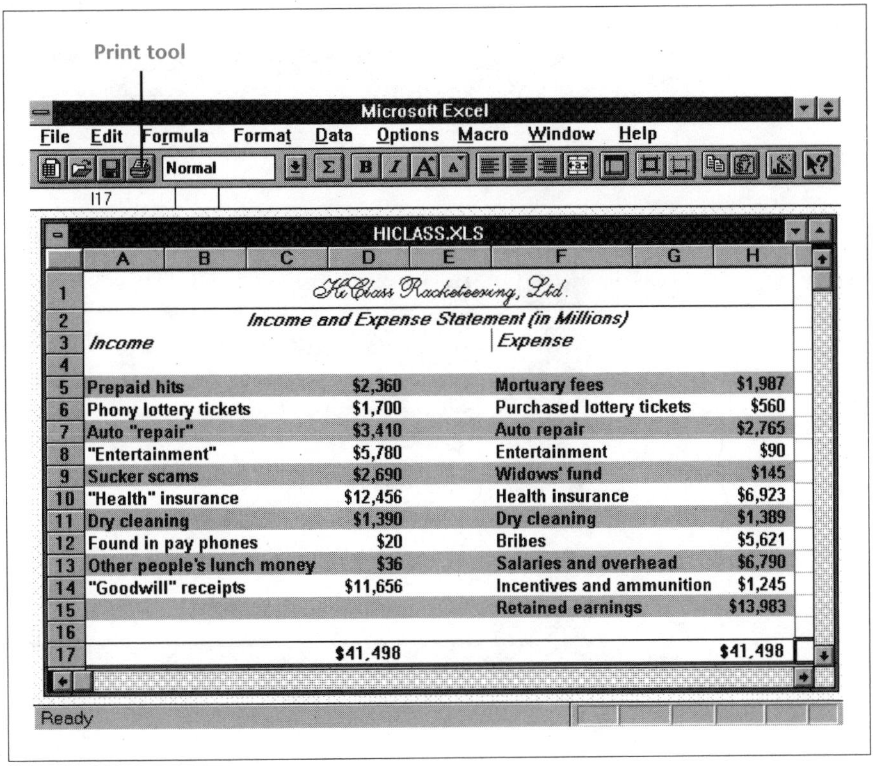

Print tool

			HICLASS.XLS				
	A	B	C	D	E	F	G	H

1				*Hi Class Racketeering, Ltd.*			
2				*Income and Expense Statement (in Millions)*			
3	*Income*					*Expense*	
4							
5	Prepaid hits			$2,360		Mortuary fees		$1,987
6	Phony lottery tickets			$1,700		Purchased lottery tickets		$560
7	Auto "repair"			$3,410		Auto repair		$2,765
8	"Entertainment"			$5,780		Entertainment		$90
9	Sucker scams			$2,690		Widows' fund		$145
10	"Health" insurance			$12,456		Health insurance		$6,923
11	Dry cleaning			$1,390		Dry cleaning		$1,389
12	Found in pay phones			$20		Bribes		$5,621
13	Other people's lunch money			$36		Salaries and overhead		$6,790
14	"Goodwill" receipts			$11,656		Incentives and ammunition		$1,245
15						Retained earnings		$13,983
16							
17				$41,498				$41,498

Ready

Clicking the Preview tool is the same as selecting File ➤ Print Preview from the menu bar. Excel gives you a sneak preview of the first page of the printout (see Figure 8.6).

If the printout will include multiple pages, you can select the Next or Previous buttons to advance or back up through the page sequence.

If you don't like what you see in the preview, select the Setup button to reopen your old friend the Page Setup dialog box. Make whatever changes you like in the Page Setup dialog box, then select OK to see your changes on the preview screen.

The resolution, or picture quality, that you get on the screen is not as sharp and fine as the printed result. To inspect parts of the preview screen more closely, move the pointer into the area of the sheet you want to see close up. As you move the pointer into the sheet, the

Printing

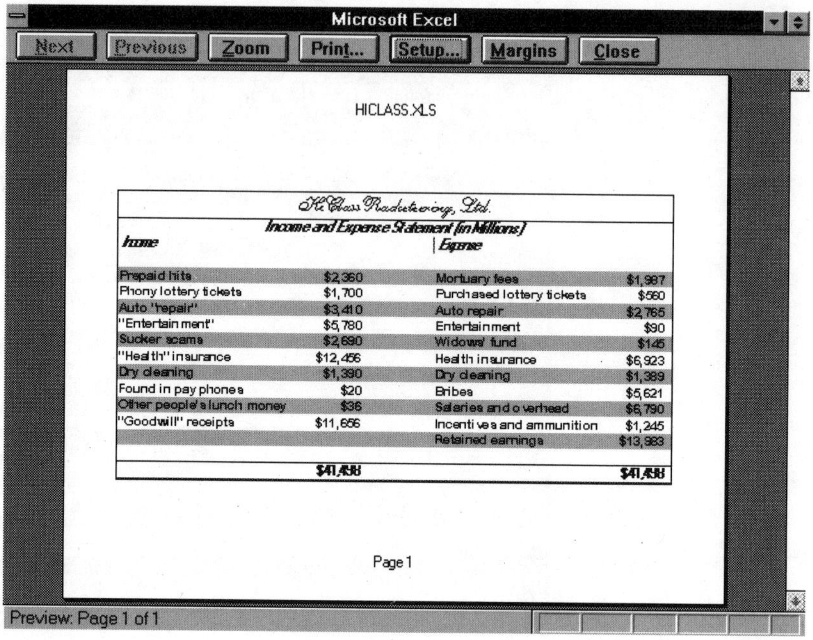

Figure 8.6:
A preview of how the sheet in Figure 8.5 will look when printed.

pointer shape will change to a magnifying glass. Click once and Excel will enlarge the view in that area. Click again and Excel will restore the full view of the sheet. If you want to move around in an enlarged view, select the Zoom button and adjust the scroll bars.

You Can Be Greedy about Your Margin

Excel lets you adjust the margins of the printed page right on the preview screen. Select the Margins button, and a collection of *handles* will appear in the display, as shown in Figure 8.7.

The handles connected by long lines represent the page margins. Move the pointer to a margin line and drag to change the position of the sheet on the page.

Figure 8.7:
When you select the Margins button in the Preview window, handles appear around the edges of the display.

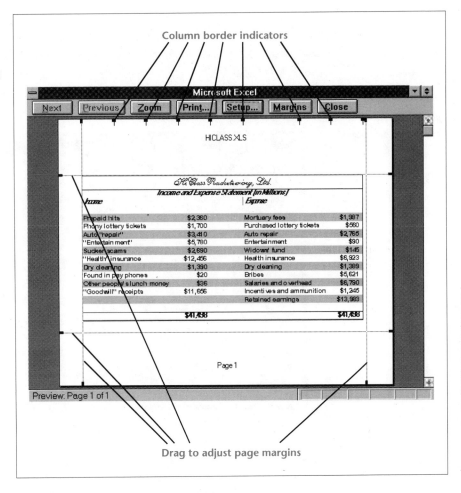

Dragging the margins of the previewed sheet affects the Margins settings in the Page Setup dialog box. Instead of dragging the margins, you can type numeric settings here, as long as you haven't checked the Center Horizontally and Center Vertically boxes:

Printing

Back in the Preview window, select the Close button if you (whoops!) need to edit the sheet before printing. If you like what you see, go ahead and select the Print button. The Print dialog box will appear, as shown in Figure 8.8.

Figure 8.8:
The Print dialog box

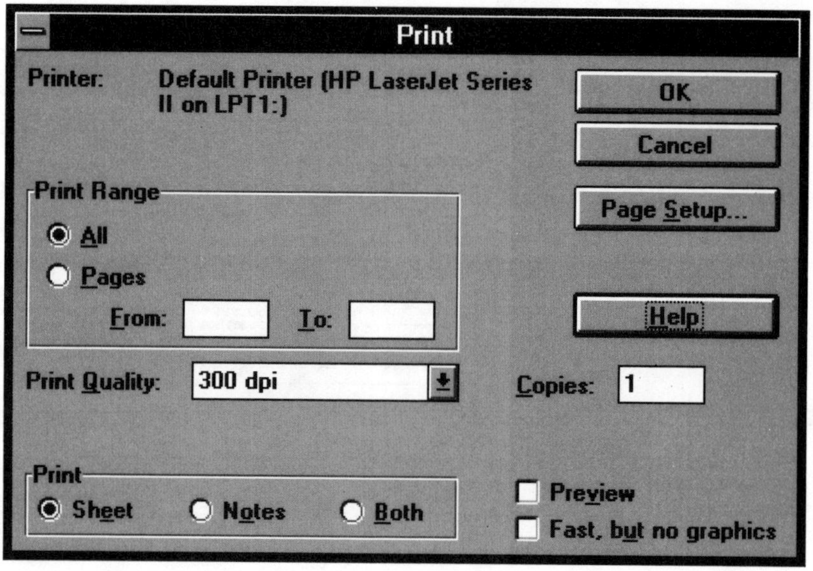

To print multiple copies, type a number in the Copies box. Print Quality depends on what your printer can do (dpi = dots per inch). Checking Preview will return you to the preview screen when you select OK—not much point in doing that. But you can mark Fast if you want to print a draft quickly. Excel will print just the stuff in your sheet with no frills. To start printing, select OK, or, if you're using a Mac, choose Print. (To read about the Notes option, have a look at Chapter 12.)

You Don't Have to Show It All

Sometimes you want to tell only part of the story (you tease). To select a portion of a sheet for printing, highlight the block of cells you want to print. Then, select Options ➤ Set Print Area from the menu bar, or click the Set Print Area tool (found on the Utility Toolbar):

The edges of the print area will appear in the sheet as dotted lines. Whenever you select Print, Excel will print just the portion of the sheet inside those lines. This setting is saved in the sheet file, so it will be there whenever you reopen the sheet.

To choose a different print area, just repeat the command. To print the entire sheet, select it all (just click the button between the row and column headings), then choose Options ➤ Remove Print Area. (You will only see this command in the menu if the entire sheet is selected.)

For World Travelers: Views, Scenarios, and Reports

Excel has some features that are sure to please managers who like to see the same stuff lots of different ways.

You can select a block of cells (or a drawing or chart) in a worksheet and define it as a *view*. A view is still part of the document, but it can contain different print settings or even hidden cells. Make your selection, then choose Window ➤ View. Now select the Add button. Type a name for the view and select OK. To see a view, choose Window ➤ View, select the name you gave it, and choose the Show button.

A view *is a separate set of print settings or hidden cells that is stored with the worksheet it is based on.*

A *scenario* is like a view, but it can have different data from the original sheet, or even different formulas. The purpose of a scenario is to show alternatives (*what if* or "just s'pose").

To create a scenario from a sheet, select the cells in the sheet that will have changeable stuff in them. Then choose Formula ➤ Scenario

Manager and select the Add button. Type a name for this scenario, and type alternate values for each of the changeable cells listed. Select OK, then choose Close. To look at a scenario, select Formula ➤ Scenario Manager, the name of the scenario, then the Show button.

*A **scenario** is an alternate set of data values or formulas that can be applied to a sheet to show the outcome of a different set of assumptions or circumstances.*

Views and scenarios can be combined in *reports*. These reports can be named and then printed as a group with a single command. To create a report, select File ➤ Print Report. Select the Add button. Type a name for the report, and pick the views and scenarios you want to include. For each combination, select Add, and finally select OK. To print the report, select File ➤ Print Report, pick the report name, and select the Print button.

*A **report** is a named collection of worksheet views and scenarios that can be printed as a group using the command File ➤ Print Report.*

Tangled in Your Sheet? Collapse It!

Excel offers a nifty way to get a very large sheet onto your very small computer screen. This feature of Excel is easier to demonstrate than it is to explain, so I'll show you how it works.

If you want to follow along at your own computer, open the sample worksheet BUDGET.XLS, which is found in the subdirectory EXCEL\ EXAMPLES (see Figure 8.9). (On the Mac, it's the BUDGET sheet in the EXCEL:EXAMPLE folder.) This sample budget is a typical kind of large sheet. It has summary lines (shown in bold) that recap the detail (shown as columns below the bold totals).

The sample budget sheet contains a multilevel set of views, created with the command Formula ➤ Outline. Each level of detail is represented by a numbered set of buttons in the top left corner of the window. The vertically stacked buttons numbered 1 through 4 are the

Figure 8.9:
The sample budget
worksheet

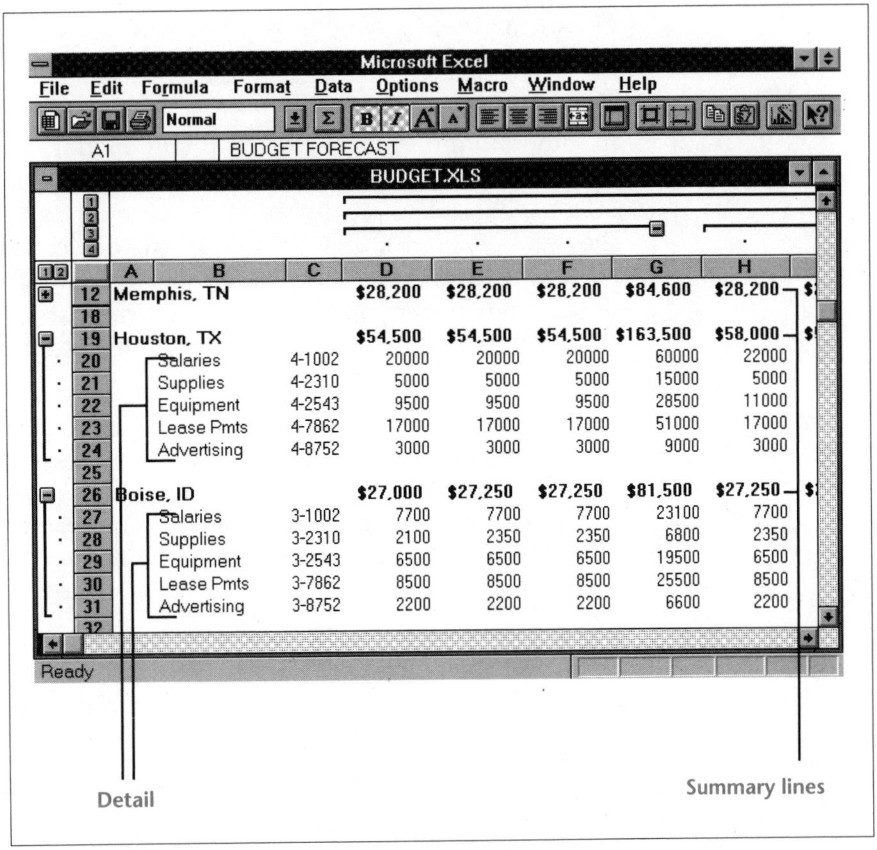

Microsoft Excel

File Edit Formula Format Data Options Macro Window Help

A1   BUDGET FORECAST

BUDGET.XLS

	A	B	C	D	E	F	G	H
12	Memphis, TN			$28,200	$28,200	$28,200	$84,600	$28,200
18								
19	Houston, TX			$54,500	$54,500	$54,500	$163,500	$58,000
20	Salaries		4-1002	20000	20000	20000	60000	22000
21	Supplies		4-2310	5000	5000	5000	15000	5000
22	Equipment		4-2543	9500	9500	9500	28500	11000
23	Lease Pmts		4-7862	17000	17000	17000	51000	17000
24	Advertising		4-8752	3000	3000	3000	9000	3000
25								
26	Boise, ID			$27,000	$27,250	$27,250	$81,500	$27,250
27	Salaries		3-1002	7700	7700	7700	23100	7700
28	Supplies		3-2310	2100	2350	2350	6800	2350
29	Equipment		3-2543	6500	6500	6500	19500	6500
30	Lease Pmts		3-7862	8500	8500	8500	25500	8500
31	Advertising		3-8752	2200	2200	2200	6600	2200
32								

Ready

Detail

Summary lines

Printing

column-level selections. The side-by-side buttons numbered 1 and 2 are
the row-level selections:

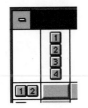

You can click the button for the level of detail you want to see—for
columns, for rows, or both. Button 1 is always the top, or grand-total,
level. The higher the button number, the greater the detail in that view.

There's another set of buttons that does the same thing:

In some situations, these buttons might be more convenient to use than the numbered buttons. Click any button that has a minus sign (–) on it to collapse, or see the summary view of, that level. Any level that shows a button with a plus sign (+) is already collapsed. Click the plus to expand that level and see its detail. For example, if you were to click the collapse button to the left of row 19 in Figure 8.9, rows 20–24 would go into hiding. (The Utility Toolbar also includes tools for collapsing, expanding, and hiding an outline.)

The result of the Formula ➤ Outline command depends on the way you've built your sheet. You will only see a Collapse button where you have a range of detail that ends in a summary total. For a sheet to be collapsible in both directions, it must have totals for rows as well as totals for columns.

What you see on the screen is what you get when you print. Once you've outlined a large sheet with the Formula ➤ Outline command, you can control the level of summary—and how much detail is shown on the printout—by clicking the little buttons.

What a bargain—handy worksheet stuff and self-improvement in the same book! Read all about Excel's shortcuts (Chapter 9), spelling checks (Chapter 10), charting (Chapter 11), and worksheet notes (Chapter 12).

BECOMING A MORE EXCEL-LENT PERSON

Chapter 9

SHORTCUTS FOR THOSE HAIRY SITUATIONS

Murphy's Work Ethic: Doing something in the most tedious and difficult manner is only required when you're learning it in school.

THIS CHAPTER IS about working smarter, not harder. No bullsheet. Let's go.

If you're working on a PC, don't wait around for Windows to give you permission to start the program. Just type win excel *at the DOS C:> prompt and get right to it!*

Go Straight to Your Cell

The quickest way into a jail cell is to leave home without your driver's license. Here's the quickest way into a comfy Excel cell: Double-click the name of the document in the Windows File Manager (see Figure 9.1). (On a Mac, you can double-click a document on the desktop.) This method of opening a file works for sheets (.XLS files on the PC), macros (.XLM), charts (.XLC), and workbooks (.XLW).

Figure 9.1:
You can start Excel and open a document in a jiffy by double-clicking the name of the Excel document.

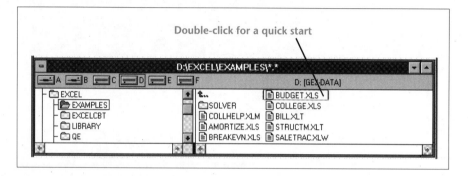

Here's another shortcut, which you can even use to open several documents at once. You must have the File Manager file listing and the Excel program icon or window displayed on the screen at the same time. Drag the document file name from the File Manager listing and drop it on the Excel program icon or open application window (see Figure 9.2). This will work when the program icon is shown in a program group or when it appears at the bottom of the screen, indicating that the application has been minimized.

With this neat trick, there are two methods you can use to select several files to open at once. To choose a group of adjacent files, hold down the Shift key while you click the top and the bottom file names in the group. To add individual, nonadjacent files to your selection, hold down the Ctrl key as you click the name of each file. Names of selected files will appear in reverse colors. Next, drag the group to the program icon or window, as described above.

Figure 9.2:
You can start Excel and open one or more documents by using this drag-and-drop method in File Manager.

D:\EXCEL\EXAMPLES*.*

A B C D E F   D: [GEJ-DATA]

D:\
ALEX
BIBLIO
EXCEL
  EXAMPLES

t..
SOLVER
COLLHELP.XLM
AMORTIZE.XLS
BREAKEVN.XLS

BUDGET.XLS
COLLEGE.XLS
BILL.XLT
STRUCTM.XLT
SALETRAC.XLW

Selected 3 file(s) (53,734 bytes)   Total 9 file(s) (126,570 bytes)

Microsoft Excel

... to here   Drag files from here...

If you find yourself always working on the same stuff, you can set up Excel so that the same document is opened automatically every time you start the program. On a PC, in File Manager or in DOS, just copy or move the document file into the subdirectory EXCEL\XLSTART. If you're using a Mac, move the file into the SYSTEM:PREFERRED EXCEL STARTUP FOLDER (4). Template files are an exception. The templates stored here don't open right away. However, Excel will list them each time you select File ➤ New.

Lost? Press the Magic Key!

If you become stumped, confused, or otherwise bewildered in the midst of performing a command or operation in Excel, just press the magic key—F1 (⌘-\ on the Mac). The Help contents screen will appear, and you can pick your topic.

There's an even quicker way to get help on a specific task. When you are trying to do something that has you stymied, press Shift-F1 on the PC or ⌘-Shift-? on the Mac. This triggers what programmers are fond of calling *context-sensitive help*. In plain English, Excel takes note of the command or operation you are attempting, finds that topic in the Help system, and opens it for you to read in the Help window.

If you're using a PC, when you're done reading the Help topic, you can get it on paper by selecting File ➤ Print Topic from the Help window menu bar, or you can select File ➤ Exit to resume working in Excel.

Shortcuts

Special Help for Lotus Eaters and Multiplan Manipulators

Excel is like a hard-working evangelist, not wishing that anyone should perish on account of old, misguided habits that are difficult to break. If you were formerly a hardened user of 1-2-3 or Multiplan, Excel forgives you.

For help with any particular command or operation while you're working in Excel for Windows, select Help ➤ Lotus 1-2-3 or Help ➤ Multiplan, depending on your previous spreadsheet indoctrination. (If you're using the Macintosh version, select Window ➤ Help For 1-2-3 Users. There's no Multiplan Help for the Mac, though.)

In Excel for Windows, Lotus users can opt to receive instructions as notes or to watch reverently as Excel translates 1-2-3 commands into selections from its own menus. Just double-click each part of the 1-2-3 command syntax as it is presented to you. For example, if you choose Demonstration mode, Excel will show the 1-2-3 command

```
Worksheet/Global/Format/Fixed/2 (then OK)
```

as the series of menu selections and dialog boxes that would appear if you were to select

```
Format ➤ Style ➤ Normal ➤ Define ➤ Number ➤ 0.00
```

Multiplan Help is even more straightforward. Just select Help ➤ Multiplan, type a Multiplan command string, and select OK. Excel will cheerfully translate the command for you. (The Lotus 1-2-3 Help window on the Mac works much like Multiplan Help in Windows.)

Don't Dial 411: Here's the Information

Not so many years ago, when phone companies were trying to cope with the growing number of calls to directory assistance, spokesperson Mariette Hartley appeared in TV ads suggesting rather insistently, "Look in the book first!" Now, there's an idea whose time has passed. People today expect answers at the touch of a button.

Sensitive to your need for instant gratification, those nice people at Microsoft gathered the answers to the most frequently asked questions about Excel and stuck them *inside the program*. Here's how to get the information.

On a PC, from the Excel menu bar, select Help ➤ Product Support. (On the Mac, choose Window ➤ Help and select Product Support near the top of the Help window.) A list of topics will appear. From the list, select Answers To Common Questions. Here in one place you'll find the 20 most frequently asked questions about Excel. If you find your question, click the word Answer listed after it, and Microsoft will share its wisdom with you. When you're done, select File ➤ Exit from the Help window menu bar on a PC, or click the window's close box on the Mac.

Save Your Work, Save Yourself

Computers have excellent memories when they are awake. But shut off their power, and they have instant amnesia. In fact, if your computer experiences even a momentary glitch in electrical power, the stuff in your sheet will go to data heaven, whence there is no reentry except through your fingers!

To safeguard your typing and all the hard work you've made Excel do, you must save your stuff in a computer disk file.

So many ways to save

There are several ways to save a sheet to disk. All have the same ultimate result—storing your sheet as a file. So save however you want. Just save early and save often!

To save the active document window (the sheet you're currently working on), you can click the Save File tool:

Alternatively, you can select Save from the File menu, or just press Shift-F12 (⌘-S on the Mac).

If this is the first time you have saved the sheet, the Save As dialog box will appear (see Figure 9.3). This is where you will create and name a new file.

Figure 9.3:

The Save As dialog box appears the first time you select File ➤ Save with a new document and any time you select File ➤ Save As.

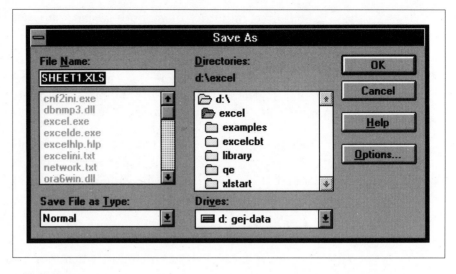

Select OK to accept the rather unimaginative name that Excel has picked (SHEET1 in Figure 9.3, or Worksheet1 if you're using a Mac), or type a different name in the File Name box (the Save Worksheet As box on the Mac). Then select OK. (If you're working in Windows, you must name the file in eight letters or fewer, with no blank spaces.)

In Excel for Windows, the .XLS file extension means that the file holds an Excel sheet. The extension is a way of telling Windows and Excel what type of stuff is stored there and which program created it. You don't have to type the extension; Excel will insist on this part of the file name and will add it whether you like it or not.

If you change the file type in the Save File As Type drop-down list box, Excel will insist on a different extension to match your selection. For example, if you select WK3 to indicate a Lotus 1-2-3 worksheet file, Excel will translate your Excel sheet into Lotus stuff and add the extension .WK3.

What's with Save As?

Once you've saved a sheet for the first time and created its file, you won't see the Save As dialog box anymore when you choose File ➤ Save or its equivalent. Excel knows where the file is and what it's called, and it just updates the disk, replacing the old file with the new.

If you select File ➤ Save As (or press F12 on the PC keyboard), the Save As dialog box will appear. There you can type a different file name and even specify a different storage location for it on the disk. (For tips on navigating the perilous waters of your disk directories, see Chapter 3.)

Murphy's Law of Data Salvation: *Use File ➤ Save when you're updating a file and don't mind at all that the old stuff will be overwritten, or replaced. Use File ➤ Save As to create a new file, saving the current sheet to disk with the option of renaming it. If you use Save As to rename a file, you will end up with separate files for the old version and the new version.*

You can save a collection of sheets together as a workbook *file (PC files will have the extension .XLW). In Excel-speak, this is called* binding *the sheets. Use the command File ➤ Save Workbook. Read all about it in Chapter 3.*

You AutoSave for a Rainy Day

Excel has an automatic file-saving feature called *AutoSave*. You must install AutoSave before you can use it.

Installing AutoSave

From the menu bar, select Options ➤ Add-Ins. Excel will open the Add-In Manager dialog box. Select the Add button. The File Open dialog box will appear, displaying a list of files in the subdirectory EXCEL\LIBRARY. To load the macro, double-click the file name AUTOSAVE.XLA. (On the Mac, the equivalent folder is EXCEL:MACRO LIBRARY and the file name is AUTOSAVE.)

Once you have loaded the AUTOSAVE macro, the Auto Save option will appear in the Add-Ins Installed listing in the Add-In Manager dialog box (see Figure 9.4). Select the Close button to resume working in Excel.

Shortcuts

Figure 9.4:

The Add-In Manager shows all the ready-made add-in macros (.XLA files on the PC) that have already been loaded into Excel and are ready to use.

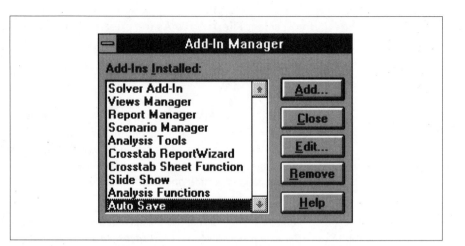

Setting up AutoSave

AutoSave includes a number of options. You should pick the ones you want before the program starts recklessly writing files to your disk of its own accord.

From the menu bar, select Options ➤ AutoSave. (This item will only appear if you did the Add-In installation described in the previous section.) The AutoSave dialog box will appear, as shown in Figure 9.5.

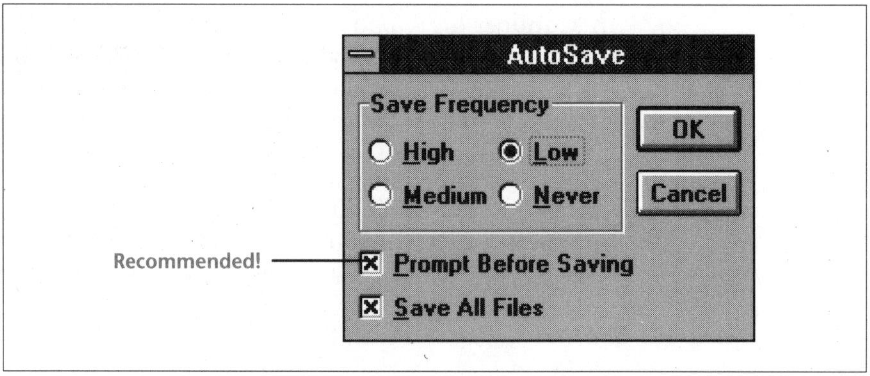

Figure 9.5:

In the AutoSave dialog box, you can select options for timed, automatic saving of documents to disk.

Select one of the following option buttons to control how often Auto-Save ought to save:

High   Every three minutes

Medium   Every nine minutes

Low   Every 30 minutes

Never   Not at all. This turns the feature off, but leaves it installed so that you can reactivate it with the Options ➤ AutoSave command.

Mark the Save All Files check box if you want AutoSave to save all open files. If you leave this box unchecked, Excel will save only the window you're currently working in.

If you want Excel to ask your permission each time it saves, mark the Prompt Before Saving check box (this is a good idea). Before saving, Excel will prompt you with a confirmation box like this:

AutoSave

Save changes in 'Sheet1'?

[**Save**]   [**Skip**]   [**Cancel**]

The automatic file save feature can be a mixed blessing. If you use it, I recommend that you choose the Prompt Before Saving option so that you can control when files are replaced. In my experience, anything that's both automatic and potentially destructive is an excuse for Murphy to work overtime. The danger is that AutoSave will automatically save your mistakes as well as your inspirations, thus obliterating what may be the only good copy of your file.

If you insist on activating timed AutoSave without warning, do yourself a favor and have Excel save the old version of the current sheet each time. Select File ➤ Save As and then choose the Options button. In the Save Options dialog box, select Create Backup File, then choose OK. With both this option and AutoSave turned on, Excel will save the current sheet periodically as SHEET1.XLS (the DOS file name), retaining the prior version each time and renaming it SHEET1.BAK.

Shortcuts

Of Macros and Add-Ins

AutoSave is a *macro,* or a set of "canned" instructions that Excel will do on command, reducing a big task to a couple of clicks or keystrokes. *Add-ins* are ready-made macros that are supplied with the program. You can add any of them by following the procedure described in this section. On a PC, add-in macros are stored in special sheet files with the extension .XLA.

You can start recording your own Excel macro with the command Macro ➤ Record. Play it back with Macro ➤ Run. On a PC, macros you create yourself are stored in sheet files with the extension .XLM.

Macros for higher math are available in a collection called the Analysis Tool-Pak. You can get at these with the command Options ➤ Analysis Tools.

Psssssst! What's the Password?

Excel can't protect you on dark and stormy nights, but it can protect your stuff. You can order Excel to prevent someone else (or even you) from changing your data.

Protecting the stuff in your sheet

To protect a document from alteration—*but not from being opened*—select Options ➤ Protect Document. The Protect Document dialog box will appear:

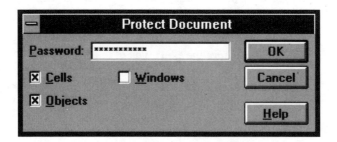

You can type a password—up to 255 characters long—in the Password box. The password is optional, but if you enter one here, the program will ask you to type it exactly—including lower- and uppercase lettering—if you try to change the protection status of the sheet. (You won't see the password as you type. On a PC, an asterisk (*) will appear in place of each character (bullets appear on the Mac). That's so nosy people can't read over your shoulder as you compose your secrets.)

These are the options in the Protect Document dialog box (a fourth option, Contents, is available for protecting all the sheets in a workbook):

Cells Excel locks the values, formulas, and formats in cells so that they can't be changed. This affects only cells that have been formatted as Locked. Usually that's all the cells in the sheet, since the Normal style includes the Locked option. To change the protection status of a cell or block of cells, select Format ➤ Cell Protection.

Objects This option applies to graphic objects, such as drawings and charts, as well as to imported or embedded objects, such as bitmaps and multimedia files. For more about drawing and charting, see Chapter 11. To bone up on object linking and embedding (OLE), read Chapter 12.

Windows This option prevents users of a file from controlling its document windows. The control boxes (or close boxes) of the windows will not appear, so the windows can't be moved, resized, or hidden. You might use this option if you created a form that you always wanted Excel to display at a certain size.

You can include the Locked and Hidden options in cell formatting. A locked cell is protected only when you turn on file protection with the command Options ➤ Protect Document. If a cell is hidden, the formulas in that cell cannot be viewed. If you select a hidden cell that contains a formula, only the result will appear in the cell and in the formula bar. This means that anyone viewing the sheet will not know which cells contain formulas or what calculations they perform.

You can use the Locked cell protection option selectively to create sheets that other people can use as forms to be filled in. In a protected sheet, use the Format ➤ Cell Protection command to specifically unlock the blank cells that will be filled in by the user of the form. When working in such a sheet, users can move from one unprotected blank cell to another by pressing Tab.

When you type a password in the Protect Document dialog box and select OK, the Confirm Password dialog box appears:

```
┌─────────────────────────────────────────────────┐
│ ▬           Confirm Password                      │
├─────────────────────────────────────────────────┤
│ Reenter protection Password.        ┌──────────┐ │
│                                     │    OK    │ │
│ ┌─────────────────────────────┐     └──────────┘ │
│ │ ***********                 │     ┌──────────┐ │
│ └─────────────────────────────┘     │  Cancel  │ │
│                                     └──────────┘ │
│                                     ┌──────────┐ │
│                                     │  Help    │ │
│                                     └──────────┘ │
└─────────────────────────────────────────────────┘
```

In this dialog box, you must retype the password exactly as you typed it the first time. If you screw up, Excel will complain, "Confirmation password is not identical." When you acknowledge this by selecting OK, the Protect Document dialog box will reopen so that you can try it again until you get it right.

If you leave the Password box blank, anyone will be able to use the Options ➤ Unprotect Document command to remove protection from the sheet and make changes to it. You might use this simpler approach if you just want to prevent the final version of a sheet from being altered accidentally.

Slamming the door on file access

You can also apply password protection to restrict access to a file. With this type of password protection, the file itself will be locked, rather than just its data, and you will need to type the password to open it in Excel.

To lock a file with a password, choose File ➤ Save As. The familiar Save As dialog box will appear on your screen. Select the Options button to open the Save Options dialog box, shown in Figure 9.6.

Type a password in the Protection Password box to restrict the opening of the file to people in the know. Another option is to type the same or a different password in the Write Reservation Password box. If you do, this password will be required before Excel writes any updates to disk, preventing unauthorized changes.

Figure 9.6:
You can apply
password protection
to the opening of
files, to updeates, or
to both.

Save Options	
☐ Create **B**ackup File	OK
┌ File Sharing ───────	Cancel
Protection Password: `****`	
Write Reservation Password: `******`	Help
☐ **R**ead-Only Recommended	

If you mark the Read-Only Recommended check box, Excel will advise users of a file that they should open it by marking the Read Only option in the Open dialog box. Read-only access is just what it says—users will be able to read the file, but they won't be able to write changes to it. The Read-Only Recommended notice is just a warning. To prevent write access, you must assign a write-reservation password, as described above.

As with sheet-protection passwords, Excel will ask you to retype any password you enter as a confirmation before it installs the lock.

Excel's password-protection feature is so secure that if you forget a password that you've installed, not even the mighty Microsoft Corporation can help you get your data back.

Those Cryptic Encrypted Files

When you apply password protection to an Excel document for file access, it does not become locked in the sense that its contents cannot be viewed. If you're curious, you can use an editor such as Windows Notepad to open the file and inspect the stuff inside. But it will look like garbage. Excel uses the password as an *encryption key* to garble the stuff so completely that only performing the process in reverse can restore the data to readable form. This is much more effective and burglar-proof than data-protection schemes that merely require an access code to get the location of the file on disk.

Shortcuts

You AutoSelect a Nicer Cell

Excel's AutoSelect feature provides a quick way to jump across or down a sheet or select an entire row or column. To use AutoSelect, move the cell pointer to the edge of the active (current) cell until its shape changes to an arrow tip. Then, do any of the following:

☞ Double-click the right cell border to jump to the last cell in the row.

☞ Double-click the bottom cell border to jump to the last cell in the column.

☞ Hold down the Shift key while double-clicking the right edge or bottom of a cell to select the entire row or column.

When using AutoSelect to select a row or column, you may not always get the results you're after. If columns or rows contain blank cells, Excel will pick everything in the column or row up to and including the last *blank* cell before it encounters another cell with stuff in it. In this case, AutoSelect thinks the cell after the empty cells is the start of a different range and stops there (see Figure 9.7).

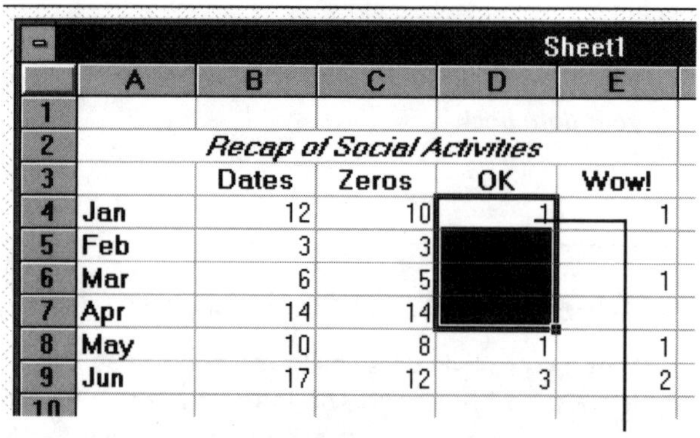

Figure 9.7:
Here's a less-than-spectacular demonstration of the AutoSelect feature, showing that it isn't always so smart.

	A	B	C	D	E
1					
2		*Recap of Social Activities*			
3		Dates	Zeros	OK	Wow!
4	Jan	12	10	1	1
5	Feb	3	3		
6	Mar	6	5		1
7	Apr	14	14		
8	May	10	8	1	1
9	Jun	17	12	3	2
10					

Sheet1

When you double-click the bottom edge of this cell, AutoSelect picks up everything up to the next nonblank cell (D8 in this case).

Let Us Put You in One of These Well-Used Autos

Some Excel features specifically designed to be time-savers are named with the Auto- prefix:

☞ AutoSave

☞ AutoSelect

☞ AutoSum

☞ AutoFill

☞ AutoFormat

AutoSave and AutoSelect are covered in this chapter. To discover Auto-Sum, which adds the stuff in a range, see Chapters 1 and 2. AutoFill, which copies stuff and can increment it as well, is also covered in Chapter 1. AutoFormat, which applies ready-made cosmetics to your stuff, is demonstrated in Chapters 1 and 7.

There's More than One Way to Rip a Sheet

Variety is the spice of life. It takes all kinds to make a world. Some say tomato—well, you get the idea. As its humble contribution to the variety of human experience, Excel offers all kinds of different ways of achieving the same result.

Murphy's Law of Alternatives: The person who watches you work and smiles must know an easier way.

When in doubt, tickle your mouse

A particularly quick way to get results in the Windows version of Excel is to click the *right* mouse button instead of the left. (On the Mac, press ⌘-Option and click.) Depending on what you're doing at the time,

Shortcuts

some kind of *shortcut menu* will appear:

☞ If the pointer is on a cell or a block of cells, an editing menu will appear.

☞ If the pointer is on an object, such as a chart, a different editing menu will appear, displaying commands that apply to the selected object.

☞ If the pointer is in the toolbar, a selection of toolbars will appear.

In any of these menus, you can make your selection by holding down the right mouse button, dragging, and releasing the mouse button when the command you want is highlighted. Or, you can move the pointer to your selection and click either the left or the right mouse button. If you've read Chapters 1 through 5, you've already seen some of these shortcut menus in action.

Blessed are the mouseless

You don't need a mouse to work in Excel (although mice are cute, industrious, and they don't eat much). If your mouse escapes, dies, or is otherwise unavailable, there are several ways to get what you want by pressing keys instead. For this reason, you might say that the mouseless hold the keys to the kingdom of Excel.

☞ To choose commands from the menu bar, first press Alt to activate the highlight. Then use the → and ← keys to move among the selections. Press ↵, ↑, or ↓ to open the pull-down menu of the highlighted selection. Press the ↑ or ↓ key until the command you want is highlighted, then press ↵ to select it.

☞ Another way to do menu-bar commands is to press Alt, then press the key of the underscored letter in the menu item. For example, to select Edit ➤ Cut, press Alt, then E, then T. (Excel ignores the difference between upper- and lowercase here.)

☞ Yet another alternative is to press the *shortcut key* (often a combination of keys) for the command you want. In Windows, if a command has a shortcut key, the shortcut is shown in the pull-down menu to the right of the command. For example, to select File ➤ Print in Excel for Windows, you can press Ctrl-Shift-F12 (all three keys at once).

Some functions and shortcut-key combinations use the F11 and F12 keys. But some keyboards only have the set F1–F10. Don't fret. You can press Alt-F1 for F11 and Alt-F2 for F12.

In any dialog box, you can press Tab or Shift-Tab to move forward or backward among the selections. To reset option buttons and move up and down in lists, press the arrow keys. To mark or unmark check boxes, press the spacebar. In most cases, you can press ⏎ to select the OK button or Esc to select the Cancel button.

For a complete list of PC keyboard alternatives, select Help ➤ Contents ➤ Keyboard Guide. On the Mac, select Window ➤ Help ➤ Keyboard Guide.

These Wizards Make House Calls

Microsoft features with names ending in -Wizard automate long and sometimes complex procedures, presenting them as straightforward selections in a series of windows. In Excel, this approach can be found as ChartWizard and Crosstab ReportWizard. See Chapter 11 to learn how to build graphs with ChartWizard. See Chapter 14 for information on analyzing data in tables with Crosstab ReportWizard.

Don't Do It Sinatra's Way!

Okay, he did it his way. You do it yours. You can customize Excel so that it suits the way you work, even if you like to work as little as possible.

Display options

To reset the options for the way sheets appear in the document window, select Options ➤ Display. The Display Options dialog box will appear.

Of these settings, perhaps the most important is the Formulas check box. If it's marked, formulas will appear in cells instead of values. This option is especially useful when you're checking the logic of a sheet. (See Chapter 5 for testing strategies.)

Shortcuts

Changing the Objects buttons to something other than Show All might make Excel go faster while you're editing, especially if you put lots of graphics in your sheet.

Calculation options

Normally, Excel recalculates the entire sheet each time you press ↵ or click ✓ to put stuff into a cell. As your sheets grow larger, all this calculating can slow the program down, and actually it's unnecessary until you want to see the results.

To reset automatic recalculation, select Options ➤ Calculation. The Calculation Options dialog box will appear. You can reset calculation to Automatic Except Tables (omitting blocks of tabular data from automatic recalculation) or Manual (calculating only when you press F9 (⌘-= on the Mac) or select the Calc Now button in this dialog box).

The Iteration options refer to the number of passes Excel makes to resolve circular references. (See Chapter 5.) The check boxes labeled Sheet Options control compatibility with other types of worksheet files.

Workspace options

You can reset other options that affect the way Excel handles your stuff on the screen by selecting Options ➤ Workspace. The Workspace Options dialog box will appear.

One of the Workspace options is the Fixed Decimal check box. If marked, this option will automatically put a decimal point in number values that you type. If you mark the check box, you can enter the number of decimal places that will be shown. You can override the Fixed Decimal option when you're working by typing the decimal point in a number value when you're entering it.

Another important option here is R1C1, an alternative cell reference scheme. R1C1, which I discuss in Chapter 4, is needed in some cases for compatibility with other spreadsheet software.

Working Out with Custom Toolbars

Recall that you can display any of the ready-made toolbars by selecting Options ➤ Toolbars or moving the pointer up to the toolbar, clicking the right mouse button on the PC (or pressing ⌘-Option and clicking on the Mac), and selecting the name of a toolbar from the pop-up menu.

There are actually many more tools available than appear on these toolbars. To add or remove tools from a ready-made toolbar, select Options ➤ Toolbars, select the name of the toolbar, and choose the Customize button. Then follow the procedures in the section titled "The Do-It-Yourself Formula Toolbar" in Chapter 4.

Shortcuts

Chapter 10

SPELL IT OUT—THEY'LL GET YOU OTHERWISE

Murphy's Recurring Nightmare: The one word you get wrong in a report has always been the pet peeve of your boss—ever since she quit her job as an English teacher in disgust after a spelling bee.

SOME SKILLS THAT are absolutely crucial to success in business are never taught in school. Even MBAs who can do depreciation and amortization analysis standing on their heads have to learn the hard way.

For example,

☞ Answer the phone by giving your name, the name of your company, or both. If you add "How may I help you?" your co-workers will not think you are a suck-up. They'll assume you have had prior business experience.

☞ Proofread everything that you write on the computer (including worksheets), correct any misspellings, and reprint. Submitting hand-corrected drafts as finished work is a sure way to get marked as a rookie.

While Excel can't help you with your phone etiquette, it will cheerfully check your spelling for you. Keep reading to find out how your trusty math slave can also help you get an "A" in English.

A computer spelling check is no substitute for proofreading. In the gap between these two similar processes, Murphy loves to play.

Excel's spelling checker will find nothing wrong with this sentence:

```
I no you love me to.
```

Putting aside the question why anyone would have this in a worksheet, you might assume that the intended message is, "I know you love me too." The other possible interpretations (or misinterpretations) are mysteriously erotic, but nevertheless unclear.

Check Your Spelling, but Carry On Your Luggage

Getting Excel started on a spelling check is easy enough. And you don't necessarily have to finish what you start.

If you know how to use the spelling checker in Microsoft Word or in any other Windows or Macintosh application, you can probably skip this chapter. The differences in the spell-checking features are minor.

To check the text in a worksheet (or in a macro sheet), select any cell and choose Options ➤ Spelling from the menu bar. To check the text in a chart, select the chart window and choose Chart ➤ Spelling. Or, bypass the menus entirely by clicking the Check Spelling tool, which lives in the Utility Toolbar:

Adding ABC✓ to Your Favorite Toolbar

Clicking the Check Spelling tool actually involves more work than using the menu commands, unless you have installed the tool in a toolbar that happens to be handy when you need it. The Check Spelling tool is normally in the Utility Toolbar. To get at the tool, you can move the pointer up to the Standard Toolbar, click the right mouse button (if you're using a Macintosh, press ⌘-Option and click), then select Utility from the pop-up menu. You can then click the ABC✓ tool to get things going. But that's a lot of clicking.

To add the Check Spelling tool to your favorite toolbar, select Options ➤ Toolbars (or choose Toolbars from the pop-up menu). Select the name of the toolbar (the usual one is named *Standard*), then select the Customize button. The Customize dialog box will appear. Select Utility from its Categories list, and the tools in that category will appear on the right. Drag the tool labeled ABC✓ into your favorite toolbar, and select the Close button to resume working in Excel.

For more on dragging tools into a toolbar, see "The Do-It Yourself Formula Toolbar," in Chapter 4.

What Gets Checked?

You can bail out of a spelling check at any point by selecting the Cancel button in the Spelling dialog box. But I'm getting ahead of myself. Besides, there are better ways to control what gets checked:

☞ If you select a single cell (any cell) in a sheet, Excel will check all the text in that sheet. This includes not only text label data, but also

    ☞ Headers and footers

Check Spelling

☞ Text in embedded charts and Excel chart documents

☞ Text boxes (which you created with a drawing tool)

☞ Notes you wrote to yourself (see Chapter 12)

☞ Text in buttons (find out what those are in Chapters 12 and 13)

☞ If you highlight a word in stuff that is currently displayed in the formula bar, Excel will check only that word:

> X ✓ Massachusetts Fund

☞ If there is stuff in the formula bar, none of the stuff is highlighted, and the formula bar buttons are showing (the formula bar is active), Excel will check all the words in the selected cell—and only in that cell.

☞ If you select a range (a block of cells) in the sheet, Excel will check only the stuff in those cells.

☞ No formulas will be checked—ever, including any text that is generated by a formula. (Like, what's the point?)

☞ If contained in your selection, the stuff in hidden cells or in the collapsed portions of outlined sheets will also be checked. (So, for the purposes of spell checking, your secret stuff isn't really hidden.)

If you select a single cell before you start the spelling checker, the spelling checker will proceed from that cell to the end of the sheet. At that point, if there is stuff in the cells above the selected cell, Excel will ask, "Continue checking at beginning of sheet?" Pick Yes to check the remaining words, No to bail out.

So What Are You Going to Do about It?

The spelling checker compares the words it finds to the entries in its internal dictionary, which is a special kind of text file. The first word that the spelling checker cannot find in the dictionary will appear in the Spelling dialog box, as shown in Figure 10.1.

Figure 10.1:
If a word has no match in the internal dictionary, it will appear as the Not In Dictionary entry in the Spelling dialog box.

```
┌─────────────────────────────────────────────────────────────┐
│ ▬                         Spelling                            │
├─────────────────────────────────────────────────────────────┤
│ Not in Dictionary: Harbour                                    │
│                                                               │
│ Change To:    │Harbor                    │  ┌────────┐ ┌─────────┐│
│               ┌──────────────────────┐▲   │ Ignore │ │Ignore All││
│               │Harbor                │    └────────┘ └─────────┘│
│ Suggestions:  │Harbors               │    ┌────────┐ ┌─────────┐│
│               │Harbored              │    │ Change │ │Change All││
│               │Harborer              │    └────────┘ └─────────┘│
│               │Headboard             │    ┌────────┐ ┌─────────┐│
│               │Heartburn             │▼   │  Add   │ │ Cancel  ││
│               └──────────────────────┘    └────────┘ └─────────┘│
│                                           ┌────────┐ ┌─────────┐│
│                                           │Suggest │ │  Help   ││
│ Add Words To:  │CUSTOM.DIC        │ ▼     └────────┘ └─────────┘│
│                                      ☐ Ignore Words in         │
│                                            UPPERCASE           │
│                                      ☒ Always Suggest          │
│ ───────────────────────────────────────────────────────────── │
│ Cell Value: Harbour                                           │
└─────────────────────────────────────────────────────────────┘
```

Becomes available if Always Suggest is off

On a PC, the main dictionary file is shared by all Microsoft Windows applications and can be found in the subdirectory WINDOWS\MSAPPS\PROOF. The file name of the version for American English is MSSP_AM.LEX. Don't bother opening or trying to edit it. The stuff it contains is in compressed binary form.

On a Mac that is running System 7, the folder that holds the dictionary files is SYSTEM:EXTENSIONS:MICROSOFT:SPELLING.

Normally, the spelling checker's best guess (the closest match in the dictionary) will appear in the Change To box. Other near matches will appear in the Suggestions list.

The standard dictionary for software shipped within the United States is American English. So, if you're doing stuff for a British audience, you'll need a different English dictionary. For example, the American dictionary will accept theatre, but it will balk at favour. Dictionaries for other languages, as well as specialized dictionaries of medical jargon and legalese, are available from Microsoft Customer Support (or so they say).

Check Spelling

Change or Change All?

To accept the suggested Change To entry, select the Change button. To pick one of the other suggestions, select it in the list, then select Change and the checking will continue. Or, if you like one of the suggestions, just double-click it and you won't have to select Change or Close.

If you don't see the word you want in the Suggestions list and you know the correct spelling, you can retype the word or edit the entry in the Change To box, then select Change.

To change all the appearances of the same word (except for words that have unusual capitalization), select the Change All button instead of the Change button. If you do this, the program will not ask you to confirm each replacement: It will do them all automatically when you're not looking.

To stop checking before the entire document or selection has been checked, select the Close button. Only words you changed up to that point will be affected.

Ignore or Ignore All?

If you're sure there's nothing wrong with the original word, you can select the Ignore button. The spelling checker will skip *this occurrence* of the word. If you select the Ignore All button instead, the program will accept all instances of the word in the current document that are spelled exactly the same and that have no capitalization inside the word (or that have the same internal capitalization as the first word). The Ignore All button is particularly useful for accepting proper names in a sheet.

Cancel or Close?

The label on the Cancel button will change to Close if you select Change, Change All, or Add. You must then select Close to exit the dialog box. The appearance of the Close button indicates that a change has been made to the document or to the custom dictionary.

Use a Quicker Checker

The Spelling dialog box includes two check boxes for options that can make the spelling-check process go faster. The way you mark these options when the Spelling dialog box first appears will affect the rest of the spelling pass, unless you change the option when the dialog box reappears with the next word not found in Excel's dictionary.

Don't bother with acronyms

If you mark the Ignore Words In UPPERCASE check box, the spell-checking program will skip words that are in all capital letters. This is a good way to exclude acronyms (such as the useful label SWAG for scientific wild-assed guess) and abbreviations such as IRS (you know who they are).

To suggest, or not to suggest

Normally, the Always Suggest check box is marked, meaning that the spelling checker will automatically display near matches in the Suggestions list.

Searching through its dictionary for suggestions can be time-consuming for Excel. To speed things up, you can turn the Always Suggest option off. Then if you want to see a list of suggestions for a particular word, you can select the Suggest button.

To see additional suggestions, select the word in the Suggestions list that comes closest to the word you want, then select the Suggest button again. Excel will display a new list of word choices.

Other Goofs Excel Will Find

In addition to unconventional spellings, Excel will find some other kinds of typographical errors. For example, it will get upset if there is a repeated word:

    the the

And it does not like internal or nonstandard capitalization:

MicroSoft

(The correct spelling is "Microsoft.")

Hey, If You Don't Like It, Write Your Own Dictionary!

This brings me to the most dangerous little button in the Spelling dialog box:

This button works like Ignore All, but with a big difference: Not only will the spelling checker skip the word forevermore—it will also add the word to a separate dictionary. There it will be enshrined as gospel, to be ignored until the end of time in future spelling checks of *any* Microsoft application document.

Be very sure that the word shown in the Change To box is not misspelled before you select Add. This can be tricky if the word is a technical term, jargon, or slang. For example, the words "workstation" and "filename" are now accepted as single words. Don't assume, therefore, that "fileserver" is okay. (The closest suggestion from Excel's dictionary is "philanderer"!)

Each time you select the Add button, you are making an entry in the custom dictionary file CUSTOM.DIC (the file name in DOS). You can build other custom dictionaries by typing a different file name in the Add Words To box.

You can build a custom dictionary by selecting the Add button each time you want to add a term, or you can create a text file that contains all the unusual spellings, terms of jargon, and proper names that you want to use. Just make sure to save the file in the WINDOWS\MSAPPS\PROOF subdirectory (SYSTEM:EXTEN-SIONS:MICROSOFT:SPELLING on the Mac).

Custom dictionaries in Windows, which you create for your own spellings (or misspellings, as you wish), must have the file extension .DIC. Stuff in these files is ANSI text, which you can open and edit with a text editor such as Windows Notepad. So if you select Add accidentally, you can open up your custom dictionary file and delete the word you inadvertently added.

And Be Sure to Thank Excel

When Excel has finished running the spell-checking program, it will report, "Finished spell checking entire sheet." It wants a thank you. You must select OK before you resume your work.

Chapter 11

SOMETIMES YOU HAVE TO PAINT THEM A PICTURE

Murphy's Law of Illustration: The weaker your math, the prettier your graphics must be.

LET'S FACE IT. Charts are sexier than numbers. Don't fight it, just learn it. Charting is easy because there's a wizard inside Excel who lives to do your charts.

The Wizard Is Smart, but You Must Be Wise

With Excel's ChartWizard, turning stuff in a worksheet into graphs is as simple as click, click, click. The challenge for you is to be picky about the data. That requires genuine, old-fashioned human perspicacity.

You see, the ChartWizard has no idea which stuff in your sheet would be most *meaningful* as a graph. That's where your judgment comes in. Most of the time, putting all the data in a sheet into a single chart is disastrous. There's just too much stuff. Instead, you need to select a few rows or columns that show related trends, basic proportions, or fundamental relationships.

A row or column that contains numbers for plotting is a *data series*, or data set. Your purpose in making it into a chart is usually to show the audience a pattern in the data, such as rising sales, increasing market share, or swelling optimism.

In a sense, charting is a way of showing more information about less stuff. Get the right stuff, and you can let the ChartWizard worry about making it pretty.

In terms a statistician would love, the purpose of making a chart is **data reduction.** *That is, a well-made chart summarizes your stuff visually. In the notion of reduction, there's a helpful hint to chart makers: Simplify!*

The simplicity that a chart can achieve is a powerful tool in the hands of a determined businessperson. When you make a business presentation, your objective is to get a result. If you're unsure what that result should be, you'd better postpone the meeting until you know what you want to achieve. The idea is to show your stuff, ask for a decision, and leave as quickly as possible—before anyone can think of an awkward question.

Murphy's Advice to Presenters: Give it to them short and sweet. Then get out of the room!

The Short Story of the Amazing ChartWizard

There are four basic steps to producing a chart in Excel:

1. Select the stuff in your sheet that you want to plot. Include the columns or rows containing the number values, as well as any text labels you have for those columns or rows.

2. Click the ChartWizard tool, which is at the right end of the Standard Toolbar:

3. The pointer will change to small cross-hairs. Drag a rectangular area in the sheet to hold the chart.

4. The ChartWizard will show you some options in a series of dialog boxes. Answer the Wizard's questions (usually this involves clicking a miniature picture of the option you want). After making a choice in each dialog box, select the Next button. In the last dialog box, select OK.

To select several columns or rows that are not adjacent to one another, hold down the Ctrl key as you click each one.

There's a lesson here: It takes a Wizard to keep things this simple!

That's really all you need to know to get started. It might be more fun to play with the ChartWizard's options than to read the rest of this chapter. Then, again, you might find that the Wizard has some tricks up its sleeve.

Getting Wise to the Wizard

Here's an example that recaps the questions the ChartWizard will put to you. The example illustrates some of the frills that you might want to include in your own charts.

Let's start with the stuff in Figure 11.1.

Figure 11.1:

There's too much stuff even in this small sheet to make a chart that's simple enough to be effective. The plot will have more visual impact if you select one or two sets of data that show a trend.

ChartWizard tool

Microsoft Excel

File   Edit   Formula   Format   Data   Options   Macro   Window   Help

Normal

A3

MURPH1.XLS

	A	B	C	D	E	F	G	H	I	J
1	**Murphy's Wrecking Company**									
2	*"You Build It, We Smash It"*									
3		Q1	Q2	Q3	Q4	Year				
4	Income	$1,200	$1,400	$1,600	$1,340	**$5,540**				
5	Expenses	$800	$950	$1,100	$989	**$3,839**				
6	Profit	$400	$450	$500	$351	**$1,701**				
7	Taxes	$92	$104	$115	$81	**$391**				
8	Net Profit	$308	$347	$385	$270	**$1,310**				
9	ROI	39%	36%	35%	27%	**34%**				
10										
11										
12										
13										

Selected data range can include chart labels

A good chart for presentation would plot the Income and Expense rows, so I've selected these rows in Figure 11.1. Notice that I also selected the column headings in the third row. The ChartWizard will automatically use these headings as axis labels.

Once you've selected the stuff you want to plot, click the ChartWizard tool. The crawling ants will march around your selection. Next, drag an area in the sheet that will hold the chart, as shown in Figure 11.2.

Excel will compose the chart to fit the area you drag. For best chart composi-tion—including labels that don't look too crowded—drag the lower-right corner of the rectangle off the bottom of the screen. The display will scroll as you do this, permitting you to select a bigger area. The bigger area will give the Wizard more room to make a pretty chart.

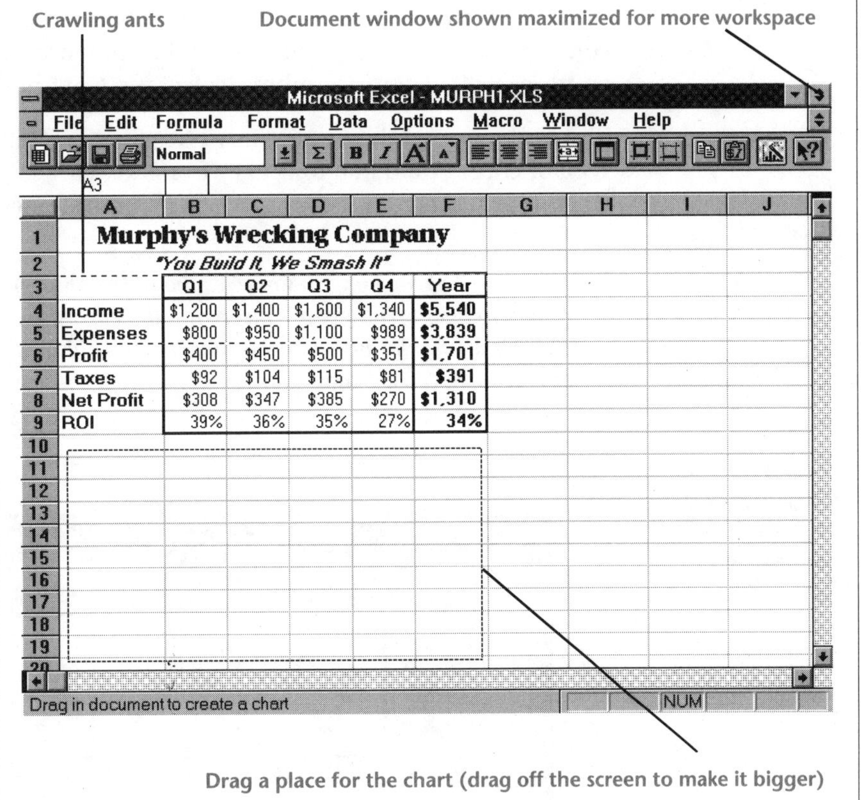

Charting

Figure 11.2:
After clicking the
ChartWizard tool, drag
a rectangle for the
chart.

Crawling ants   Document window shown maximized for more workspace

Microsoft Excel - MURPH1.XLS

File   **Edit**   **Formula**   **Format**   **Data**   **Options**   **Macro**   **Window**   **Help**

Normal

A3

	A	B	C	D	E	F	G	H	I	J
1	**Murphy's Wrecking Company**									
2	*"You Build It, We Smash It"*									
3		Q1	Q2	Q3	Q4	Year				
4	Income	$1,200	$1,400	$1,600	$1,340	$5,540				
5	Expenses	$800	$950	$1,100	$989	$3,839				
6	Profit	$400	$450	$500	$351	$1,701				
7	Taxes	$92	$104	$115	$81	$391				
8	Net Profit	$308	$347	$385	$270	$1,310				
9	ROI	39%	36%	35%	27%	34%				
10										
11										
12										
13										
14										
15										
16										
17										
18										
19										
20										

Drag in document to create a chart   NUM

Drag a place for the chart (drag off the screen to make it bigger)

When you release the mouse button after dragging the chart area, the
ChartWizard will ask its first question (Step 1 of 5):

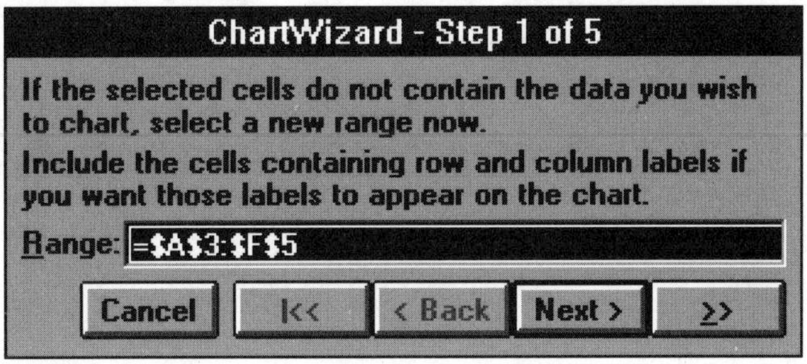

ChartWizard - Step 1 of 5

If the selected cells do not contain the data you wish
to chart, select a new range now.

Include the cells containing row and column labels if
you want those labels to appear on the chart.

Range: **=$A$3:$F$5**

| Cancel | |<< | < Back | Next > | >> |

The ChartWizard is just confirming that the range you have selected in the sheet is the range you want to plot. Notice that the ChartWizard courteously reminds you that it will happily use your labels in the chart, as well as your numbers. Select the Next button to continue.

The next question the ChartWizard has for you (Step 2 of 5) is about the type of chart you'd like to make. To make a selection, click one of the miniature charts the ChartWizard presents (see Figure 11.3).

In the Step 2 dialog box, the ChartWizard will recommend the Column chart type by preselecting it. This doesn't mean that the Wizard knows best and you should take this advice. It's just that the column chart (also called a bar *graph) is the most commonly used chart type.*

Figure 11.3:
The ChartWizard's Step 2 dialog box lets you choose from a variety of chart types.

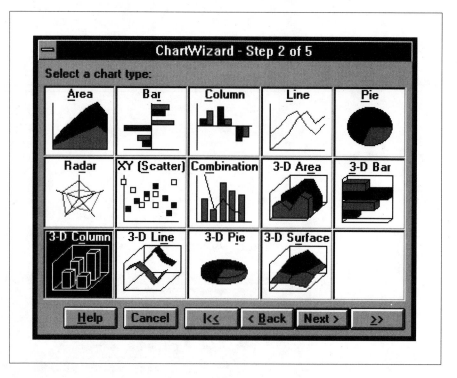

Charting

Select the Next button to continue. The next dialog box that appears (Step 3) shows some variations of the chart type you selected in Step 2:

ChartWizard - Step 3 of 5

Select a format for the 3-D Column chart:

| 1 | 2 | 3 | 4 | 5 |
| 6 | 7 | | | |

| Help | Cancel | |<< | < Back | Next > | >> |

Click one of the chart types, then select Next.

If the ChartWizard guessed correctly, a chart very similar to the one you want will appear in the Sample Chart box in the Step 4 dialog box (Figure 11.4). However, in some cases, the ChartWizard will have things all turned around. You can reset the option buttons to put them right.

Select the Next button to continue. The Step 5 dialog box shows the sample chart again, with additional option settings on the right (Figure 11.5). If you reset the Add A Legend option or type labels in any of the Titles boxes, the ChartWizard will update the chart in the Sample Chart box to reflect the changes.

When you select OK to close the Step 5 dialog box, the finished chart will appear in the sheet (Figure 11.6).

The ChartWizard has infinite patience. It will never hold you to any of your decisions. While you're working in any of the Step dialog boxes, if you decide you should have answered a previous step differently, select the Back button instead of Next. The ChartWizard will return you to the previous dialog box, in which you can select a different option. Go back as many steps as you like and make changes from that point forward, or select the Cancel button and start again from scratch.

Figure 11.4:

If the data items in the sheet have been transposed as data series or labels in the sample chart, you can assign them correctly by resetting the option buttons on the right side of the Step 4 dialog box.

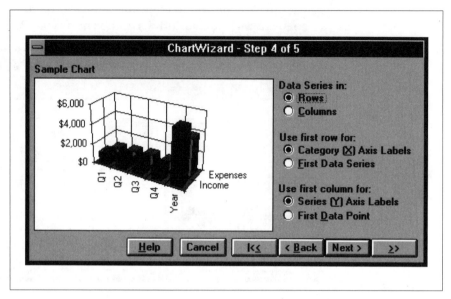

Figure 11.5:

In the last ChartWizard step, you can specify an optional legend and enter titles for the chart and its axes. Compare the approximation in the Sample Chart box to the result in Figure 11.6.

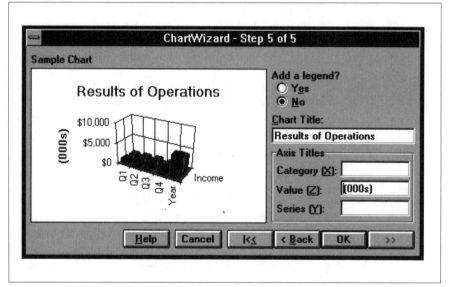

Figure 11.6:
The result of answering
the ChartWizard's five
essential questions

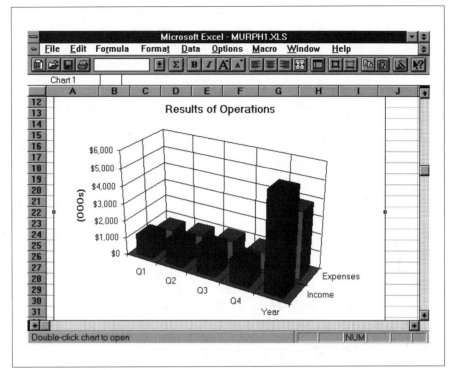

Charting

Embedded Charts
Are Comfy in Your Sheets

A chart that you create inside a worksheet document (as described in the section above) is called an *embedded chart*.

You can also create a chart as its own document. Start by entering and selecting the data you want to plot in a worksheet. From the menu bar, select File ➤ New. The New dialog box will appear. Select Chart from the list of document types and then select the OK button.

The data you selected in the sheet will be plotted immediately as a chart, without any interrogation from the ChartWizard. Instead, Excel will apply a set of preselected options. As a result, you will find yourself looking at a neatly plotted, but rather plain, column chart.

You can change the appearance of this chart just as you can modify an embedded chart. Read the next section for instructions.

If you created a chart as a separate document with the File ➤ New command, you must choose File ➤ Save to save it as a separate chart file (the PC file extension is .XLC).

Editing the ChartWizard's Work

You don't have to be satisfied with the chart the Wizard gives you. To edit a chart, move the pointer to it and double-click. The chart will open for editing in its own document window.

Finding objects in a chart

After you have opened the chart window for editing by double-clicking the chart, click one of its corners:

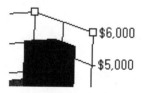

A small, hollow square (called a *handle*) will mark your selection. This is how you select objects for editing. By clicking different places in the chart, you can select grid lines, columns, axis titles, and so on.

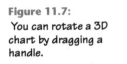

Give the chart a whirl

If you've created a 3D chart like the one in the example, you can rotate it by dragging. With the corner of the chart still selected, as described above, click the hollow handle again. The handle will become solid, indicating that you can now move the chart *as a whole*.

Drag one of these solid handles and watch what happens. The view of the chart changes to an outline, as shown in Figure 11.7. You can rotate this 3D outline to any position you like.

The purpose of rotating the 3D chart in this case is to position the Expenses bars in front so that they are not hidden by the taller Income bars. See the improvement in Figure 11.8.

Figure 11.7:
You can rotate a 3D chart by dragging a handle.

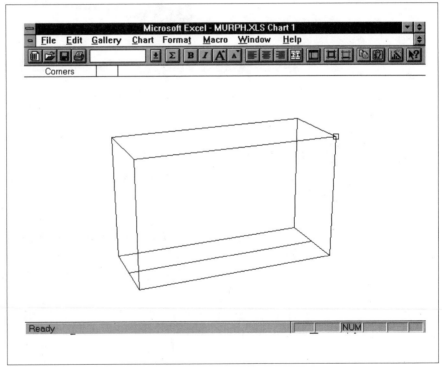

Here's the result of rotating the 3D chart. The view of the bars is improved. However, note that the x axis now runs from right to left rather than from left to right, as most audiences would expect.

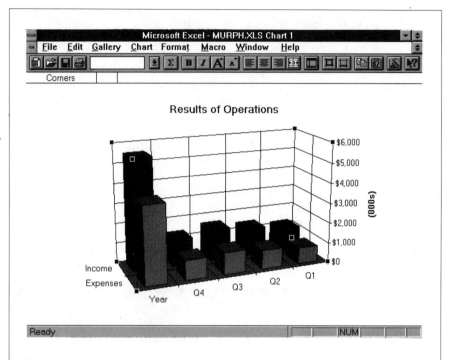

Dabbling in Color

Inevitably, you—or your boss—will want to change the colors in your chart. When it comes to color, everybody's an expert, and no two people agree.

In the example chart pictured earlier in this chapter, Excel made what looks like a dumb mistake. It plotted the Income bars in red and the Expense bars in green. Normally, you'd expect to see it the other way around. Fortunately, changing the colors is a snap with Excel.

To change the color of a data series plot, open the chart (by double-clicking it), then click again on the plot you want to change. If you have selected the plot of a data series—such as a set of bars or points, a line, or an area—by clicking on it in the chart, the series will be indicated in the cell reference box by the letter S (for data series), followed by the number of the series in the chart. (The first series is S1, the second is S2, and so on.) In the formula bar, you will see the formula reference for the series, which uses the SERIES function name:

| S1 | =SERIES(MURPH1.XLS!$A$4,MURPH1.XLS!$B$3:$F$3,MURPH1.XLS!$B$4:$F$4,1) |

In the example above, the worksheet and cell references in the SERIES formula are link references to the source worksheet. For more about external data links, see Chapter 13.

As another confirmation of your selection, hollow handles will appear around the plot. In the example, handles appear at the tops of the first and last bars in the data series.

Once the plot is selected, a quick way to change the color is to open the Drawing Toolbar and click the Color Palette tool:

You can cycle among the 16 solid colors available in the Color Palette by clicking the Color Palette tool repeatedly.

You can also change the color of a selected plot (and its pattern) by issuing a command. On a PC, click the right mouse button (if you're using a Mac, press ⌘-Option as you click the graph), and select Patterns from the pop-up menu, as shown in Figure 11.9. (Alternatively, you can select Format ➤ Patterns from the menu bar.)

The Patterns dialog box will open (see Figure 11.10). Here you will find options for the border (outline) of the plot, as well as for the fill, or the color and pattern inside the border.

To pick a different color for your plot, reset the Area option in the Patterns dialog box to Custom. Then, from the drop-down boxes, select a color from the Foreground box and an optional pattern (requiring a second Background color) for the plot. (If the pattern is solid, only the Foreground selection will be used.) When you select OK to close the dialog box, the plot will appear in the new color you chose.

Figure 11.9:
You can change the color or pattern of a selected data series plot by clicking the right mouse button (⌘-Option on the Mac) and choosing Patterns from the pop-up menu that appears.

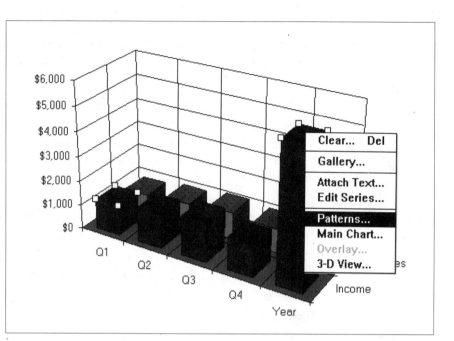

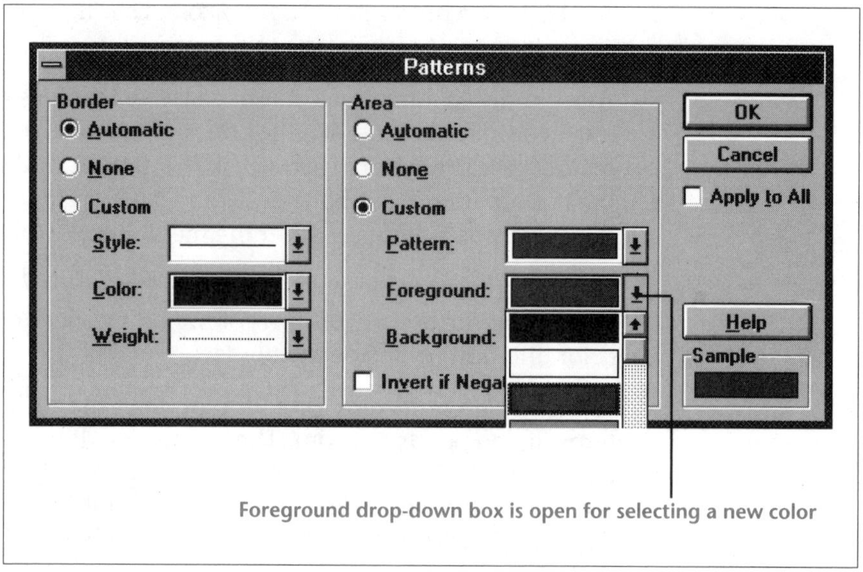

Figure 11.10:
The Patterns dialog box

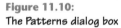

Foreground drop-down box is open for selecting a new color

Excel also lets you change the colors of grid lines, axis labels, chart titles, and so forth. The procedure is the same: Just click the object with the right mouse button (⌘-Option on the Mac), make the appropriate selection from the pop-up menu, and change the options.

Other Optional Stuff

Other chart options that people get finicky about are axis labels and grid lines.

You can hide the labels of any axis by opening the chart and selecting Chart ➤ Axes. The Axes dialog box will appear. Turn off the check box of any axis for which you don't want the labels to appear, and select OK.

To hide grid lines selectively, open the chart and choose Chart ➤ Gridlines. Turn off the check boxes of the major or minor grid lines you don't want to display, then select OK. (Major grid lines are at scale divisions. Minor grid lines, if used, subdivide those divisions.)

There isn't space in this humble book for the unabridged version of the chart story. I admit that all the menu commands and options aren't covered. But believe me, there's enough here to keep you busy making attractive charts. If you're curious about a command I've left out, move the menu highlight to it and, if you're using a PC, press Shift-F1. (Mac users press ⌘-Shift-?.) Help is on the way.

Browsing in the Chart Gallery

You can view a list of chart types by selecting Gallery from either the menu bar or the pop-up menu. These chart types are the same choices that the ChartWizard showed you previously. If you have second thoughts about your chart design, you can issue the Gallery command and make the poor Wizard generate a different type of chart.

If you want, the ChartWizard will use one of your own masterpieces as a model for future charts. Having created and selected said masterpiece (so that handles surround it), select Gallery ➤ Set Preferred from the menu bar. Then, whenever you're working in an open chart window, you can select Gallery ➤ Preferred, and the ChartWizard will imitate your previous stellar effort.

When you're done editing an embedded chart, select File ➤ Close from the chart's menu bar to resume working in the sheet. When you do this, you will see the chart positioned in the sheet where you originally dragged the rectangle, right after clicking the ChartWizard tool. To reopen the chart, just double-click it.

Excel provides a special set of tools in the Drawing Toolbar so you can doodle to your heart's content. However, only three of these tools will function in the window of an embedded chart: the Arrow tool, the Text Box tool, and the Color Palette tool. To use the other drawing tools, select File ➤ Close to close the chart window. Then you can use the rest of the tools to draw over the chart in the worksheet window.

Showing Off with Slides

Since everybody's an electronic media freak these days, Excel lets you show worksheets, charts, and all kinds of other stuff as screens in an electronic slide show. You can create a sequence of this stuff for presentation without printing out a single thing.

To create a single slide (that you will later group with other slides in a show), select the stuff in a sheet that you want to exhibit. (If you want to use a graphic that appears in a sheet, select the cells *underneath* it.) Then choose Edit ➤ Copy.

Select File ➤ Open. The Open dialog box will appear. Select Templates in the List Files Of Type box (MS Excel Templates on the Macintosh), and change to the subdirectory EXCEL\LIBRARY\SLIDES. (The Mac folder is EXCEL:MACRO LIBRARY: SLIDE SHOW.) Select the file name SLIDES.XLT and choose OK (choose SLIDE SHOW on the Mac).

A slide show worksheet will appear on your screen, with the cell highlight in the Slide Image column. Select the Paste Slide button (found just beneath the column A heading in the Slide worksheet). The Edit Slide dialog box will open. Select an effect for the transition between screen displays (such as a fade or a dissolve) and other options, then select OK.

Charting

If you want to create a show that runs all by itself after the user starts it, select the Timed option. Enter a time in seconds to tell Excel how long to display each slide on the screen before automatically advancing to the next slide.

The selected stuff will appear in the slide show listing, as shown in Figure 11.11. You can repeat the process of copying stuff and pasting it into this sheet to build a sequence of screens for your slide show. When you're done, select File ➤ Save to save the show.

To run a show, first you need to get a slide show file (such as SLIDES1) by selecting File ➤ Open. When the slide show list appears, click the Start Show button. Unless you used the Timed option to create a continuously advancing show, you can advance the display to the next screen by clicking the mouse button.

Figure 11.11:
Here the Murphy's Wrecking Company worksheet is pasted into the listing for an electronic slide show.

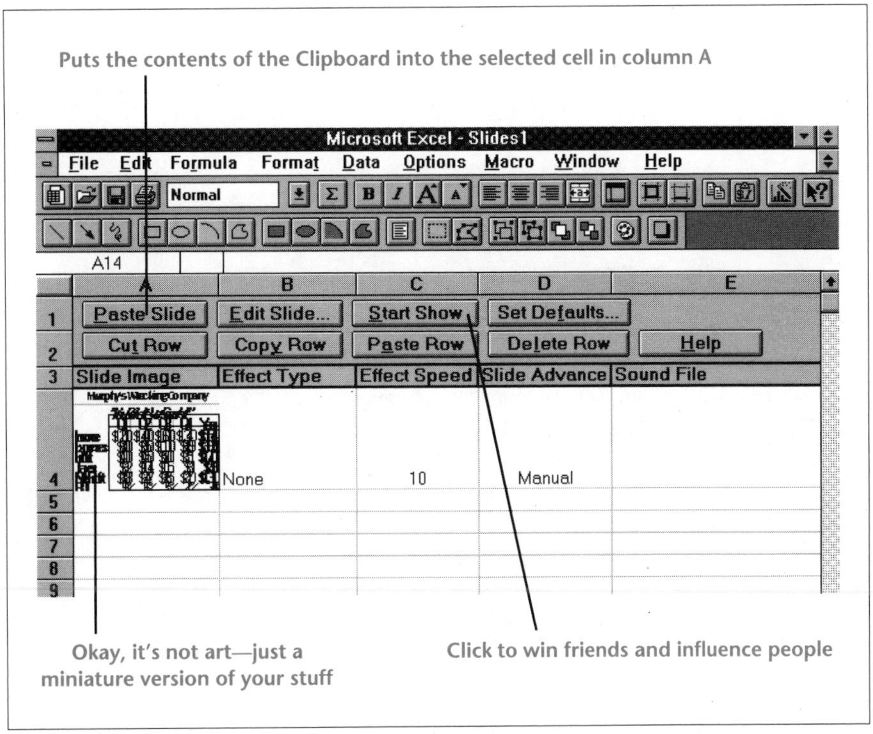

Puts the contents of the Clipboard into the selected cell in column A

Okay, it's not art—just a miniature version of your stuff

Click to win friends and influence people

Chapter 12

DO YOU WRITE NOTES TO YOURSELF?

Murphy's Psychiatric Diagnosis: In some people, paranoia is just a heightened state of awareness.

WRITING NOTES To yourself doesn't mean you're crazy. It can be a way of covering yourself in case your sheet hits the fan.

This chapter is about writing notes to yourself. But it's also about the larger topic of adding all kinds of helpful information to a worksheet file. There are two main reasons to make a worksheet *self-documenting*:

☞ If you return to the worksheet after a length of time, you will probably need some memory-jogging to remember how you constructed it. In particular, you must be able to understand the logic of its formulas quickly.

☞ If you share a worksheet file with a project team or workgroup, other people who have to use or modify it should be able to understand its logic.

Reminding Yourself What You Did

In Excel, *notes* are comments that you can hide in sheets. Notes are not normally visible on the screen, and they aren't usually printed with the sheet. They are useful as a means of justifying yourself in case someone interrogates you about the way you built your sheet.

To create a note, first select the cell that will hold it. Then, from the menu bar, select Formula ➤ Note. The Cell Note dialog box will open (see Figure 12.1). Type the text of your note in the Text Note box. When you get to the end of a line, the text will automatically drop down, or wrap, to the next line. If you want to insert a break between lines or between paragraphs, press Ctrl-↵ (or ⌘-Return on the Mac) where you want the break to appear. When you're finished writing the note, select OK to close the Cell Note dialog box.

The clue to your buried note is a little square. (On color monitors, whether or not they're in Russia, it's the little Red Square.) This *note indicator* appears in the top right corner of the cell that holds the note (see Figure 12.2).

If a cell already contains a note, you can just double-click it to open the note for reading or editing. Or, you can repeat the Formula ➤ Note command.

Leaving a Trail of Enticing Notes

When you're working in the Cell Note dialog box, just select the Add button to bury another note in the sheet. Select the cell in the sheet where you want to put the note (or type the cell address or name in the Cell box). Drag over the text of the previous note in the Text Note box and type the text of the new note in its place.

Figure 12.1:
Excel lets you write notes to yourself and bury them in the sheet.

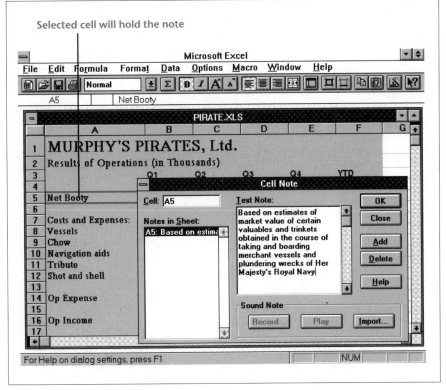

Selected cell will hold the note

Figure 12.2:
The little square in the upper-right corner of the cell tells you there's a note hiding there.

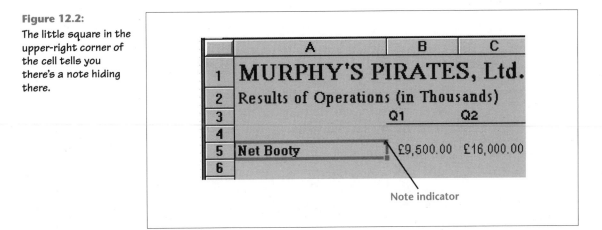

Note indicator

Notes

To continue leaving a trail of enticing notes, choose the cell where you want to bury the note, write your next installment, and select the Add button again (see Figure 12.3).

Figure 12.3:
To continue leaving a trail of notes, select the cell that will hold another note, type the note, and then select the Add button.

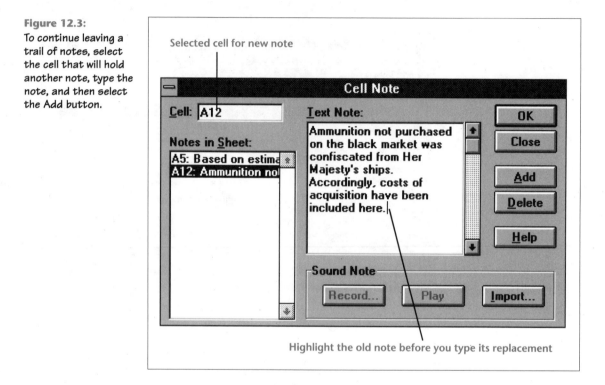

Now, Where Did I Put That Note...?

That little note-indicator square is a dead giveaway to where your secret stuff is buried. If you want to make it really secret, you can hide the indicators as well as the note text.

From the menu bar, select Options ➤ Workspace. The Workspace Options dialog box will appear. Clear the Note Indicator check box and select OK. The little squares will disappear from your sheet. (You can restore them at any time by repeating the command and marking the same check box.)

If you hide the note indicators, the notes will still be there—and they'll reappear, even if somebody else double-clicks the cell by accident.

It's not a good idea to hide the note indicators in your only copy of a sheet. If you forget where you buried the notes, you could be double-clicking all night trying to unearth them.

Instead, create a separate copy of the sheet file. Hide the note indicators in the copy, and use that file if you need to share the sheet with curious third parties.

Make Recordings for Posterity

If your computer is equipped for sound recording, the Record and Play buttons will be available in the Cell Note dialog box:

To make a sound recording, as an alternative to a text note, select the Record button. The Sound Recorder program will open. Its control buttons work just like an audio tape recorder (see Figure 12.4).

Figure 12.4:
The Sound Recorder buttons work just like tape recorder buttons.

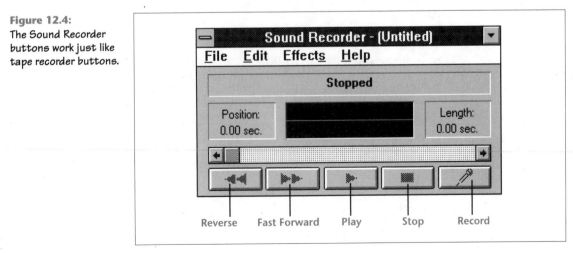

Click the Record button to start recording, the Stop button to stop. Select File ➤ Save to save the sound recording as a file, File ➤ Exit to close the Sound Recorder, and OK to close the Cell Note dialog box.

To play back a sound note, just double-click the cell that holds it, or select Formula ➤ Note and then select the Play button in the Cell Note dialog box.

Wrapping a Gift of Text in a Little Box

Another way to document your sheets is to create notes that aren't hidden but that anybody can read. You can do this using a *text box*. Text that you create as a text box is part of the sheet; the text will appear on the screen and in printouts.

To create a text box, first you need to open the Drawing Toolbar: Move the pointer up to the toolbar at the top of the screen and click the right mouse button. (On the Mac, press ⌘-Option and click the toolbar.) Then select Drawing. The Drawing Toolbar will appear on your screen:

To create a little box with text inside it, click the Text Box tool:

The pointer will change to small cross-hairs. Drag a place in the sheet to indicate the location and size of the text box.

A flashing vertical bar will appear inside the text box. Type your text. When you're done, click anywhere *outside* of the text box (see Figure 12.5).

Figure 12.5:
To create a text box, click the Text Box tool, drag the box in the sheet, type the text, then click anywhere outside the box.

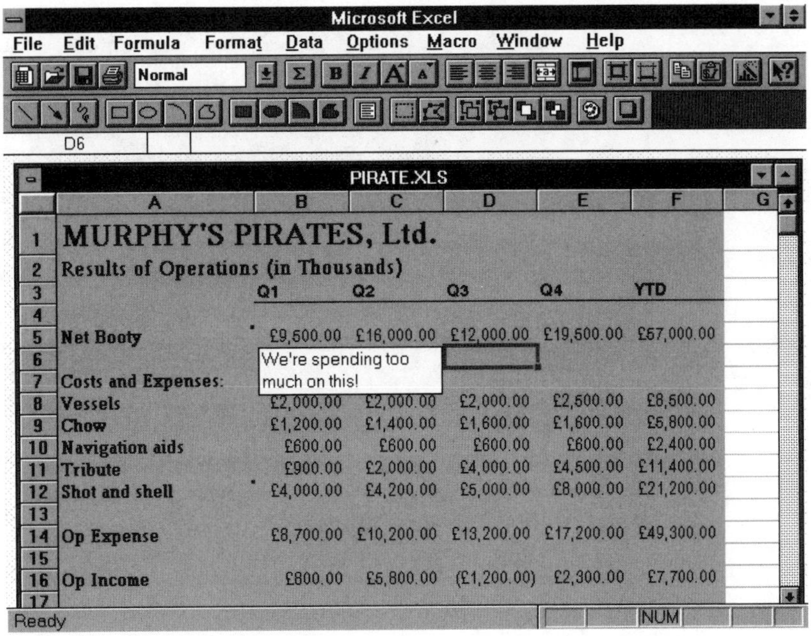

Notes

Shooting Arrows of Desire

It's not much use having an informative little box containing text unless you can show precisely what it's referring to. This is where arrows are helpful.

To draw an arrow from a text box (or from any other point, for that matter) to any other point in the sheet, click the Arrow tool in the Drawing Toolbar:

The pointer will change to small cross-hairs. Drag it from the point where the tail of the arrow will begin, and release the mouse button at the arrow tip (see Figure 12.6).

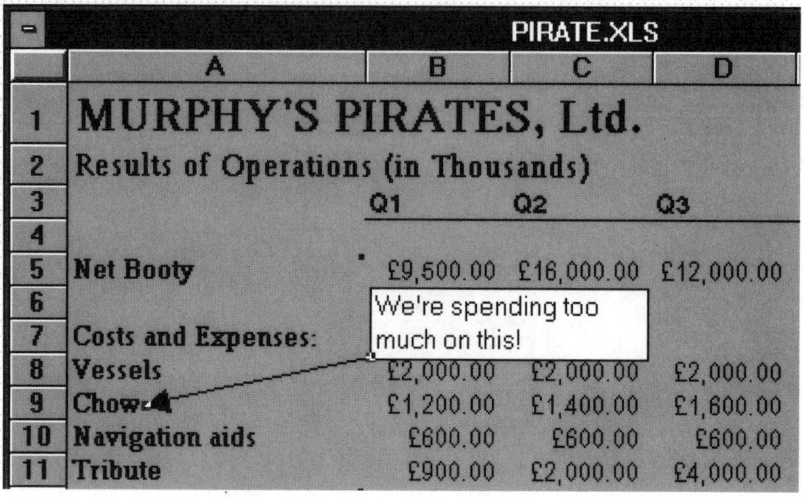

Figure 12.6:
You can use arrows to
connect a text box with
the cell it refers to.

	A	B	C	D
1	**MURPHY'S PIRATES, Ltd.**			
2	**Results of Operations (in Thousands)**			
3		**Q1**	**Q2**	**Q3**
4				
5	**Net Booty**	£9,500.00	£16,000.00	£12,000.00
6		*We're spending too much on this!*		
7	**Costs and Expenses:**			
8	**Vessels**	£2,000.00	£2,000.00	£2,000.00
9	**Chow**	£1,200.00	£1,400.00	£1,600.00
10	**Navigation aids**	£600.00	£600.00	£600.00
11	**Tribute**	£900.00	£2,000.00	£4,000.00

PIRATE.XLS

Go Ahead, Push My Buttons

One of the many magic tricks of Windows is OLE ("ohlay!"), short for
the intriguing term *object linking and embedding*. OLE allows the serious
self-documenter to put related documents into a worksheet file in such
a way that he or she can get at and edit all of the documents in one
place.

For example, the sheet containing the results of operations of Murphy's
Pirates might be part of a written report titled, "Piracy on the High
Seas: A Growth Industry for the Sixteenth Century." That report might
be written in a Windows word processing application, such as (let's pick
one of Excel's kissing cousins) Microsoft Word.

With OLE you can insert that Word document into your sheet as a *button*. Click the button, get the report. It's that easy.

In technical terms, an embedded object is called a package. *The term* button *in Excel can also refer to a graphic control button that you create with the Button tool and assign to a macro. In either case, clicking (or double-clicking) the button triggers the program (or the program and document) it represents.*

Here's how to create this type of button. Select the cell in the sheet that will become the location of the button. (A blank cell in an empty area of the sheet will do nicely.) From Excel's menu bar, select Edit ➤ Insert Object. The Insert Object dialog box will appear. From the Object Type list, select Word Document (you must have Microsoft Word installed, of course):

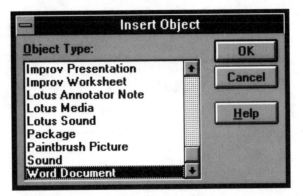

When you select OK to close the Insert Object dialog box, a Word document window will open (see Figure 12.7). This is where you can author your report.

When you're done composing your report in Word, select File ➤ Update from Word's menu bar to put the document into your sheet. Finally, select File ➤ Exit to close the Word program. (On the Mac, click the program's close box.)

The embedded object will appear in the sheet like this:

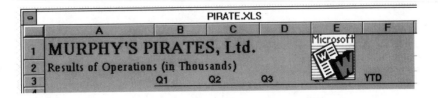

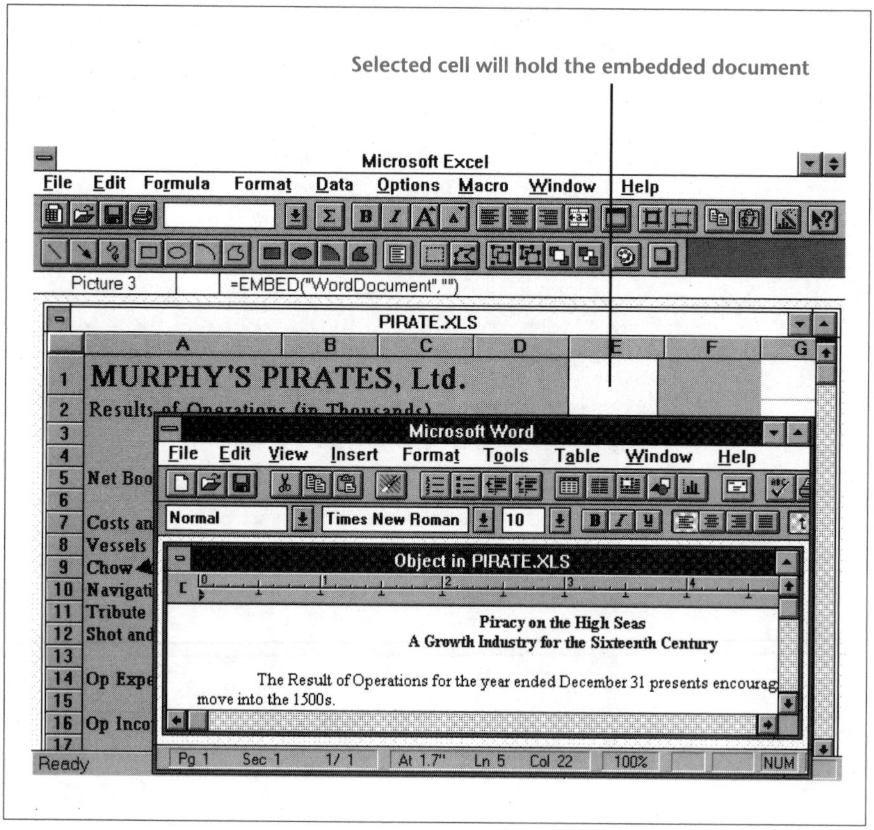

Figure 12.7:
You can use OLE to insert a word processing document— as well as other types of objects, such as graphics and sound— into an Excel worksheet.

When you double-click the object in the sheet, Word will open and show you the report.

You can use this technique to bury all kinds of other objects in your sheet—including graphics and multimedia objects—from any application that supports OLE. You'll see a list of OLE applications each time you select Edit ➤ Insert Object.

Name It, It's Yours

In Chapter 2, I give you the Excel-lent suggestion of giving names to the ranges in your worksheet. It's just downright simpler to understand and remember what EXPENSES means than it is to look back to see what the stuff in cells B14:F14 is all about.

Actually, you can use the Formula ➤ Define Name command (as described in Chapter 2) to give names to single cells and to formulas, as well. It just depends on what you've selected when you do the command.

Naming cells and ranges will make any formulas that refer to them much easier to understand. Compare the poetry of

    =INCOME-EXPENSES

to the obscurity and devilishness of

    =B5:F5-B14:F14

Excel doesn't want you to work any more than absolutely necessary. It can pick up the labels in a column or row automatically and use them as range names. Just select a range that includes the labels as well as the data that will be named by those labels. Then choose Formula ➤ Create Names. The Create Names dialog box will appear. Mark the check box that will tell Excel where to find the names in your selection. (See Figure 12.8.) Then select OK.

To see or edit the names you've created and their address references, select Formula ➤ Define Name.

Book Yourself into a Binding Situation

As I explain in Chapter 3, you can save a collection of worksheets together as a *workbook* file (.XLW extension on the PC). This is called *binding* the sheets, and it's a wise way to keep related stuff together so you know where to find all required sheets for a task and you can get at all the stuff quickly. It's also the best way to store and manage communal sheets that eat each other's stuff, or share data. More about data sharing and links between sheets in the next chapter.

Figure 12.8:

To pick up labels in the sheet as range names, select a range that includes both the labels and the data, choose Formula ➤ Create Names, mark the appropriate check box, and select OK.

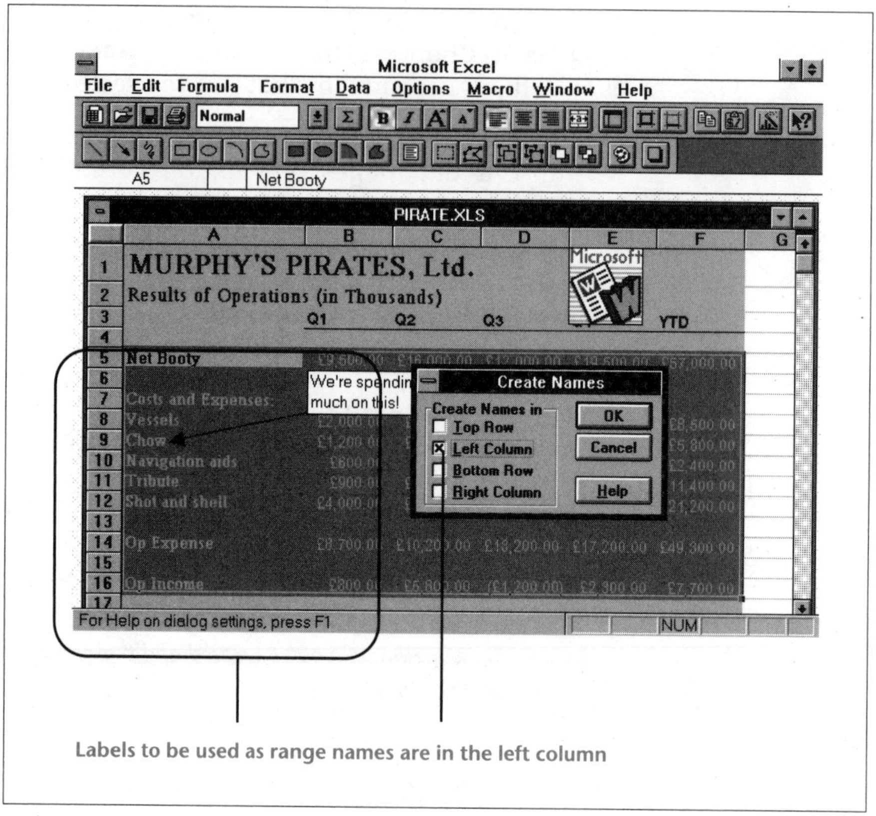

Labels to be used as range names are in the left column

PART 5

Don't let the geeks and propeller-heads intimidate you. They don't own this turf. You're just a few clicks away from exchanging your stuff with other programs and computers, and even with yourself, if you're into that (Chapter 13). Find out how easy it is to sort your stuff any which way in Chapter 14, and celebrate by letting one of Excel's wizards show you to a nice table. For your enjoyment, the whole smorgasbord of Excel tips is laid out in Chapter 15, with handy cross-references to the foregoing goings-on.

WHO SAID THIS STUFF IS HARD?

Chapter 13

SHARING CAN BE FULFILLING

Murphy's Principle of Data Exchange: Good organization overcomes. Poor organization succumbs. For people who go it alone, guess which kind comes naturally.

I KNOW YOUR mother told you to share your stuff. Excel can help you do that. In fact, there are even some good selfish reasons for exchanging data between worksheets and between applications.

Two of these selfish reasons are *convenience* and *accuracy*. It's often convenient to type a piece of data just once and have Excel put it into all the sheets that use it. This is also the most accurate way of entering stuff—after all, retyping it is another invitation to let Murphy into your life.

Sharing Your Stuff with Me, Myself, and I

Consider this selfish example: Let's say that you have three worksheets that need the same piece of data. The piece of data is the amount of a check you wrote on January 2 for a miscellaneous business expense. You need to enter this same stuff in three different sheets:

☞ You need to record it in the check register of your checkbook so that you don't spend the money twice.

☞ You'll want to include it in the Miscellaneous column of your employee expense report so that you can get reimbursed for it.

☞ Since you're also the company accountant, you must enter the item in a listing of other miscellaneous expenses for the month. (At the end of the month, you'll carry the total of these expenses to another sheet, the company's general ledger—but that's another book entirely.)

For a more meaningful sharing experience, you might want to bone up on the topic of 3D sheets as it is elucidated in Chapter 3. While you're at it, have a look at the section on workbooks that follows it. This is another Excel-lent technique used in the examples in this chapter.

Three sheets to the wind

The Excel sheets in which you want to record the amount of the check are called CHECKS, EXPENSE, and MISC. To work with all of these sheets at the same time, first you do the File ➤ Open thing three times—once for each file. To view the sheets on the screen in three horizontally layered windows, select Window ➤ Arrange ➤ Horizontal. Figure 13.1 shows how they look—thin, trim, and ready for action.

Book 'em!

Since you'll often have to use these three sheets together, it makes sense to bind them in a workbook file (.XLW extension in DOS). With the three sheets open, choose File ➤ Save Workbook. The file name JANUARY seems appropriate, since all of the sheets are for that accounting period.

Figure 13.1:
These three sheets must use the same piece of data—the amount shown in cell C4 of the CHECKS sheet.

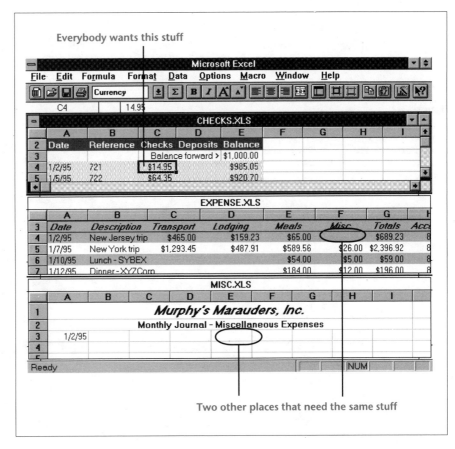

Linking sheets without sewing

To pick up the check amount and pass it to the other sheets, you need to take it through the Clipboard. Select the cell that holds the data (in this case, C4 in the CHECKS sheet) and choose Edit ➤ Copy. The friendly crawling ants will march around your selection.

Switch to the sheet on the receiving end and select the cell where you want to put the stuff. (If you're being assisted by your mouse, just click the cell.) Next, from the menu bar, select Edit ➤ Paste Link. The stuff will be copied from the Clipboard into the selected cell. In addition, the stuff will be linked to the sheet it came from.

Sharing Data

In Figure 13.2, the amount $14.95 has been pasted and linked to cell F4 in the EXPENSE sheet and to cell E3 in the MISC sheet. If at any time you change the data in cell C4 of the CHECKS sheet, it will be changed in all of the sheets and cells to which it is linked.

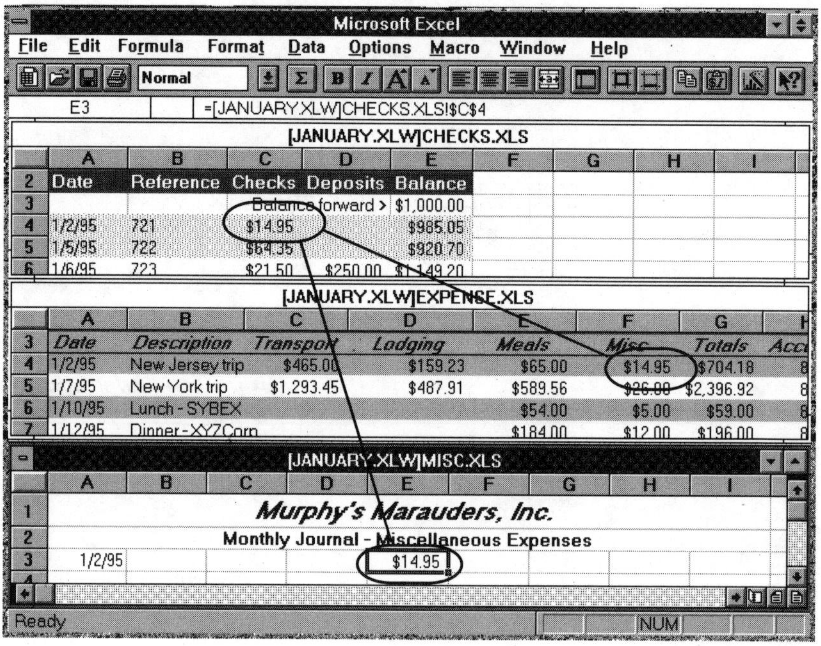

Figure 13.2:
The Copy and Paste Link commands let these three sheets share a single piece of data.

You can select other cells, perhaps in other sheets, to receive linked data. As long as the diligent ants continue to crawl around your stuff, you can select the receiving cell and choose Edit ➤ Paste Link.

Types of Excel documents that you can link are worksheets, worksheets within workbooks, charts, and macro sheets. A chart that is embedded in a worksheet is automatically linked to that worksheet.

Linking the Bigger Stuff

In the preceding example, a number value from a single cell is paste-linked into solitary cells in other sheets. You can also link entire ranges, including all their data and formulas. If the linked stuff is a range, or a block of cells, it must be the same size and shape in each of the linked sheets.

When you use Paste Link to insert stuff in another sheet, you need only select the first (top left) cell in the range that will receive the stuff. The original range will then be copied exactly into the other sheet.

When you paste-link a range, Excel inserts the stuff in the other sheet as an array formula. For the short skinny on array formulas, see Chapter 5.

Playing with Your New Set of Links

Once you've got links between your sheets, you need to understand how they will work, now and until you break them.

In Excel-speak, the original sheet that holds a piece of linked data is called the source worksheet, *and any sheet that receives linked data is called a* dependent sheet.

Here are some general guidelines about the care and feeding of nefarious links:

☞ If you edit a linked piece of data in the source sheet, it will be changed automatically in all the *open* dependent sheets to which it is linked. This is another good reason to put the linked sheets in a workbook so that you can open them together.

☞ If you edit the linked piece of data in the source sheet when a dependent sheet is closed, the next time you open the file, Excel will ask, "Update references to unopened documents?" If you say No, the link will still be there, but the data might not be current.

Sharing Data

☞ If you try to edit a linked piece of data in a dependent sheet, you will sever the link to the sheet you're working in, and the change will only appear in the dependent sheet.

☞ Always save source files first, then save the dependent files. This assures that links are current and that the latest version of the source worksheet has been calculated before the data gets passed to the dependent sheets.

☞ Believe me, your life will be simpler if you store worksheet files that are linked to one another in the same directory. That way, if you move the files, the links will still operate as long as all the files continue to be in one directory.

☞ If you insist on putting linked sheets in different directories, you must use a special link syntax. (See "Test Your Technical Aptitude," later in this chapter.)

Call It What You Will, It's a Meaningful Relationship

In Windows, exchanging data "on the fly" among open applications is called *dynamic data exchange,* or DDE. An enhancement of DDE came along with Windows 3.1. Since then, the enhanced process has been called *object linking and embedding,* or OLE. Technically, DDE is the L in OLE. (There's an example of object embedding—the E part—in Chapter 12.)

In DDE terminology, the source worksheet is the *server* and the dependent worksheet is its *client*. In OLE, the source worksheet is the *source* and the dependent worksheet is the *destination*. In Apple System 7, the source application is the *publisher*, a dependent application is the *subscriber*, and a shared document is an *edition*. These are all different ways of saying the same thing.

In Windows and in System 7, server-client, source-destination, and publisher-edition links can exist among different applications, as well as among different Excel documents. However, some applications are picky about what they do. Some prefer only to donate data, others prefer to receive it. The marvelously accommodating Excel will swing either way.

Linking Cells in the Same Sheet

You can use Paste Link to insert a linked copy of a piece of data or a formula elsewhere in the same sheet. When you do this, Excel simply puts the absolute address of the source cell into the dependent cell as a formula.

For example, suppose you wanted to use a subtotal in two places on the same sheet, as shown in the restaurant bill in Figure 13.3. The cell that holds the original stuff is B6. Having selected this cell, you can do the Edit ➤ Copy and Edit ➤ Paste Link commands as described above to put a linked copy of the same stuff into cell B9. The result is that Excel puts this formula in cell B9:

=$B$6

Notice that if you had used Paste instead of Paste Link, the *value* in B6 would have been copied, not the linked reference to the cell. With Paste Link, if the value in B6 were to change, it would also change in B9.

Figure 13.3:
The subtotal appears twice in this sheet. You can use Copy and Paste Link to insert a link reference into the dependent cell.

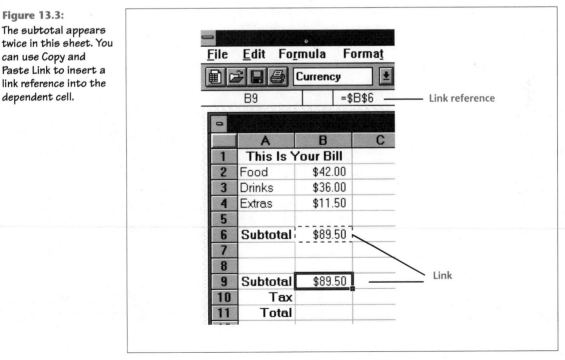

Sharing Data

Linking cells within the same sheet is still a link for practical purposes; however, because the data is not being passed through the Clipboard, it is not the same kind of external data link that can exist between files.

Test Your Technical Aptitude: Try Link Syntax

When you paste-link stuff into a dependent worksheet, Excel inserts an *external reference formula* into the receiving cell.

This formula must follow a special syntax for external data links. If you're going to fool around with this stuff, it might help to understand what all the funny characters in the syntax mean.

Normally, you won't have to fool with the link syntax unless you need to edit the file or cell references of sheets that are not currently open. Even then, a more "foolproof" approach would be to open the sheets, simply repeat the Copy and Paste Link commands, and let Excel worry about the syntax. However, knowing the elements of the syntax can help you pinpoint where all that linked stuff is coming from. This might be useful in tracing the logic of a set of formulas across multiple sheets.

Here's a familiar example

Let's go back to the example about your check for miscellaneous expenses. Figure 13.4 shows the reference that appears in the formula bar in Figure 13.2.

The syntax for the same reference may look different from this example—especially if the source worksheet isn't open or if it's not in the same directory as the active sheet. Compare Figure 13.4 to Figure 13.5.

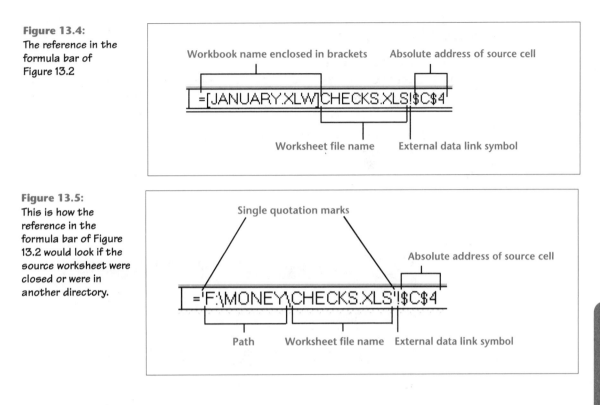

Figure 13.4:
The reference in the formula bar of Figure 13.2

Workbook name enclosed in brackets   Absolute address of source cell

=[JANUARY.XLW]CHECKS.XLS!$C$4

Worksheet file name   External data link symbol

Figure 13.5:
This is how the reference in the formula bar of Figure 13.2 would look if the source worksheet were closed or were in another directory.

Single quotation marks

Absolute address of source cell

='F:\MONEY\CHECKS.XLS'!$C$4

Path   Worksheet file name   External data link symbol

Single quotation marks appear in the syntax when there is a *path name* in front of the source file name. (The path tells Windows and Excel how to get to the source file on the disk. In this example, F: is the name of the disk drive, and MONEY is the name of the directory that holds the file.)

On the Macintosh, the equivalent link syntax might be

    ='DISK:MONEY:CHECKS'!$C$4

Notice that the name of the hard drive is DISK and not C, colons (:) are used instead of backslashes (\) as separators, and the file name has no extension.

Sharing Data

Inspect those links

Curious whether the active worksheet has links to organized crime? Just select File ➤ Links, and any external links will appear in the Links dialog box, shown in Figure 13.6.

If the Links command is dimmed in the File menu, your search is over: There aren't any links in the current sheet.

Figure 13.6:
The Links dialog box

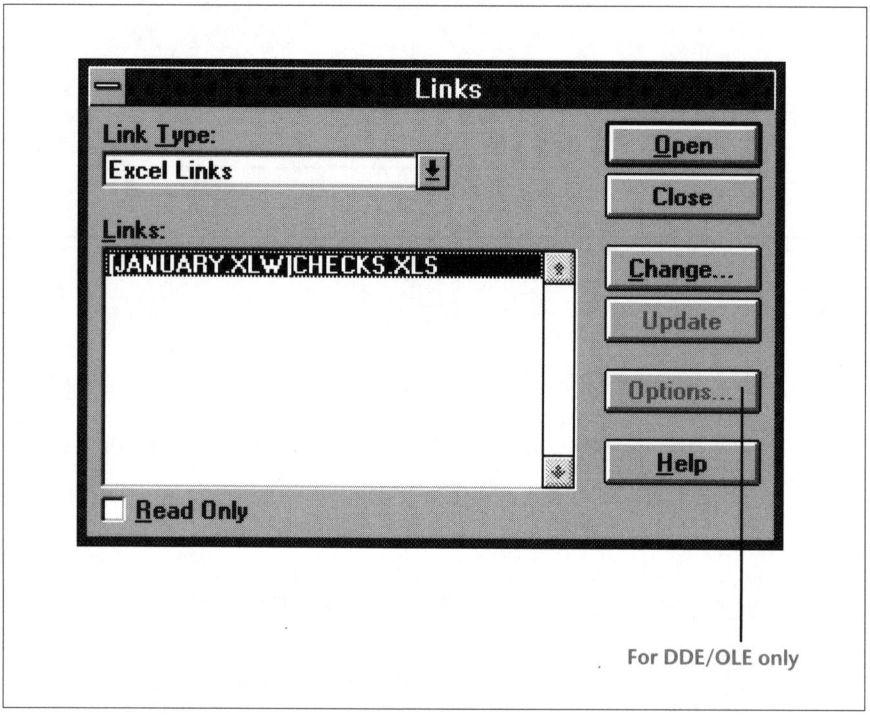

The Options button in the Links dialog box will be available only if the link refers to a DDE/OLE object from another application. Selecting the Options button opens the DDE/OLE Options dialog box. In many cases, the only option is the Automatic check box, which controls whether linked files are updated automatically. (The available options depend on the type of object.)

Forge new links

To forge a link to a different sheet (one that has been renamed or removed), select the link reference in the Links list in the Links dialog box. Then select the Change button. A file listing will appear. Select a new source file, then choose OK (Change on the Mac). (If you select the name of a workbook file, you will then have to specify which sheet in the workbook will be the source.)

From the Links dialog box, you can change the name of the source worksheet using the procedure described above. You might do this to change to a newer, renamed version of the same source worksheet or if you moved the source worksheet to a different directory. Excel will simply substitute the path and name of the sheet you select in the external link syntax, keeping the absolute address of the source cell. So, unless the new source sheet has the desired stuff at exactly the same location, the new link will make no sense whatsoever.

Sharing Data with Other Applications

An *object* is a collection of related data, such as a chart. In Windows, as well as in System 7, you have any number of ways of exchanging data, pictures, sound, and other types of objects among applications.

In many cases, anything that can be copied to the Clipboard from another application can be pasted into an Excel sheet with the Edit ➤ Paste command. Here are some special cases:

☞ If you are embedding an object in an Excel sheet, the command is Edit ➤ Insert Object. This inserts a *button* (also called an *object package*) by which you can open the application and view or edit the object from inside Excel. For an example, you can read about burying a Word document in your sheet in Chapter 12.

☞ If you are pasting some types of objects, such as pictures, whether from another Excel document or from another application, the command in the dependent sheet is Edit ➤ Paste Special. The Paste Special dialog box will open (see Figure 13.7). For some types of pictures, you have the option of inserting it as a Picture (which can be resized and edited with the drawing tools) or as a

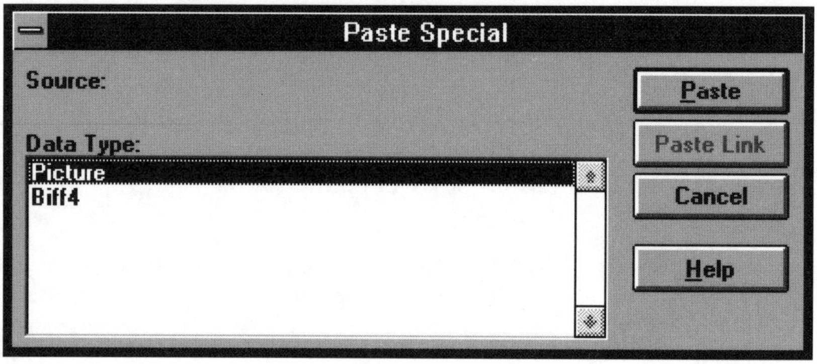

Figure 13.7:
If the stuff you're
pasting is a picture or
a multimedia object,
this dialog box will
appear when you
choose Edit ➤ Paste
Special.

Bitmap (which can be resized but not edited). If the source application will do data linking, you can select the Paste Link button in this dialog box to insert the object and establish an ongoing link. Otherwise, only the Paste button will be available. (Paste puts a copy of the object in your document without a link.)

Importing and Exporting without a License

Another way of exchanging information with other programs is by *importing* and *exporting*. This method is particularly handy when you need to share stuff with applications that are not available on your own computer. The medium of exchange is a file instead of the Clipboard.

Importing just means reading a document (usually a worksheet) that has been created by another program and translating it into Excel. Once a document has been imported, you can work on the stuff just as you work on Excel sheets.

To import a file, select File ➤ Open in Excel. The Open dialog box will appear (Figure 13.8). Select the type of file you want to import in the List Files Of Type box. If necessary, change to the drive and directory where the file is stored, then select the file from the File Name list. (The Mac procedure is much the same, but you don't have to specify the file type.)

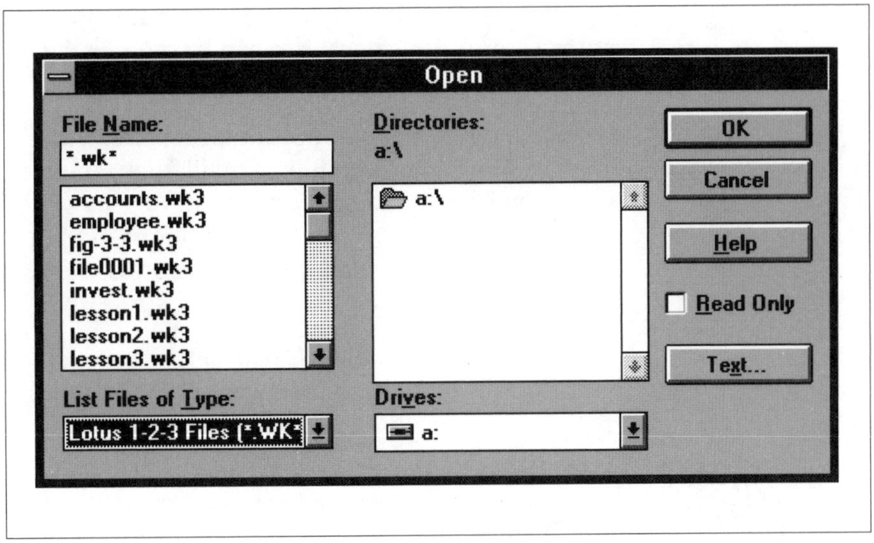

Figure 13.8:
To import a document that was produced by a different application, choose File ➤ Open, select the "foreign" file type in the List Files Of Type box (if you're using a PC), and select the file name.

Open

File Name:
`*.wk*`

accounts.wk3
employee.wk3
fig-3-3.wk3
file0001.wk3
invest.wk3
lesson1.wk3
lesson2.wk3
lesson3.wk3

List Files of Type:
Lotus 1-2-3 Files [*.WK*]

Directories:
a:\

📁 a:\

Drives:
💾 a:

OK
Cancel
Help
☐ **Read Only**
Text...

In the Windows version of Excel, if you don't see the file type in the List Files Of Type box, it's not a document that Excel can import directly. However, you might be able to translate the file to one of the types listed using the application the document was created in.

When you select OK, Excel will read the file, handling all necessary translation, and present it to you as if it were one of its own.

Importing Exotic Stuff

If you are importing a different type of worksheet, you might need to reset some of Excel's options (although Excel might reset some of them automatically). For example, on a PC, in Options ➤ Calculation, you might need to mark 1904 Date System for compatibility with Mac files. Or you might need to mark Alternate Expression Evaluation or Alternate Formula Entry for compatibility with Lotus files. If the external file uses the R1C1 addressing system, you might need to specify R1C1 in Options ➤ Workspace.

Sharing Data

Exporting an Excel worksheet means translating the worksheet and writing it as a document that can be read directly by another application, such as the dBASE database system.

Exporting a file is just importing in reverse. Begin by selecting File ➤ Save As. The Save As dialog box will open. Select the type of file you want your sheet to be converted to in the Save File As Type box. (If you don't see the type of file listed, it's not one of the types Excel knows how to translate.) Type a file name and select OK. (Again, the procedure on the Mac is similar.)

You should then be able to open this file in the other application by selecting File ➤ Open or an equivalent command.

The fact that you can import files from and export files to other applications is no guarantee that they will be useful when translated. For example, for a sheet to be usable by a database application, usually the stuff in it must be arranged as a lookup table. For a good table that's not by the kitchen, check out Chapter 14.

Beware of the Three-Dimensional Lotus People!

Three-dimensional sheets in Lotus 1-2-3 use a different addressing scheme: Each worksheet file can have many sheets. Each sheet is named by a letter of the alphabet followed by a colon. A reference to the range B2:D4 (B2..D4 in Lotus language) in the first sheet in a file (A:) would be

    A:B2..D4

If you import a 3D sheet from 1-2-3 into Excel, some interesting changes will occur. The name of the Lotus worksheet file will become the name of a new Excel *workbook*, and each lettered 1-2-3 worksheet will become a different Excel sheet that is bound in that workbook.

Here's an example using the Windows versions of 1-2-3 and Excel. A 1-2-3 worksheet file named BIGSHEET.WK3 contains three sheets, lettered A–C. Imported to Excel, the sheets are bound into the workbook BIGSHEET.XLW. The names of the sheets it contains are [BIGSHEET.XLW]A, [BIGSHEET.XLW]B, and [BIGSHEET.XLW]C.

In the Excel sheet, the reference A:B2..D4 would be

```
=[BIGSHEET.XLW]A:B2:D4
```

You need not save the new sheet files separately, since they are bound and saved in the workbook file. But if you did, the individual file names would be

```
A.XLS
B.XLS
C.XLS
```

Once again, Excel forgives you for messing with the competition. It just makes you sweat a little as you come over.

Sharing Data

Chapter 14

SORTING IT OUT (WITHOUT COUNSELING)

Murphy's Guide to Dinner Parties and Database Extraction: Ninety-nine percent of the effort is in setting up the table.

This chapter is all about arranging tasty stuff as *lookup tables* on which Excel and other programs can munch happily. A related topic also covered here is *sorting*, which involves getting Excel to do the work of rearranging stuff, usually the stuff in tables.

Lookup tables provide a handy way of storing a lot of stuff so that you can get at it quickly and easily. Specifically, a lookup table is a scheme for retrieving one piece of information based on another, related piece of information. For example, the white pages of a phone book are one big lookup table. You look for a name in order to retrieve a phone number.

Sorting the stuff in a table alphabetically—or by any other method—is something that your faithful math slave Excel will gladly do for you. So, you don't need to type stuff into a table in alphabetical order. Just stick it in any which way, and let Excel worry about rearranging it. You can even set up a *database*—a kind of multipurpose table—inside Excel by constructing it as a special kind of table in a worksheet.

The Ins and Outs of Databases

You can build a database inside Excel, as described in this chapter, or you can send out for it. Although you can put a lot of stuff into an Excel database sheet, database software can manage a lot more stuff using much the same method—arranging it in tables.

This little coincidence makes Excel the perfect partner for your favorite database program. Excel comes with an application called Q+E, which is designed specifically to hook you up to your favorite database so that you can grab stuff from it and cram it into Excel. Through Q+E, you can get data from dBASE, SQL, Oracle, and other database files and construct tables that you can then feed to Excel.

You can use this purloined stuff to build Excel worksheets that can generate all kinds of new and useful information. What's more, you can link the sheet to the database system so that Excel and the caretaker of your valuable stuff can have an ongoing and deeply meaningful relationship.

Unfortunately, there isn't enough room in this humble book to go into Q+E, but this chapter gives you a head start on the basic things you need to know about databases and Excel.

Setting a Nice Table

Figure 14.1 shows an example of a familiar kind of lookup table—a personal phone book. (Admittedly, yours might not include the same types of special information.)

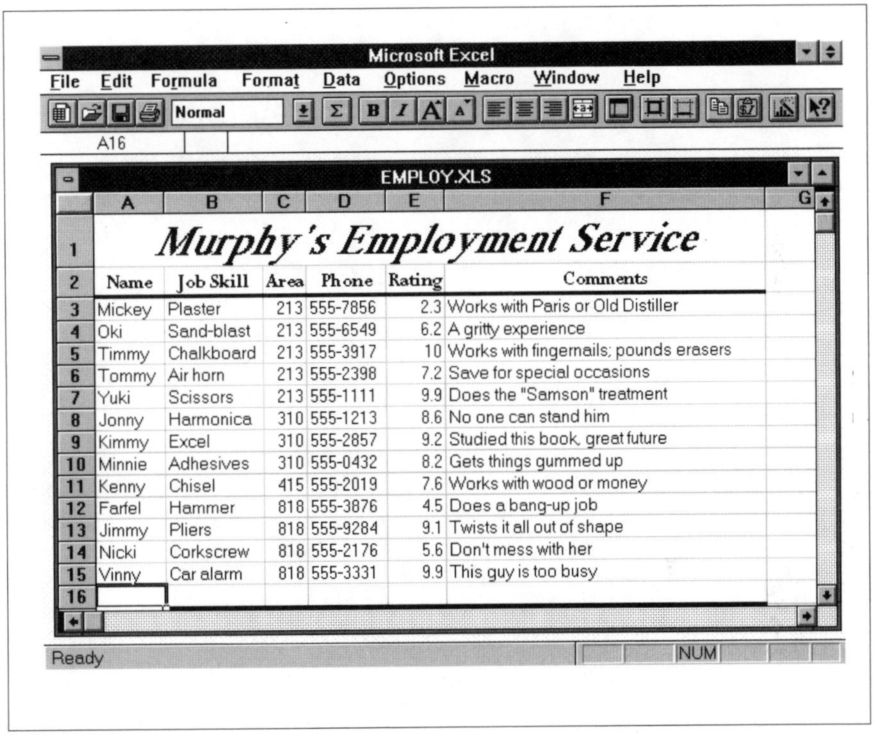

	A	B	C	D	E	F
1	Murphy's Employment Service					
2	Name	Job Skill	Area	Phone	Rating	Comments
3	Mickey	Plaster	213	555-7856	2.3	Works with Paris or Old Distiller
4	Oki	Sand-blast	213	555-6549	6.2	A gritty experience
5	Timmy	Chalkboard	213	555-3917	10	Works with fingernails; pounds erasers
6	Tommy	Air horn	213	555-2398	7.2	Save for special occasions
7	Yuki	Scissors	213	555-1111	9.9	Does the "Samson" treatment
8	Jonny	Harmonica	310	555-1213	8.6	No one can stand him
9	Kimmy	Excel	310	555-2857	9.2	Studied this book, great future
10	Minnie	Adhesives	310	555-0432	8.2	Gets things gummed up
11	Kenny	Chisel	415	555-2019	7.6	Works with wood or money
12	Farfel	Hammer	818	555-3876	4.5	Does a bang-up job
13	Jimmy	Pliers	818	555-9284	9.1	Twists it all out of shape
14	Nicki	Corkscrew	818	555-2176	5.6	Don't mess with her
15	Vinny	Car alarm	818	555-3331	9.9	This guy is too busy
16						

Figure 14.1: You can arrange data in a lookup table for quick retrieval.

This particular table is set up to look up stuff by row. Starting with a name entry in the left column, you would look in the same row to find the corresponding job skill, area code, phone number, performance rating, and comments.

Sort Your Sock Drawer— and Still Have Time to Go Out!

In an Excel lookup table, the stuff you must already know when you start your search is called the *compare value*. For example, if I wanted to look up Nicki's phone number, "Nicki" would be the compare value for that search.

Sorting the table for easy lookup

To be able to use the sample table to look up stuff by name, the compare values must be in the first column *in ascending order*—from A to Z in this case. If the compare values aren't arranged that way, you must have Excel sort them for you before you can use the table. Start by selecting all of the data in the table. (Include the compare values in the first column as well as the data that goes with those values, but exclude the title of the sheet and the column labels.) In the example, the range A3:F15 must be selected.

From the menu bar, select Data ➤ Sort (see Figure 14.2). The Sort dialog box will appear (Figure 14.3). Choose whether to sort by rows or by columns. In this case, the stuff on each person is arranged in a row, so the data must be rearranged by rows.

The address of the cell that holds the first compare value must be entered in the 1st Key box. Excel tries to do this for you, and you will see the ants crawl around the cell it has picked. You can click a different cell if you want to, or type a different address in the 1st Key box. You must also select either the Ascending or Descending option. I already told you it had to be ascending, and Excel has made that choice for you, as well.

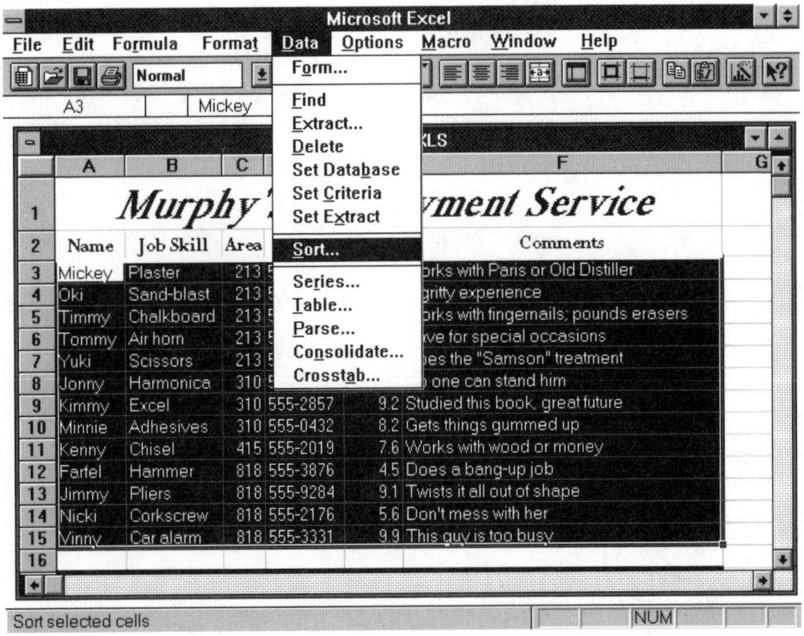

Figure 14.2:
To sort data, select it
and then choose Data
➤ Sort.

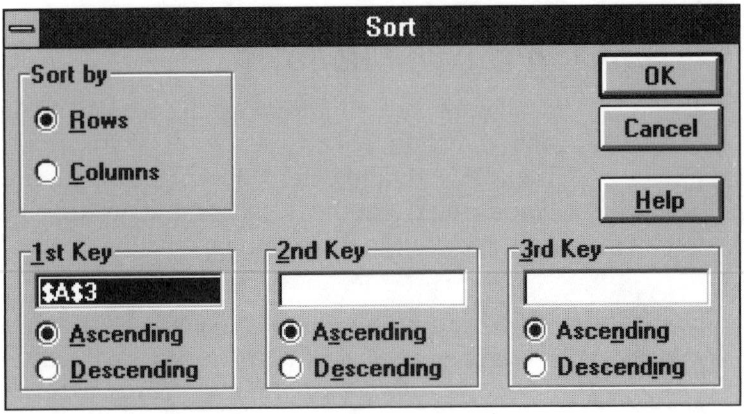

Figure 14.3:
The Sort dialog box

The 2nd Key and 3rd Key boxes are for values that will be used to sort additional levels. For example, if there were two last names Smith, you would want to tell Excel where to find the first names so that Smith, Alva gets placed before Smith, Kate. Similarly, you would need the third key if there were likely to be two or more people in the list named Smith, Alva. You might then use a column that held entries of Ms. or Mr., or ZIP code, or some other key for sorting out all those Alva Smiths.

In the small table shown in Figures 14.1 and 14.2, the only duplications are area codes. Second or third keys would be necessary only if the area code were used as the first key.

Having set the options in the Sort dialog box, select the OK button to make Excel go to work. In a wink, Excel shuffles the list so that its rows are arranged alphabetically by name (see Figure 14.4).

If you don't like the result of a sort, select Edit ➤ Undo Sort immediately after the sort, before doing anything else.

If compare values are not text, Excel determines ascending order as follows: If the values are numbers, the order starts with negative numbers, counts upwards to zero, then continues counting upward through the positive numbers. If logical values are used, FALSE comes before TRUE.

Sorting for the helluvit

Of course, you might have other reasons to sort stuff besides arranging it in a lookup table. For example, if you selected the same table, chose Data ➤ Sort, and entered E3:E15 as the first key in descending order, Excel would sort the people by their ratings, with the best performers on top.

The Data ➤ Sort command permits you to select as many as three keys. You can sort on more than three keys by repeating the command and specifying the other keys. However, if you sort in several passes, sort in reverse order: Sort with the low-level keys (least important) first, the highest-level (most important) keys, such as last name, last. But on each pass, make the most important key in that pass the first key (1st Key).

Figure 14.4:
In Excel, a lookup table must list its *compare values* (in this case, the key in the first column) in ascending order. If the stuff is names, as shown here, that's from A to Z.

	Microsoft Excel					
File	Edit	Formula	Format	Data	Options	Macro	Window	Help

A16

EMPLOY.XLS

	A	B	C	D	E	F	G
1	*Murphy's Employment Service*						
2	Name	Job Skill	Area	Phone	Rating	Comments	
3	Farfel	Hammer	818	555-3876	4.5	Does a bang-up job	
4	Jimmy	Pliers	818	555-9284	9.1	Twists it all out of shape	
5	Jonny	Harmonica	310	555-1213	8.6	No one can stand him	
6	Kenny	Chisel	415	555-2019	7.6	Works with wood or money	
7	Kimmy	Excel	310	555-2857	9.2	Studied this book, great future	
8	Mickey	Plaster	213	555-7856	2.3	Works with Paris or Old Distiller	
9	Minnie	Adhesives	310	555-0432	8.2	Gets things gummed up	
10	Nicki	Corkscrew	818	555-2176	5.6	Don't mess with her	
11	Oki	Sand-blast	213	555-6549	6.2	A gritty experience	
12	Timmy	Chalkboard	213	555-3917	10	Works with fingernails; pounds erasers	
13	Tommy	Air horn	213	555-2398	7.2	Save for special occasions	
14	Vinny	Car alarm	818	555-3331	9.9	This guy is too busy	
15	Yuki	Scissors	213	555-1111	9.9	Does the "Samson" treatment	
16							

Ready   NUM

If You Don't Know It, Look It Up

Excel has some handy ready-made functions you can use to order your math slave to go fetch stuff in a lookup table. VLOOKUP, or vertical lookup, works in tables that are arranged like my example—Excel has to scan the first column vertically for the stuff you want. HLOOKUP works in tables that are arranged so that Excel has to scan the first row. And there's another function called LOOKUP that can scan every which way—but let's stick with the same example and use VLOOKUP.

Here's another illustration that getting good results is largely a matter of setting a table properly. For VLOOKUP to work correctly, the compare value must be in the first column, and records must be sorted in ascending order (A to Z). For HLOOKUP to work, the compare value must be in the first row, also with records sorted in ascending order.

Remember too that you can sort records by any field in any position, not just the compare value, as the examples in this chapter do.

Look again at my address book table. One common everyday task would be to pick a name, get a phone number. Figure 14.5 shows how to do it.

Figure 14.6 gives you a closer look at the formula in cell D19 of Figure 14.5. Notice that the syntax, or way of writing the formula, must include

☞ an equal sign (=)

☞ the name of the function (VLOOKUP)

☞ the address of the cell that holds the compare value (A19)

☞ the range that contains the table (A3:F15)

☞ the number of the column that holds the phone numbers (4)

Figure 14.5:

Based on any name typed into cell A19, the VLOOKUP formula in cell C19 returns the area code, and a similar formula in cell D19 returns the phone number.

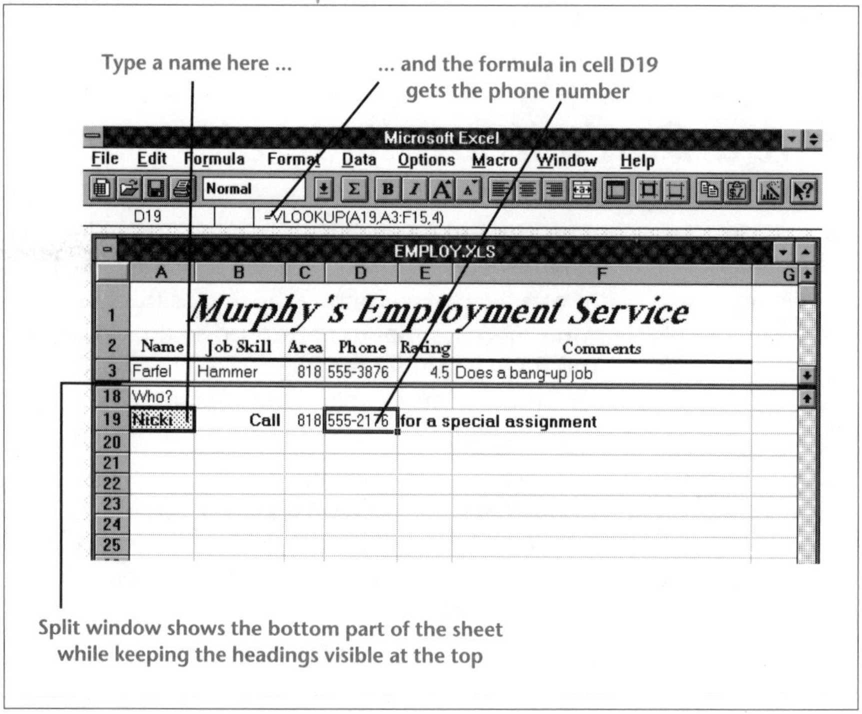

Type a name here ...

... and the formula in cell D19 gets the phone number

Murphy's Employment Service

	A	B	C	D	E	F	G
2	Name	Job Skill	Area	Phone	Rating	Comments	
3	Farfel	Hammer	818	555-3876	4.5	Does a bang-up job	
18	Who?						
19	Nicki		Call	818	555-2176	for a special assignment	
20							
21							
22							
23							
24							
25							

Split window shows the bottom part of the sheet while keeping the headings visible at the top

Figure 14.6:

The formula in cell D19 of Figure 14.5

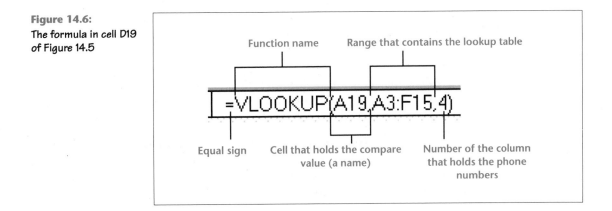

As always, the arguments you feed to the function must be enclosed in parentheses, and they must be separated by commas. (If none of this sounds familiar, have another look at Chapter 4.)

Although it doesn't appear in the illustrations, there's another VLOOKUP formula in cell C19 that fetches the area code. It's identical to the one in cell D19, except that it orders Excel to look in column 3, not 4:

```
=VLOOKUP(A19,A3:F15,3)
```

HLOOKUP works exactly the same way, but the compare values must be in the first *row*. In my example, each person would be in a different column. So, the last argument in the HLOOKUP syntax would be the number of the *row* you want Excel to scan.

Your Table's a Lamp Base, Mine's a Database

In Excel, a database is a special kind of sheet. It has the same purpose as files created by database programs—to make it possible to store and retrieve a large amount of stuff in a variety of ways. However, the arrangement of a database sheet is very specific in Excel and is not necessarily the same as that of other databases you might be familiar with.

Tables

An Excel database is very similar in arrangement to a lookup table. A lookup table can have related stuff either in rows or in columns. But in a database sheet, each set of related stuff, or each *record*, must be arranged in a single *row*. An advantage to setting up a table as a database instead of as a lookup table is that the database is more flexible. There are just many more ways you can work with the stuff it contains.

The first row of the database must contain column labels. The column labels are the *field names* Excel will use to look for stuff. Figure 14.7 shows an example. (A *field* is a category of stuff. In a database table, a field is a specific column or row. For example, one field might hold the street address for each record in a phone book database.)

Calculated field

Leave an empty (but formatted) row for expanding the database

The last column in this sheet (G) contains formulas for multiplying the hourly rate of each worker by the number of hours worked to calculate a value for gross pay. (The formula in cell G6 appears in the formula bar.) Fields such as this one are called *calculated fields*. Calculated fields contain formulas that do calculations on other fields in a database.

Go ahead, call it a database

Having arranged a table like Figure 14.7, you can get Excel to treat it as a database with a single command. Start by selecting the table, including the column labels. In this case the database is the range A2:G16. (The last, blank row is included to allow for expansion of the database.) With the table selected, choose Data ➤ Set Database. (On the Mac, the Set Database dialog box will appear.) Excel will assign the range name DATABASE to your selection. Now you can order Excel to fetch stuff in many different ways from your new database.

A database can be as big as a single Excel sheet. That's pretty big—as many as 256 columns and 16,384 rows.

Sort it any which way

Having set up a database, you can make Excel rearrange its records (sort the rows) by choosing Data ➤ Sort, as described previously in this chapter. But it's even easier than doing a sort on any old table. You can sort by any field in a database just by entering its field name in the 1st Key box.

When you use the Data ➤ Sort command to sort a database, do not include the row with the column labels (field names) in your selection. You should also omit from your selection that empty row you added for expanding the database in the future.

Tables

Raiding Your Database for Tasty Stuff

Having set up a database in your sheet, you can have Excel find, fetch, or even get rid of records. It will do this based on one or more conditions, or *criteria*, that you specify.

To get stuff out of your database, you need to set up two more ranges in your sheet, a *criteria range* and an *extract range*, as shown in Figure 14.8.

The criteria range has just two rows: The top row is a set of field names, and the bottom row has empty cells beneath each name. The field names must be the same as those in your database, although you need not include the names of fields you don't want to look into. In the example, the criteria range is A21:G22.

Figure 14.8:
To fetch stuff from your database, you need a *criteria range* to take your order for stuff and an *extract range* to hold the records that Excel finds based on those criteria.

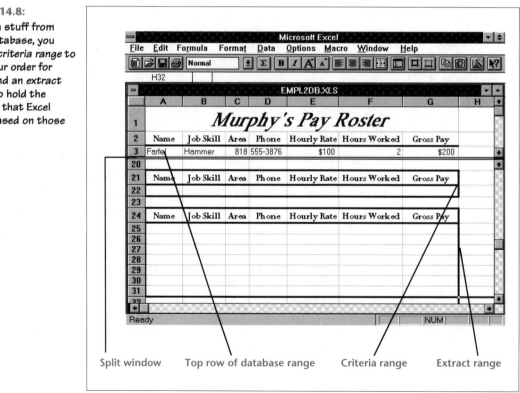

Split window   Top row of database range   Criteria range   Extract range

The extract range must have the same set of labels as the database, because Excel will insert records (row entries in the database) below them. The extract range will hold all the records Excel can find that match the conditions you enter in the criteria range. In the example, the extract range is A24:G31.

To create the headings for criteria and extract ranges, copy the column labels in the database using the drag-and-drop method: Select the labels, then move the pointer to the edge of the selection until it changes to an arrow icon. Hold down the Ctrl key as you drag the selection into the row that will hold the copied labels.

Having copied (or typed) the labels for the criteria and extract ranges, you need to tell Excel where those ranges are:

☞ To create the criteria range, select the labels (field names) and the blank row beneath the labels. Then choose Data ➤ Set Criteria. Excel will assign the range name CRITERIA to those rows.

☞ To create the extract range, select the labels (field names) and a number of blank rows beneath them. (Include as many rows as the number of records that might be retrieved.) Then choose Data ➤ Set Extract. Excel will assign the range name EXTRACT to those rows.

You can enter several criteria (or conditions) in the criteria range. A criterion can also be a calculation (usually a logical comparison), as shown in the following data extraction example.

Finding stuff

Finding stuff in the database involves just the criteria range, not the extract range. To find the first record that holds a specific value for a field, type that value under the appropriate label in the criteria range. For example, to find the first record in Murphy's listing with a phone number in the 310 area code, you would type that value in the criteria range, as shown in the following example.

Name	Job Skill	Area	Phone	Hourly Rate	Hours Worked	Gross Pay
		310				

With your criteria entered, select Data ➤ Find. Excel will move the cell highlight to the first record that matches the criteria you entered. To find the next record, select Edit ➤ Repeat Find.

Be Logical, or Not

You can use the following logical operators in your criteria:

=	equal to
>	greater than
<	less than
>=	greater than or equal to
<=	less than or equal to
<>	not equal to

If you leave a criteria field blank, Excel will place no restrictions on that field. If you enter an equal sign (=) followed by a blank, only records that contain a blank in that field will match. If you enter <> followed by a blank, only records that do not have a blank in that field will match.

A leading equal sign is optional for entries in the criteria range if you just want a single match value. For example, you can enter 310 for the Area instead of =310. Excel assumes the equal sign. Also, you need not enclose text entries in quotation marks—unless you want to be picky about upper- and lowercase letters.

Excel ignores the difference between uppercase and lowercase letters in criteria. To restrict a search to text that is capitalized a certain way, enter it in quotation marks as a text value that is capitalized exactly the way you want it:

```
="ChartWizard"
```

For this type of exact matching, the equal sign *and* the quotation marks are required.

Extracting stuff

In addition to finding records that match your criteria, Excel copies those records into the extract range you created. For example, to find and extract all the records of people who have hourly rates greater than $100 and who worked one hour or more, you would type the following logical comparisons in the criteria range:

Name	Job Skill	Area	Phone	Hourly Rate	Hours Worked	Gross Pay
				>100	>=1	

Next choose Data ➤ Extract. The Extract dialog box will appear:

Extract

☐ **U**nique Records Only

OK

Cancel

Help

If you'd like to prevent getting duplicate copies of records that might appear several times in the database, mark the Unique Records Only check box. Then select OK to begin the extraction. Excel will put all of the matching records into the extract range, as shown in Figure 14.9.

Be sure to include enough rows in the extract range to hold the number of records that Excel might find. If you haven't included enough rows, Excel will report, "Extract range is full," and you will only get some of the records that match. To correct this and get all the matching records, you will have to redefine the extract range with more rows, then redo the Data ➤ Extract command.

The brief examples in this chapter barely scratch the surface of the uses of database criteria and the types of conditions and calculations that you can use as criteria.

To get the scoop on this stuff, select Help ➤ Contents ➤ Databases ➤ Defining A Criteria Range ➤ Using Comparison Criteria.

Tables

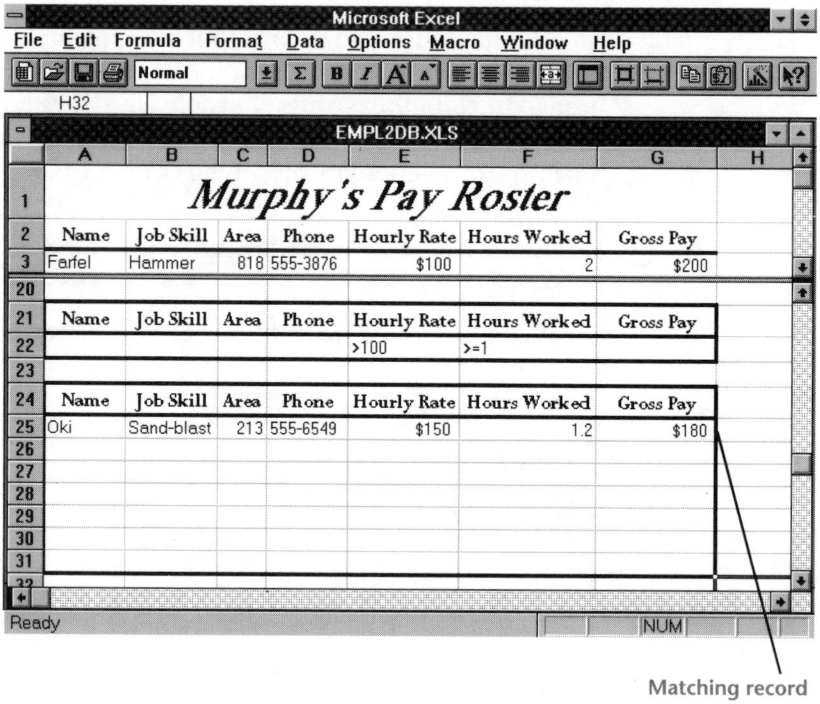

Figure 14.9:
Excel copies the
records that match
the criteria you enter
into the extract range.

Matching record

Summoning a Wizard for Cross Tabulation

In Chapter 11, I introduce you to the ChartWizard, a special program that handles charts in Excel. Excel also has a resident wizard that generates reports from tables. This built-in guru has the honorific title Crosstab ReportWizard. There's just enough space left in this chapter for a modest demonstration of its prodigious skills.

Look again at Murphy's Pay Roster. Suppose the boss would like to set up a report that will show whether the hourly rate has anything to do with the number of hours each freelance contractor got to work. (You can probably guess the result, but apparently the boss wants to prove it. Sound like anyone you know?)

Generating this kind of information involves *cross-tabulating* the stuff in the table. You don't have to know how to do a cross tabulation, though. The Crosstab ReportWizard will lead you through the process step by step.

To start with, you must define the table as a database using Data ➤ Set Database, as described previously in this chapter. (To use all the records, be sure the criteria range is blank.) Then, to summon the wizard, choose Data ➤ Crosstab. The Crosstab ReportWizard will display the first of a series of questions on your screen: "What would you like to do?" (See Figure 14.10.) Select the button labeled Create A New Crosstab, and you're on your way.

Figure 14.10:
The Crosstab
ReportWizard's
Introduction dialog box

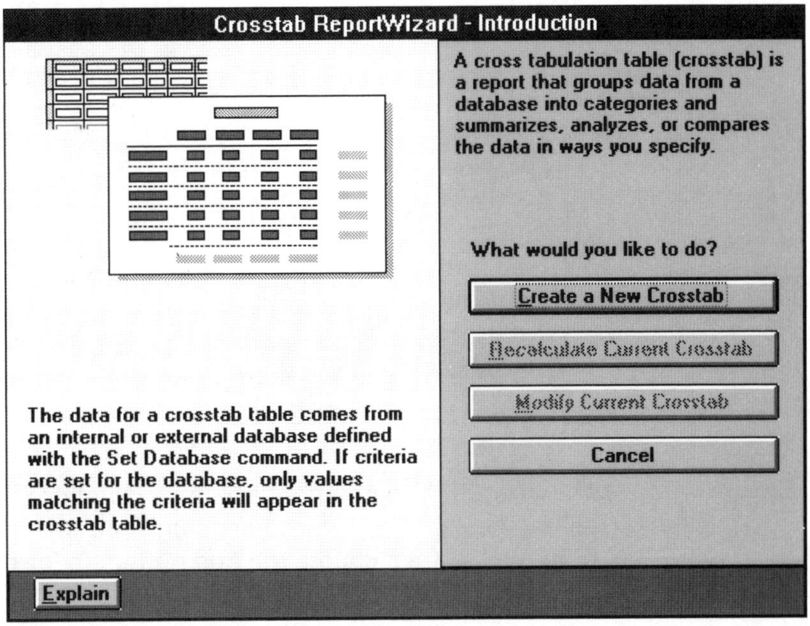

Crosstab ReportWizard - Introduction

A cross tabulation table (crosstab) is a report that groups data from a database into categories and summarizes, analyzes, or compares the data in ways you specify.

What would you like to do?

[**Create a New Crosstab**]

[Recalculate Current Crosstab]

[Modify Current Crosstab]

[**Cancel**]

The data for a crosstab table comes from an internal or external database defined with the Set Database command. If criteria are set for the database, only values matching the criteria will appear in the crosstab table.

[**Explain**]

Tables

The wizard's second question asks, "Which Database fields contain the values you want as Row headings?" In this case, select Name from the Fields In Database list, then choose the Add button (Figure 14.11). Select the Next button to advance to the next question.

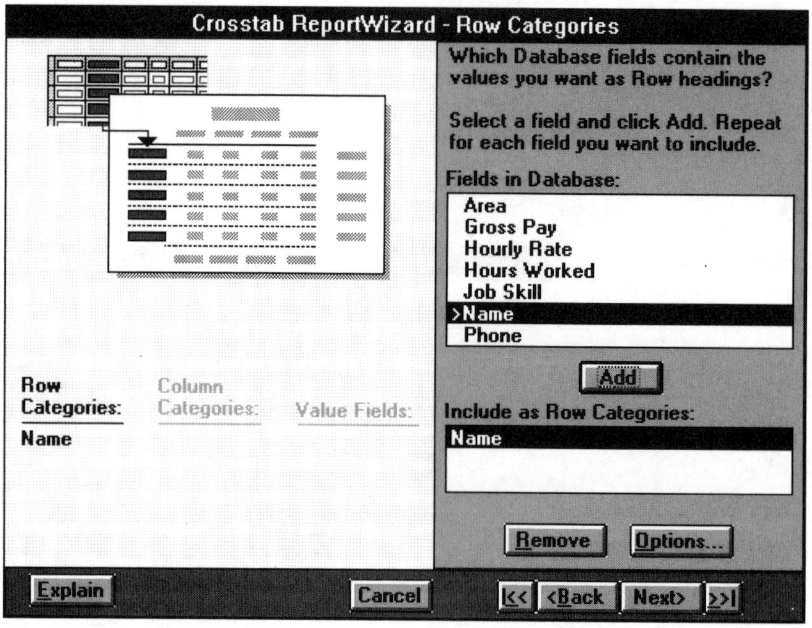

Figure 14.11:
The Crosstab
ReportWizard's Row
Categories dialog box

The wizard's third question is "Which Database fields contain the values you want as Column headings?" In this case, select Hourly Rate from the list, then choose the Add button, followed by the Next button.

Next the wizard wants to know which values should appear within the table of the new report. Select Hours Worked, then choose Add, and then choose Next.

Having taken your order for a crosstab report, with your specified row categories, column categories, and values, the wizard is ready to create the cross tabulation. Hold your breath and select the button labeled Create It. Figure 14.12 shows the result, which Excel presents as a new, outlined worksheet.

Figure 14.12:
The Crosstab
ReportWizard
generated this table,
which highlights the
relationship between
what people charged for
their services and how
much work they got.

Clicking these buttons will collapse the outlined sheet

Microsoft Excel - CTROSST.XLS

File   Edit   Formula   Format   Data   Options   Macro   Window   Help

Normal

G18

	A	B	C	D	E	F	G
1	*Sum of Hours Worked*		Hourly Rate				
2	Name	100	150	200	350	Grand total	
3	Farfel	2	0	0	0	2	
4	Jimmy	0	0	0	0	0	
5	Jonny	0	0	0	0	0	
6	Kenny	3.5	0	0	0	3.5	
7	Kimmy	0	0	0	0	0	
8	Mickey	0	0	0	0	0	
9	Minnie	0	0	0	0	0	
10	Nicki	0	0	0	0	0	
11	Oki	0	1.2	0	0	1.2	
12	Timmy	0	0	0	0	0	
13	Tommy	0	0	0	0	0	
14	Vinny	0	0	0.5	0	0.5	
15	Yuki	0	0	0	0	0	
16	Grand total	5.5	1.2	0.5	0	7.2	
17							
18							

Ready   NUM

Appearance formatting has been applied to sheet title and headings

As you might expect, the cross tabulation shows that the people who
charged the least ($100 per hour) got the most work, the $150 people
worked fewer hours, the $200 people even fewer, and the $350 people
died of boredom.

*Since Excel presents the crosstab report in a separate sheet, select File ➤ Save
Workbook to bind the database sheet and the report into a workbook file for easy
reference.*

Murphy's Law, Revisited

As the law at the beginning of this chapter suggests, what you can get out of a table or a database depends largely on how you set it up. And that goes double for cross tabulations.

In your quest to get the wizard to do your bidding, I suggest that you work backwards: Start with what you want to know. That is, define the crosstab results first and think about the things you want to include in the report. Then, think about the stuff you need to gather to calculate that stuff. End by designing the table that you will feed to the wizard. But always remember...

Murphy's Rule of Order: After you have it all arranged, an anonymous someone in upper management will want to see it inverted.

Chapter 15

SOME EXCEL-LENT ADVICE

Murphy's Advice: If it works, don't fix it.

Murphy's Warning: If it's fixed, don't work it or it will break.

Murphy's Conclusion: If you call in sick, it will work perfectly until you get back—then it will break.

WRAPPING UP THIS little volume is a summary of cogent things I have learned from experience or otherwise stumbled upon—some after unprovoked attacks by Murphy's minions. Following each is a reference to the chapters where you can find further cautionary notes.

Try Help First...

If you find yourself baffled, select Help ➤ Product Support ➤ Answers To Common Questions. For help with a specific command or procedure, start to do it (issue the command) and press the F1 key.

For help on the Mac, select Windows ➤ Help ➤ Product Support ➤ Answers To Common Questions. For context-sensitive help, press ⌘-/.

Basic Training for New Recruits

Following are some things you just gotta know about entering and editing stuff in worksheets.

Number formatting

Numbers that you type into cells cannot have letters mixed in. However, number values can include

```
Currency symbols ($100)
Commas separating thousands (1,000,000)
Leading plus or minus signs (+ or − in front of the
number)
Decimal points (100.00)
Slashes (/) or hyphens (−) in dates (1/2/99 or 1-2-99)
Percent signs (%) after percentages
Scientific notation (1E+08 in Excel-speak means 1.0 × 10⁸)
```

For more about number formats see Chapters 1, 2, and 6.

Text

If your stuff is not a number, Excel will think it's text. Text can be anything, and often is. (See Chapter 1.)

Copying stuff

Drag the fill handle of a selected cell to copy its contents into adjacent cells (the fill handle is the solid plus sign in the lower-right corner of an active cell):

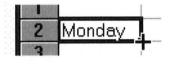

Depending on what you've selected, Excel might increment the copies as well. For example, you can drag Monday all the way to Friday. (See Chapters 1 and 2 on AutoFill.)

Moving stuff by drag-and-drop

To move a selected cell or block of cells, place the pointer at the border of the cell highlight so that it changes to an arrow symbol. Drag the arrow to move the stuff, as shown in Figure 15.1. (See Chapter 6.)

Copying stuff by drag-and-drop

If you do the move thing as described above but you hold down the Ctrl key while you're doing it, Excel will copy the stuff into the place where you drop it. (See Chapter 6.)

Figure 15.1:
To move a block of selected cells, place the pointer at the border of the highlight so that it changes to an arrow symbol, then drag the arrow wherever you want to move the stuff.

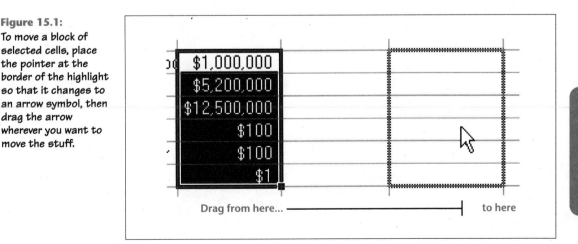

Tips

Clearing stuff

To delete just the data (values or formulas) from a selected cell or block of cells, drag the fill handle upward, back over the selection. (See Chapter 1.)

Figure 15.2:
To clear the data from selected cells, drag the fill handle upward, over the selection.

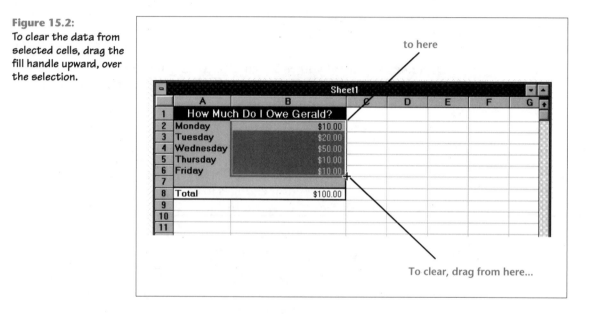

Using AutoSum without getting hurt

To generate a total, you can select a cell and double-click the AutoSum tool...

...but only if the selected cell is at the foot of a column or at the end of a row and you want to add all the numbers in that column or row.

Otherwise, click AutoSum *once*, and drag the line of crawling ants around the group of cells you want to add. Then press ↵ or click the Confirm (✓) button. (See Chapters 1 and 2.)

Never mind and undo it

If at almost any time you don't like what you did, choose Edit ➤ Undo or press Ctrl-Z to undo it *before you do anything else*. To restore what you did, choose Edit ➤ Redo. Some things can't be undone—that's life. (See Chapter 6.)

Give yourself some room

Double-click the right border of a column heading or the bottom border of a row heading, and Excel will adjust the width of the column or height of the row to fit the stuff in its cells (see Figure 15.3).

Figure 15.3:
You can double-click the right border of a column or the bottom border of a row heading to make Excel adjust the column or row width to accommodate the data.

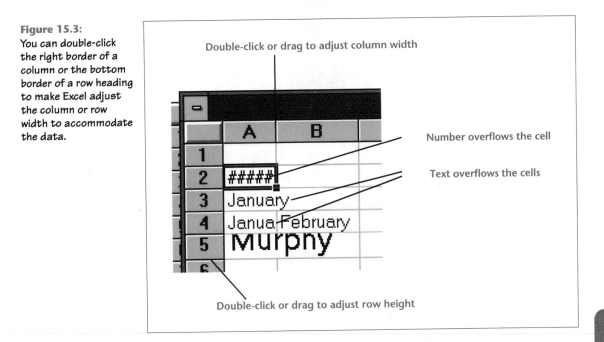

Double-click or drag to adjust column width

Number overflows the cell

Text overflows the cells

Double-click or drag to adjust row height

This shortcut is especially handy when you see the dreaded pound signs (#######) in a cell, indicating that the cell is too narrow to display the number inside it. (See Chapter 6.)

Tips

Change your stuff, change your life

If you want to edit some stuff in your sheet, select it on a PC by clicking it (or dragging the pointer over a block of cells), then click the *right* mouse button. (On the Mac, press ⌘-Option as you click.) A shortcut menu will appear displaying the commands that apply to the type of object you've selected (Figure 15.4). (See Chapter 9.)

Figure 15.4:
You can display a shortcut menu by clicking the *right* mouse button. (Mac users press ⌘-Option as you click.)

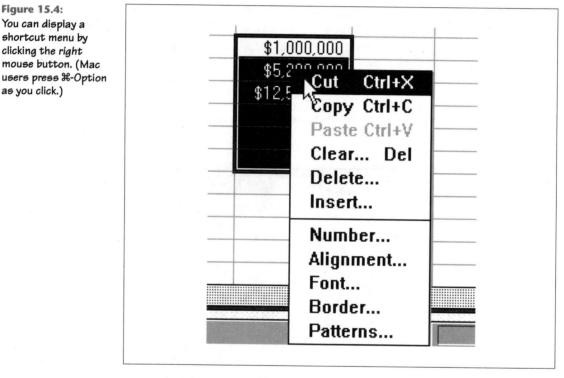

Juggling sheets for your own amusement

Use Edit ➤ Copy and Edit ➤ Paste to copy stuff between different open worksheets. Use Edit ➤ Copy and Edit ➤ Paste Link to copy stuff between open sheet files so that the data and its copies are happily linked in an ongoing relationship. (See Chapter 13.)

Make Your Life Easier

I don't want you to do things the hard way, but if you insist, Murphy might be amused.

Splitting without headaches

Choose Window ➤ Split if you need to view the headings and the bottom of a long sheet at the same time (or the row headings and the right edge of the sheet). (See Chapter 3.)

Bind several loose sheets so they don't blow away

Store several sheets that you frequently use together in a single workbook file. (See Chapter 3.)

Use directories and folders to get organized

Create directories (or folders on the Mac) to store files for different projects or clients. Learn to navigate the file system without getting swamped. (See Chapter 3.)

Collapse those big sheets

Use the Formula ➤ Outline command on big sheets that have multiple levels of detail to collapse or expand them with a click (Figure 15.5). (See Chapter 8.)

Figure 15.5:
The + and − minus buttons let you expand and collapse an outlined sheet to display different levels of detail.

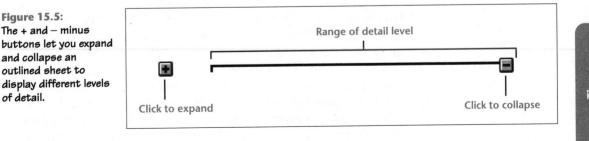

Range of detail level

Click to expand

Click to collapse

Tips

Hooray for Ohlay!

Use object linking and embedding (OLE) to embed a report narrative in the sheet it describes. (See Chapter 12.)

Make Excel Do Your Math Homework

Below are some tips on using formulas and functions (ready-made formulas) to give orders to your faithful math slave.

Murphy's Eight Great Steps to Success beneath the Sheets

This is the Reader's Digest version of my advice in Chapter 5—truths that became apparent to me only after many visits from the ubiquitous Murphy.

1. *Pick the right function for the job.* Beware of differences between functions that have similar purposes (ROUND and TRUNC, AVERAGE and MEDIAN, to name some of the worst offenders).

2. *Watch for common sources of error.* Avoid division by zero, rounded or truncated values used in multiplication formulas, and circular references.

3. *Make sure to feed a function everything it wants.* Enclose text values that are used as arguments in quotation marks, but don't use quotation marks on range names or on TRUE or FALSE. Use parentheses in matching pairs. If you're not sure what arguments a function needs, press Ctrl-A after typing the equal sign and the function name in the formula bar.

4. *Use the right stuff.* Make sure that arguments refer to cells or ranges that hold the values needed by the function. Use range names for clarity, but don't assume that the name refers to the correct range until you recheck it. Select the range you think is named and look in the cell reference box (top left of the screen) to see if the name appears there. Don't name a formula unless you fully understand its math. Use absolute and relative addressing correctly to prevent errors that might creep in if you edit the sheet later.

5. *Test each formula.* Watch for error messages (there's a list of them in Chapter 2) and incorrect results. Revise your formulas until the sheet works as expected.

6. *Test the sheet.* Generating graphs from ranges in the sheet can be a quick visual check on the reasonableness of results. (See Chapter 11.)

7. *If you make changes to the sheet, recheck and retest it.*

8. *If you think Excel goofed, think again.*

If you need to test a sheet that contains a lot of formulas, you might try an Excel Add-In macro called the Worksheet Auditor. To install the Auditor on a PC, select Options ➤ Add Ins ➤ Add and then select the macro file AUDIT.XLA. To start the Auditor, select Formula ➤ Worksheet Auditor ➤ Generate Report.

To install the Worksheet Auditor on a Mac, select the Worksheet Auditor add-in macro file. To start the Auditor, select Formula ➤ Worksheet Auditor ➤ Generate Audit Report.

Address for success

In formulas, use relative addresses (A1) unless you want to make sure that a formula will always use the same address, even if the formula is copied or moved into another cell (absolute: $A$1). (See Chapter 4.)

Make Yourself Look Pretty and Presentable

If you're going to put in an appearance, make it good. Here are some tips on dressing up your sheet when the company's coming.

You really AutoFormat that sheet

Click the AutoFormat tool to get dressed up in your sheet in time to catch the movie:

Tips

Chapter 7 offers lots of other tips on improving your appearance.

Look before you leap, preview before you print

Hold down the Shift key as you click the Print tool to get an on-screen preview of your printout. When you do this, the icon changes to the Preview tool. (See Chapter 8.)

Get centered

To compose printouts quickly, mark the Center Horizontally and Center Vertically check boxes in the Page Setup dialog box (choose File ➤ Page Setup). (See Chapter 8.)

Don't sit still for portraits

If you do lots of letters and memos in portrait orientation but usually want your worksheets in landscape, set up your printer for portrait orientation in the Windows Control Panel and in any word processing applications, but change the orientation in Excel to landscape for the current document by selecting File ➤ Page Setup. (See Chapter 8.)

Pfunny pfonts?

If you're having font trouble in Windows, try this: Choose Main ➤ Control Panel ➤ Fonts ➤ TrueType and mark both check boxes: Enable TrueType Fonts and Show Only TrueType Fonts In Applications. This setting will apply to *all* Windows applications. (See Chapter 8.)

In a hurry to go out?

Click the Print tool...

and live happily ever after!

Stay Out of Trouble

The following tips may help you bar Murphy from your door, or at least make it that much tougher for the old devil to get in!

You AutoSave—or not

If you set up AutoSave for automatic timed saving of sheets to disk, please choose the Prompt Before Saving option so that you can control the overwriting of existing files. (See Chapter 9.)

These passwords are _very_ secure!

If you apply password protection to a sheet or to a file, keep the password in a safe place. If you forget the password, you're really and truly out of luck. Even Bill Gates and all his gurus at the mighty Microsoft won't help you get your stuff back. (See Chapter 9.)

Check it, but get proof

Use the Check Spelling tool to catch misspellings in text:

But remember—the spell-checking program is no substitute for old-fashioned proofreading. (See Chapter 10.)

Tips

Read this before you hit the Add button

In the Spelling dialog box, you can select the Add button to build a custom dictionary for jargon, technical terms, and proper names that you use frequently. But don't add words to this dictionary unless you are absolutely certain that they are spelled correctly. (See Chapter 10.)

Writing notes to yourself isn't crazy

Document your work in case your sheet hits the fan. But don't select the Hide option for the note indicators in your only copy of a sheet, lest you forget that they're there and neglect to turn them back on (Figure 15.6). (See Chapter 12.)

Figure 15.6:
Note indicators show
you which cells have
note text attached to
them.

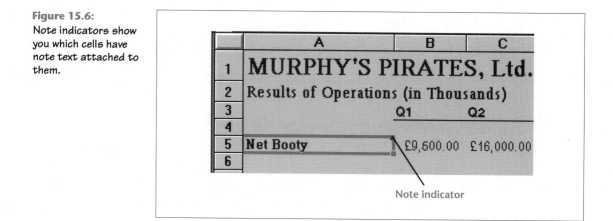

Note indicator

Charts can be pretty or pretty awful

The secret to getting the ChartWizard to make useful charts is picking a range that reveals a meaningful pattern or trend in the data. (See Chapter 11.)

Get linked, but not snarled

You can use data links to create 3D sheets (stacks of sheets in a workbook) that work like a single many-layered sheet. Before you try this, read "Playing with Your NewSet of Links" in Chapter 13.

Get What You Want!

You can't always get what you want? Tell Mick Jagger he's out of touch with the Excel generation.

Show yourself to a nice table

Create a lookup table to store and retrieve related stuff like names and phone numbers. If you want to be able to look up and grab stuff everywhichways, create the table as a database instead.

The usefulness of the information you get out of a table (lookup or database) depends mostly on how well you set it up. (See Chapter 14.)

Murphy's grab bag

Before departing with a wan and somewhat suspicious smile, Murphy left this assortment of goodies. Care to try one?

☞ In your worksheet, leave an extra formatted column or row—empty of data but including all required formulas—that you can copy to expand the sheet quickly.

☞ Use templates as fill-in-the-blank forms for sheets that you reuse or that you submit periodically (File ➤ Save As ➤ Template on the PC; Options ➤ Template on the Mac). Save template files in the XLSTART subdirectory so that you can grab one quickly whenever you select File ➤ New. (On the Mac, the folder is System: Preferences:Excel Startup Folder (4).)

☞ Don't use a single complicated formula if several simpler formulas in different cells will do the same job.

Tips

☞ Use text labels liberally to identify number values in your sheets.

☞ Give cells and ranges descriptive names. This will make the formulas using the names easier to understand. By naming the cell that holds the original formula, you might also name formulas that are used by other formulas. Beware that using a name in place of a formula can obscure its underlying math.

☞ Sprinkle your sheets liberally with cell notes to explain to yourself and to others how the sheet was constructed and what its formulas do.

☞ Use text boxes with arrows to call out required inputs or items needing special attention.

☞ Highlight stuff that is calculated by formulas (variables) in a different color.

☞ Use cell protection to control which stuff in a sheet can be changed or edited by another user of the sheet.

☞ Save your work, and save often (File ➤ Save). The next power glitch could have your name on it.

And in Conclusion...

I'd like to share with you my favorite of Murphy's laws. It may give you some comfort, especially when presenting the results you have labored so mightily to produce with Excel.

Murphy's Law of Self-Confidence: Make all your mistakes in a loud, clear voice. No one will know the difference.

Mega-Index

Are you ornery enough to take on The Murphy's Mega-Index?

There's a **MURPHY'S LAW OF INDEXES** too. It says that even if you list something in an index ten different ways, someone will always come along ornery enough to look for it an *eleventh* way!

If you look for some information in our index, and you do not find it listed the *first way you look it up,* let us know. We'll add your eleventh way of looking it up to future indexes AND you will earn yourself a place in Indexers' Heaven!

Throughout the index, we have used certain typographical conventions to help you find information. **Boldface** page numbers indicate primary explanations. *Italic* page numbers indicate illustrations.

Bolface page numbers indicate primary explanations.

Italic page numbers indicate illustrations.

Bolface page numbers indicate primary explanations.

Italic page numbers indicate illustrations.

Bolface page numbers indicate primary explanations.

Italic page numbers indicate illustrations.

Italic page numbers indicate illustrations.

Italic page numbers indicate illustrations.

Bolface page numbers indicate primary explanations.

Italic page numbers indicate illustrations.

Italic page numbers indicate illustrations.

Italic page numbers indicate illustrations.

Bolface page numbers indicate primary explanations.

M

magnification, of viewfinders, **64–65**
magnifying glass, mouse pointer as, 180
main directory, 73
major grid lines, 235
Manual recalculation, 208
Margin settings (Page Setup dialog box), 181
margins, adjusting in Print Preview, 180
math. *See also* formulas
  automatic calculation of, 11–12
  macros for higher, 200
MAX( ) function, 111
Maximize button, 70
maximizing windows, **70**
Maximum Change, 122
Maximum Iterations, 122
maximum size, for worksheets, 49
median, or average, 112
MEDIAN( ) function, 111, 123
medical terms, dictionary for, 215
"memavail" keyword, 85
memory
  function to report available, 85
  and multiple open windows, 60, 68
  shrinking windows and, 70
Menu bar, *5*
  Alt key to activate, 206
menus, ➤ symbol and, xxiv
messages. *See also* error messages
  "AutoFormat could not detect a table around the active cell," 150
  "Cannot resolve circular references," 121, 122
  "Confirmation password is not identical," 202
  "Could not find matching data," 53
  "Error in formula," 39
  "Extract range is full," 285

"Finished spell checking entire sheet," 219
"Parentheses do not match," 39
"Too few arguments," 123
"Too many arguments," 123
"Update references to unopened documents?," 259
mice. *See* mouse
Microsoft Windows. *See* Windows (Microsoft)
MIN( ) function, 111
Minimize button, for window, 69
minor grid lines, 235
minus sign (–)
  for numbers, 13, 292
  in SUM formula, 101
minus sign (–) button, to collapse worksheet, 186, *297*
MINUTE( ) function, 120
mistakes. *See* errors
mixing colors, 165
MOD( ) function, 104, 117
models, for charts, 235
MONTH( ) function, 120
mouse, xxv
  to add borders, 164
  clicking right button, **205–207**
  keyboard alternatives to, xxiv, 206
  to move cell highlight, 8
  for moving cell pointer, 5
mouse pointer, 7. *See also* cell pointer
  as cross-hairs, 223
  as I-beam cursor, 34–35
  as magnifying glass, 180
  vertical bar with double arrow as, *16*
  as vertical line, 34
moving
  cell highlight, 8, 128
  cells with drag and drop, 293
  charts as whole, 231
  with cut-and-paste, **132–134**
  to distant cells, **49–50**

Bolface page numbers indicate primary explanations.

Bolface page numbers indicate primary explanations.

Italic page numbers indicate illustrations.

Font, 161
Number, 143
Paste, *133*
Patterns, 164, 233, *234*
of toolbars, *168*
portrait orientation, 172, 300
positioning text. *See* alignment
positive numbers, in R1C1 addressing, 96
PostScript fonts, *161*, 162
pound sign (#), for error messages, **43–44**
pound signs (######), as overflow indicator, **43**, 131, 295
power failure, and work loss, 195
preventing
  errors, **122–125**
  scrolling in window pane, 58
Preview tool, 178, 179, 300
Previous button (Print Preview), 179
Print (File menu), 174
Print dialog box, *182*
Print Preview, **178–180**, 300
  adjusting margins in, 180
  column border indicators in, *181*
  enlarging, 180
Print Preview (File menu), 179
Print Quality (Print dialog box), 182
Print Report (File menu), 184
Print tool, 172, *179*, 300, 301
Print Topic (File menu), 193
Printer button, 21
printer driver, 166, 173
printer fonts, *161*
  problems with Windows, 178
  or screen fonts, **177–178**
  TrueType, 178
printers, 166
  color on, 166
  setup, 172
printing, 20–21, **171–186**
  block of cells, **182–183**
  centering, 175, 300

Help, 193
multipage worksheets, **175–177**
multiple copies, 182
Murphy's Law of, 172
portrait or landscape orientation, *172–173*, 175
scaling, 175, 176
setting page breaks in, 177
starting, 174
problem solving. *See* help
problems using computers, xx–xxi
  preventing, **122–125**
PRODUCT function, 102
Product Support (Help menu), 195
profits, errors projecting, xxi
Program Manager (Windows), 178
  for installing Excel, xxv
Prompt Before Saving box (Auto-Save dialog box), *198*, 199, 301
proofreading, 212
proper names, spelling check and, 216
Protect Document (Options menu), 167, 200
Protect Document dialog box, 200
publisher, 260

Q

Q+E application, 272
quotation marks (")
  for keywords in functions, 84, 123
  for labels as arguments, 84
  for text in formulas, 115, 123
QUOTIENT( ) function, **103**

R

R1C1 cell addressing, **95–97**, *96*, 208, 267
RAND( ) function, 85

Bolface page numbers indicate primary explanations.

Italic page numbers indicate illustrations.

Bolface page numbers indicate primary explanations.

Italic page numbers indicate illustrations.

Italic page numbers indicate illustrations.

Italic page numbers indicate illustrations.

Bolface page numbers indicate primary explanations.

X

× (Cancel) button, with formula
bar, 33
.XLA file name extension, 200
.XLC file name extension, 192, 230
.XLM file name extension, 192,
200
.XLS file name extension, 67, 72,
73, 192, 196
.XLW file name extension, 72,
192, 197, 249

Y

YEAR( ) function, 120
YIELD function, 118, 123

Z

zero
and AVERAGE function, 86
division by, 43–44
zoom, **64–65**
Zoom (Window menu), 64
Zoom button (Print Preview), 180
Zoom dialog box, *64*
Zoom In tool (Utility Toolbar),
65–66
Zoom Out tool (Utility Toolbar),
65–66

SYBEX

FREE BROCHURE!

Complete this form today, and we'll send you a full-color brochure of Sybex bestsellers.

Please supply the name of the Sybex book purchased.

_____

How would you rate it?

_____ Excellent   _____ Very Good   _____ Average   _____ Poor

Why did you select this particular book?

_____ Recommended to me by a friend

_____ Recommended to me by store personnel

_____ Saw an advertisement in _____

_____ Author's reputation

_____ Saw in Sybex catalog

_____ Required textbook

_____ Sybex reputation

_____ Read book review in _____

_____ In-store display

_____ Other _____

Where did you buy it?

_____ Bookstore

_____ Computer Store or Software Store

_____ Catalog (name: _____)

_____ Direct from Sybex

_____ Other: _____

Did you buy this book with your personal funds?

_____ Yes   _____ No

About how many computer books do you buy each year?

_____ 1-3   _____ 3-5   _____ 5-7   _____ 7-9   _____ 10+

About how many Sybex books do you own?

_____ 1-3   _____ 3-5   _____ 5-7   _____ 7-9   _____ 10+

Please indicate your level of experience with the software covered in this book:

_____ Beginner   _____ Intermediate   _____ Advanced

Which types of software packages do you use regularly?

_____ Accounting   _____ Databases   _____ Networks

_____ Amiga   _____ Desktop Publishing   _____ Operating Systems

_____ Apple/Mac   _____ File Utilities   _____ Spreadsheets

_____ CAD   _____ Money Management   _____ Word Processing

_____ Communications   _____ Languages   _____ Other _____
                                                                         (please specify)

Which of the following best describes your job title?

_____ Administrative/Secretarial   _____ President/CEO

_____ Director   _____ Manager/Supervisor

_____ Engineer/Technician   _____ Other _____
(please specify)

Comments on the weaknesses/strengths of this book: _____

_____

_____

_____

_____

Name _____

Street _____

City/State/Zip _____

Phone _____

PLEASE FOLD, SEAL, AND MAIL TO SYBEX

SYBEX, INC.
Department M
2021 CHALLENGER DR.
ALAMEDA, CALIFORNIA USA
94501

SYBEX

SEAL

Murphy's Little-Known Laws of Excel

Computers are supposed to make people more productive. Evidently that applies to Murphy, whose influence is multiplied by the power of automation. Here are some laws that might sound familiar to users of spreadsheet software, whether it's Microsoft Excel or Brand X.

☞ In any worksheet, the formula with a flaw in it will be in the last cell you check.

☞ It is impossible to make a worksheet foolproof because fools are so ingenious.

☞ You don't want to make a worksheet bulletproof. Better they should shoot at it and not at you.

☞ Every job quotation you calculate will take twice as long as you expect and will be half as profitable.

☞ The one item they question on your expense report will be the one for which you have no receipt.